OCCASIONAL PAPER 187

Philippines:
Toward Sustainable and Rapid Growth
Recent Developments and the Agenda Ahead

M. Rodlauer, P. Loungani, V. Arora, C. Christofides, E. G. de la Piedra,
P. Kongsamut, K. Kostial, V. Summers, and A. Vamvakidis

INTERNATIONAL MONETARY FUND
Washington DC
2000

Production: IMF Graphics Section
Typesetting: Choon Lee
Figures: Sanaa Elaroussi

Cataloging-in-Publication Data

Philippines : toward sustainable and rapid growth : recent developments and
the agenda ahead / M. Rodlauer . . . [et al.]. —
Washington D.C. : International Monetary Fund, 2000.
   p.   cm . — (Occasional paper, 0251-6365) ; no. 187

ISBN 1-55775-861-1

   1. Philippines—Economic conditions—1986– .   2. Philippines—Eco-
nomic policy.   3. Finance, Public—Philippines.   4. Monetary
policy—Philippines.   5. Banks and banking—Philippines.   I. Rodlauer,
Markus.   II. International Monetary Fund.   III. Series: Occasional paper
(International Monetary Fund) ; no. 187.
HC455.P45 2000

Price: US$18.00
(US$15.00 to full-time faculty members and
students at universities and colleges)

Please send orders to:
International Monetary Fund, Publication Services
700 19th Street, N.W., Washington, D.C. 20431, U.S.A.
Tel.: (202) 623-7430   Telefax: (202) 623-7201
E-mail: publications@imf.org
Internet: http://www.imf.org

recycled paper

Contents

Figures

Preface

This Occasional Paper takes stock of economic developments in the Philippines during the 1990s, a period of comprehensive reforms and transformation toward a dynamic emerging market economy. A notable aspect of this experience has been the country's relatively strong performance during the recent Asian crisis, under conditions that, in the past, might have derailed the economy. By the same token, the pressure of recent shocks has highlighted the remaining barriers to sustained rapid growth and development. In reviewing this experience, the paper focuses on the policies behind the favorable performance in recent years as well as the remaining reform agenda.

The paper is the product of a team effort led by Markus Rodlauer and Prakash Loungani. The team of authors, which also included Vivek Arora, Charalambos Christofides, Enrique G. de la Piedra, Piyabha Kongsamut, Kristina Kostial, Victoria Summers, and Athanasios Vamvakidis, greatly benefited from the guidance and cooperation received from Margaret R. Kelly. They also would like to thank for their helpful comments and cooperation Hamid Faruqee, Peter Isard, Henri Lorie, Wilhelmina Mañalac, Greta Mitchell Casselle, Elizabeth Milne, Sean Nolan, and Charles Woodruff. Helpful suggestions were also received from the Philippine authorities to whom a previous draft was presented for comments, and from Executive Directors who saw an earlier version in conjunction with the 1999 Article IV review of the Philippine economy. The authors are also indebted to Pihuan Cormier, Ranee Sirihorachai, and Ahang Edalatpour for assisting with numerous drafts, to Ioana Hussiada and Fritz Pierre-Louis for research, and to Martha Bonilla of the External Relations Department for editing the paper and coordinating its production and publication.

The opinions expressed are solely those of the authors and do not necessarily reflect the views of the IMF, Executive Directors, or the authorities of the countries covered in this study.

Except where otherwise indicated, the paper reflects information available through May 1999.

1 Overview and Background

Markus Rodlauer

The Philippines has received considerable attention in recent years as it "emerged" in the early 1990s from a long period of slow growth and economic imbalances, and then managed to escape the "Asian crisis" relatively unscathed. This suggests that the reforms under way since the late 1980s, and intensified in the 1990s, have paid off, and are continuing to bear fruit with the help of skillful crisis management through the recent turbulence. By the same token, the pressure of recent shocks has put the spotlight on the remaining structural weaknesses that need to be addressed for sustained rapid growth and development. The Philippines' recent experience may contain valuable lessons for emerging economies' efforts at crisis prevention and crisis management, as well as for the country's own policy choices at the threshold of the next decade. This Occasional Paper describes this experience, focusing on the elements behind the relatively strong performance in recent years as well as the remaining reform agenda.

The economic situation in the Philippines deteriorated sharply in the 1980s. Roiled by economic policy mistakes, external shocks, natural disasters, and political instability, the economy suffered two setbacks that left real per capita income at the end of the decade about 7 percent lower than at the beginning. This performance contrasted sharply with that of other countries in the region, which resulted in the latter being called "Asian tiger" economies, while the Philippines was often labeled the "sick man of Asia."

The first half of the 1980s witnessed the collapse of the regime of Ferdinand Marcos and the growth strategy pursued since the mid-1970s. Although growth averaged more than 6 percent during 1975–80, it was accompanied by a large buildup of external debt, much of it to fund an expansion of the public sector. Easy credit encouraged excessive borrowing by private firms, and protectionist industrial and trade policies caused investment to increase mainly in import-substitution and nontradable activities, undermining competitiveness. Serious governance problems, often characterized as "crony capitalism," exacerbated the vulnerabilities. A series of external shocks in the early 1980s[1] exposed these weaknesses and, compounded by domestic events,[2] led to a major crisis with default on external obligations, widespread failure of domestic banks and corporations, and a deep recession.

While the economy remained on a rocky path during the second half of the 1980s, this period witnessed important changes that paved the way for fundamental improvement in the 1990s. After growth bounced back during 1986–89 under a new government, the recovery faltered in 1990–91 with a string of natural disasters,[3] external shocks, and renewed political instability. The setback was compounded by policy slippages, including a sharp widening of the fiscal deficit, lax monetary policy, and real currency appreciation, leading to a sharp increase in the current account deficit, a jump in inflation, and a near-balance of payments crisis in 1991. The repeat "boom-and-bust" cycle also reflected structural constraints including high import dependence and a shallow domestic capital market. At the same time, however, the change in government in 1986 ushered in a new, democratic, and open political regime that, although initially plagued by instability, set the stage for the political stability achieved in the 1990s. The government of Corazon Aquino also initiated outward-looking and market-oriented economic reforms that, although implemented only partially and not without setbacks, signaled a shift in policy direction on which the comprehensive reforms of the 1990s would build.

1990–96: Reforms Bear Fruit

The 1990s have witnessed impressive economic progress in the Philippines, reflecting sound eco-

---

[1]Including the second oil price shock, a hike in world interest rates, recession in industrialized countries, and the Latin American debt crisis.

[2]These included a financial scandal in 1981 and the assassination of Ninoy Aquino in 1983.

[3]Including a major earthquake, drought, and a volcanic disaster.

nomic policies in a more favorable external environment and greater political stability. By 1996, growth had accelerated to about 6 percent; inflation was down to 5 percent; and the external position had strengthened, with rapid export growth and rising reserves. The new government led by President Fidel Ramos (1992–98) embraced a comprehensive reform strategy aimed at further opening up the economy, reducing macroeconomic imbalances, and addressing other structural rigidities. Under this program, supported since 1994 by an Extended Fund Facility (EFF) from the IMF, the fiscal deficit was brought down sharply, privatization was accelerated, and the central bank was recapitalized under a new statute. A number of important sectors were opened to new competition (including banking, telecommunications, domestic shipping, and the oil sector), and limits on foreign participation were liberalized in various sectors. Quantitative import restrictions were removed (except for rice), and the average import tariff is now about 10 percent, one-third the level of the mid-1980s.

Notwithstanding the progress made, some barriers to sustained rapid growth proved difficult to uproot, and the Philippines' arrival as a successful emerging market economy entailed new vulnerabilities. The lingering structural problems included low domestic savings; limited progress in addressing long-standing public sector issues such as weak tax collection and civil service and local government reforms; weaknesses in the banking sector; and the continued high incidence of poverty. Many of these problems reflected the legacy of the past as unequal income distribution, past heavy regulation of the economy, and the degradation of governance under the Marcos regime created powerful interest groups resisting the reform efforts designed to level the playing field. The acceleration of growth, investment, and capital inflows experienced in the mid-1990s masked these shortcomings, but also heightened the economy's vulnerability to the eventual shift in market sentiment. The de facto pegging of the Philippine peso to the U.S. dollar in late 1995 added to the risks by encouraging rapid growth of short-term capital inflows.

Thus, on the eve of the Asian crisis, the Philippine economy was vulnerable, albeit less so than the most heavily affected neighboring countries. By mid-1997, the peso had appreciated by more than 25 percent in real effective terms since 1993 (nearly 40 percent since 1990), and the external current account deficit had widened to more than 5 percent of GNP (with a trade deficit of about 13 percent). Large external borrowing in 1996, especially by banks, had raised foreign currency debt exposures, including on short-term debt which, at about $10 billion, about equaled the level of usable gross official reserves.

Private sector credit had expanded rapidly during 1995–96, including a significant rise in credit to real estate and consumption. While these developments had increased the economy's vulnerability, the Philippines was less susceptible to a sudden downturn than most other East Asian economies. In particular, the period of rapid credit expansion and debt accumulation in the Philippines was much shorter than elsewhere, resulting in lower levels of corporate leverage; major banks were well capitalized; and the structural and political reforms under way since the mid-1980s had created a more open, market-oriented, and competitive system that was able to resist the type of systemic collapse witnessed elsewhere. Both government and the private sector had significant experience with crisis management, and a flexible policy response to the unfolding crisis was facilitated by the close policy dialogue under the existing arrangement with the IMF.

1997–99: Crisis Management

From early 1997, economic conditions deteriorated as the regional downturn interacted with the country's own vulnerabilities. A decline in capital inflows and a slowdown in manufacturing output combined with sharp falls in the stock market and mounting pressures on the peso. The authorities initially responded by tightening monetary policy and by intervention to maintain the de facto peg of the peso. When this stance became unsustainable in the aftermath of the float of the Thai baht, the peso was floated on July 11, accompanied by a strengthening of fiscal, monetary, and structural policies. The new program was supported by augmentation and extension of the EFF (scheduled to expire in mid-1997), followed by a new two-year Stand-By Arrangement in early 1998.

The authorities' strategy focused initially on stabilizing the situation through relatively tight monetary and fiscal policies; as stabilization took hold, the stance shifted gradually toward supporting recovery. The program also comprised a set of key structural reforms to underpin stabilization and medium-term growth prospects. Monetary policy during this period would "lean against" pressures in the exchange market by raising interest rates, without attempting aggressively to resist market forces. Likewise, the Bangko Sentral would intervene in the exchange market to provide liquidity and restore calm during periods of extreme volatility, but refrain from large-scale intervention to defend any particular level of the rate. As the peso began to stabilize during the second half of 1998, interest rates were brought down—cautiously at first, in view of the still unsettled external environment and the relatively high rate of inflation. The monetary stance became more fully supportive of recovery in early 1999, as the turnaround in the balance of payments was firmly established and inflationary pressures abated. Fiscal policy was also adapted gradually to the slowdown in output and the associated revenue shortfall: from a precrisis target for 1998 of a fiscal surplus of 1 percent of GNP, the program was revised several times to an eventual deficit target of 3 percent of GNP. Structural reforms under the program, in addition to completing the agenda of the Ramos administration (oil deregulation, tax reform, and continued trade liberalization), focused on strengthening the banking sector and improving tax administration, both key to the stabilization and medium-term growth objectives.

Financial markets remained volatile through late 1998, reflecting both external and domestic developments. Several waves of external shocks put further pressure on the peso and equity prices. The collapse of the Korean and Indonesian economies brought the peso to a low of ₱46 per $1 in January 1998 (a 44 percent depreciation from mid-1997). After a brief recovery in early 1998, the deterioration in Japan coupled with uncertainties over the policies of the newly elected government of Joseph Estrada[4] caused a new downturn over the summer that culminated in the emerging market crisis in September[5] (with the stock market index falling below 1,200, compared with the high of more than 3,400 in January 1997). Since then, financial markets have strengthened continually, with equity prices up twofold; peso appreciation and a large increase in official reserves; and interest rates declining to below precrisis levels.

Economic activity began to stall in the second half of 1997, followed by a slight recession in 1998. After growing by 5.2 percent in 1997,[6] real GDP dropped by 0.5 percent in 1998, weighed down by a severe drought that reduced agricultural output by over 6 percent. Industry also declined (by 1.7 percent), while services remained relatively buoyant (growing by 3–5 percent). On the demand side, growth was supported by continued strong export growth (20 percent in volume terms), which was one of the key factors distinguishing the Philippines' adjustment experience from that of its neighbors. Private investment, however, fell sharply, and unemployment rose to more than 10 percent. Reflecting

the impact of peso depreciation and a drought-related increase in food prices, inflation reached 10.4 percent by year's end. In the external accounts, 1998 witnessed a dramatic turnaround in the current account, to a surplus of nearly 2 percent of GNP, on the strength of continued export growth, while imports fell sharply.

Following the upturn in financial markets, the real economy also bottomed out in early 1999. Led by a recovery in agriculture, first-quarter real GDP grew by 1.2 percent, followed by 3.6 percent growth in the second quarter, as the recovery spread to other sectors. Thus, on balance, the Philippine economy has been able to weather the regional crisis better than most of its neighbors, reflecting more favorable starting conditions as well as the pragmatic implementation of sound economic policies. That this has been achieved during a period of political transition testifies to the resilience of the Philippine economy and a broad-based consensus for sound economic policies.

Remaining Challenges

While policies pursued over the past decade have had major positive results, events over the past two years have highlighted that much remains to be done. The task is not only to restore the momentum of growth and investor confidence of the mid-1990s, but also to sustain it through policies that prevent a return to the boom-and-bust cycles of the past while ensuring the Philippines' full and competitive participation in the global marketplace. Against this background, and considering the policy agenda into the next decade, two imperatives are: to deal with the still quite pervasive legacy of the past, such as low savings, widespread poverty, accommodation of rent-seeking activities, and a weak public sector; and to manage successfully the challenges of globalization, allowing the country to fully partake of the benefits of integration while minimizing the associated risks of excessive leverage, currency overvaluation, and sudden capital flow reversals. In particular, this agenda includes:

- maintaining prudent macroeconomic policies, with emphasis on avoiding fundamental inconsistencies that risk disruptive shifts in capital flows;
- raising domestic savings and investment from the current unsustainably low levels;
- further leveling the playing field through domestic and external liberalization, as well as effective programs to assist the poor and to enhance the opportunities of the disadvantaged;
- streamlining and strengthening the public sector—a traditional "Achilles' heel" of the economy;

[4]Presidential and legislative elections were held in May 1998, and President Joseph Estrada, his government, and a new congress took office in July.

[5]Following the introduction of capital controls in Malaysia and Russia's default on part of its government debt.

[6]On a seasonally adjusted quarter-to-quarter basis, real GDP growth decelerated sharply in the second half of 1997 (to an annual rate of 1.4 percent).

- further strengthening prudential, supervisory, and debt resolution frameworks in the financial and corporate sectors (including prudential-based management of foreign currency risk);
- accelerating rural development through agricultural modernization and by encouraging the growth of small- and medium-sized enterprises in the countryside; and
- improving further the investment climate, including by strengthening governance and "economic security."

In a wider sense, successful implementation of this agenda will need to be embedded in a continuous strengthening of Philippine democracy and its institutions, to overcome elements of stagnation such as a weak judicial system; corruption in public administration; concentration of control over economic resources, the media, and the political process; and rapid population growth.

The sections that follow review a range of issues that have arisen as the Philippines has progressed from a major crisis case in the 1980s to a successful emerging market in the 1990s. Section II examines the evolution of output growth and the elements that have contributed to its acceleration in the 1990s, as well as the remaining structural barriers to sustained rapid growth. Section III reviews fiscal develop- ments and the various reforms that have been implemented to put the public finances on a sounder footing, and discusses the remaining weaknesses in public sector management that have been brought to the fore by the recent economic slowdown. Section IV considers the conduct of monetary policy, describing inter alia the evolution of the central bank from an institution with limited independence, a weak balance sheet, and underdeveloped instruments of monetary control to a modern, independent, and financially sound "Bangko Sentral." Section V describes external sector developments and prospects, reviewing the structural transformation that has occurred, and is still under way, in the external accounts; the section also evaluates external competitiveness from a variety of angles, and looks at the medium-term outlook and related policy issues. Section VI reviews the development of the banking sector in the Philippines, describing how it has "emerged" as an increasingly sophisticated market in the 1990s, while outlining the reform challenges that remain. Section VII surveys corporate governance in the Philippines, highlighting the need for progress in many areas, particularly reforming the framework for debt resolution and insolvency. A final section discusses social issues, in particular, the impact on poverty of accelerating growth in the 1990s.

II Economic Growth

Piyabha Kongsamut and Athanasios Vamvakidis

The Philippine economy has long been set apart from many of its Asian neighbors by its weaker growth performance; its performance in recent years, however, offers grounds for optimism.

- In 1950, Philippine per capita income placed it in the center of a group of its Asian neighbors; by 1996, it had slid to the bottom of the group (Figure 2.1). Relative to the United States, Philippine per capita income fell from one-seventh in 1950 to one-tenth by 1996, while all its neighbors improved—some spectacularly. Over the past three decades, per capita real GDP growth in the Philippines averaged less than 1 percent a year, compared with close to 3 percent a year in the Association of South East Asian Nations (ASEAN-3) countries (Indonesia, Malaysia, and Thailand).
- The Philippines' more recent economic performance offers grounds for some optimism; in particular, 1993–98 was marked by a performance better than the historical average, at a time when performance in the ASEAN-3 countries had slipped below historical norms (Table 2.1).
- At the height of the Asian crisis, Philippine real GDP declined only 0.5 percent in 1998 (despite a bad year for agriculture), compared with declines of 6–14 percent in the ASEAN-3 countries and Korea.

This section reviews the growth experience of the Philippines, with a view to assessing the outlook and policy requirements for rapid growth over the medium term. It presents stylized facts about Philippine economic growth, recent changes in economic performance, and the role of policies and institutions in shaping growth. Then, it describes growth performance during the Asian crisis, and presents a statistical analysis of the sources of growth, with particular focus on the contribution of trade liberalization. Lastly, it concludes with an assessment of the medium-term growth outlook.

The main findings are as follows:

- *Role of policies.* The increasingly outward-oriented and market-based policies adopted since 1986 appear to have borne fruit. Historically, the salient features of Philippine growth have been (1) its unevenness or "boom-and-bust" nature; (2) the absence of productivity gains; and (3) a distorted industrial structure (biased toward capital-intensive, import-competing production). However, the turnaround in the orientation of economic policies since 1986 appears to have yielded results in the form of (1) improved economic performance—particularly since 1993—and the resilience exhibited during the Asian crisis; (2) signs of pickup in productivity growth; and (3) some movement toward a less distorted industrial structure.
- *Sources of growth.* Statistical analysis indicates that the pickup in performance in recent years is due to increasing openness, stable investment rates, and an increase in foreign direct investment. Empirical estimates of the determinants of growth for 1970 to 1995—building on Fischer (1993) and Barro and Sala-i-Martin (1995)—show that the weaker performance of the Philippines, on average, relative to East Asian countries is due to its lower degree of openness and lower (and uneven) investment rates, including FDI. By the same token, the recent pickup in Philippine performance can be attributed to some catching up with East Asian countries with respect to these determinants.
- *Medium-term growth.* Prospects depend on maintaining the broad thrust of policies adopted since 1986, while deepening considerably the reforms in several areas. In particular, robust growth is contingent on continued trade liberalization, accompanied by a shift toward broad-based incentives and complementary investments in infrastructure; maintenance of high and stable investment rates (including FDI, but supported as well by higher domestic savings); and a low inflation environment, which in turn requires fiscal consolidation and a continuation of prudent monetary policies. Under this scenario, the estimates of potential output growth

Figure 2.1. Real GDP per Person
(Constant prices based on PPP exchange rates)¹

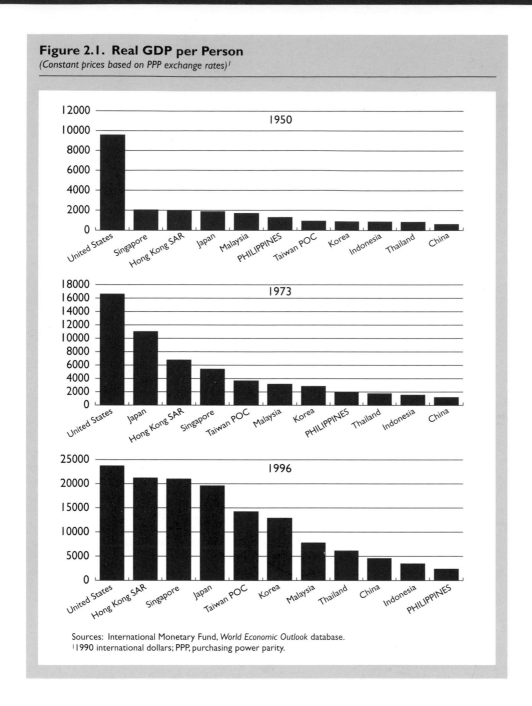

Sources: International Monetary Fund, *World Economic Outlook* database.
¹1990 international dollars; PPP, purchasing power parity.

in the Philippines range between 3.5 percent and 5 percent for 2000–05.

Role of Policies and Institutions in Shaping Growth

Stylized Facts About Philippine Growth

Growth since the 1970s has been uneven (Table 2.2). The rapid growth of the 1970s proved un-

sustainable and culminated in a sharp reversal during the first half of the 1980s. The period since has been marked by slower but somewhat steadier growth. Performance since 1994 has been particularly encouraging, with the economy achieving increasing growth rates up until the outbreak of the Asian crisis in 1997 (see the next part of this section for a discussion of the crisis period).

Despite recent progress, per capita income remains low (Figure 2.2). Per capita GDP is below its level in 1980 and only 3 percent higher than that in

Table 2.1. Growth in the Philippines and ASEAN-3: Historical Average and Recent Performance
(Percent change)

	Philippines	Indonesia	Malaysia	Thailand
Per capita real GDP growth, average 1969–98	0.8	2.6	2.9	2.6
Real GDP growth, average 1969–98	2.3	3.4	3.8	3.4
Per capita real GDP growth, average 1993–98	1.3	0.2	1.9	1.1
Real GDP growth, average 1993–98	3.0	1.5	3.6	1.9

Sources: *Penn World Tables*, updated using growth rates from World Bank; and International Monetary Fund, *International Financial Statistics* databases.

1990. The debt crisis in the early 1980s, the near-crisis in 1991, and the mixed performance in the intervening years took their toll from which the economy has yet to recover fully.

Productivity growth has historically made little—or even a negative—contribution to Philippine output growth; but there is some evidence of a pickup in recent years. Most studies indicate that total factor productivity growth in the Philippines has been negative (Table 2.3).[1] When total factor productivity growth is estimated over more recent periods, there is evidence of improved performance in the 1990s,

[1]Attempts to measure the relative contributions of factor inputs and technological progress to growth have been the focus of extensive research. In the case of East Asian economies, the most common finding is that capital accumulation has made the largest contribution, while productivity growth has made smaller but still significant contributions. Some studies suggest that almost all of the region's growth was due to capital accumulation, with productivity growth contributing almost nothing (Young (1992 and 1995); and Krugman (1994)).

Table 2.2. GDP Growth by Subperiods
(Percent change)

	Philippines	Malaysia	Indonesia	Thailand
1969–74	4.0	7.6	5.6	4.6
1975–80	3.9	6.6	5.9	5.5
1981–86	−1.3	1.5	3.4	3.4
1987–92	2.6	7.1	4.4	6.5
1993–98	3.0	3.6	1.5	1.9

Source: International Monetary Fund, *World Economic Outlook* database.

with total factor productivity growth averaging between .75 percent and 1 percent a year.

At the sectoral level, aggregate growth has been driven mainly by the industry and service sectors; agriculture has rarely contributed more than 1 percent of growth each year over the past 20 years (Figure 2.3). Agriculture still accounts for a large proportion of output, and employment in the sector remains high, at 43 percent of total employment. While other countries in the region have benefited from continuing shifts in the output and employment structure away from agriculture, the Philippines has lagged behind (Table 2.4).

Role of Policies and Institutions

As in many developing countries, government policies have played an important role in shaping the nature and extent of growth in the Philippines. In particular, government policies in the period following independence were characterized by (1) import substitution; (2) a strongly interventionist stance, as reflected in a range of fiscal incentives and directed credit; and (3) the promotion of capital-intensive industries in a labor-abundant country. Despite piecemeal attempts at reform, the above policies prevailed through the 1970s and much of the 1980s.

There were fundamental problems with these policies.[2]

- The financing for these policies was difficult to secure on a sustained basis. As a consequence, growth was uneven. The economy suffered through episodes of severe macroeconomic imbalances as manifested in balance of payments crises, large fiscal deficits, and high inflation. In

[2]Krueger (1998) provides a lucid discussion of the shortcomings of an import-substitution strategy.

Figure 2.2. GDP per Capita

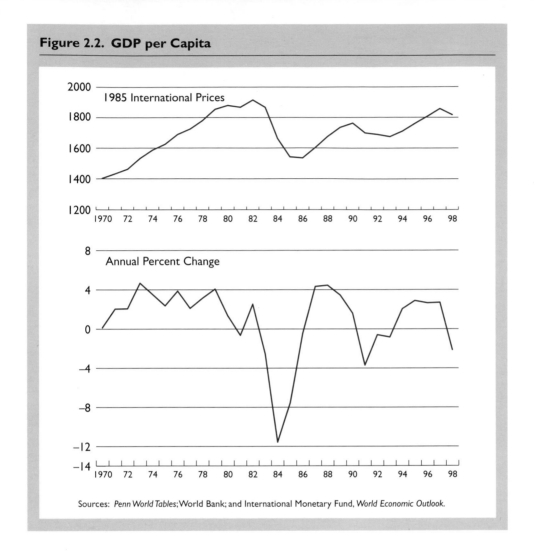

Sources: *Penn World Tables*; World Bank; and International Monetary Fund, *World Economic Outlook*.

Table 2.3. Estimates of Total Factor Productivity Growth

Source	Period	Total Factor Productivity Growth *(Annual)*
Collins and Bosworth (1996)	1960–94	–0.4
	1984–94	–0.9
Benhabib and Spiegel (1994)	1984–94	–0.9
Dowling and Summers (1998)	1961–95	0.0
	1986–95	–0.1
International Monetary Fund (1995)	1961–94	–0.8
	1994–95	1.0
Sarel (1997)	1978–96	–0.8
	1991–96	0.7

particular, the rapid buildup of external debt prior to 1982 helped feed an unsustainable boom that ended in the debt crisis.[3]

• Government intervention in the economy hindered productivity growth and the efficient allocation of resources. The trade regime was protectionist and discretionary. While there were export incentives, the policy tilt was still in favor of capital-intensive industries that could not compete in international markets. The central bank provided subsidized credit to enterprises, and later rescued them from financial difficulties. The pricing policies of marketing boards in the agricultural sector did not encourage efficient production,[4] nor did

---

[3]For a detailed economic history of the Philippines, see Dolan (1993) and Leipziger (1997).

[4]For example, two of the major export products (sugar and coconuts) were put under the control of marketing boards, which nominally were set up to help farmers but actually enriched a few businessmen. Also, price controls existed for many products.

Figure 2.3. GDP Growth by Sector
(Changes in percent of previous year's GDP)

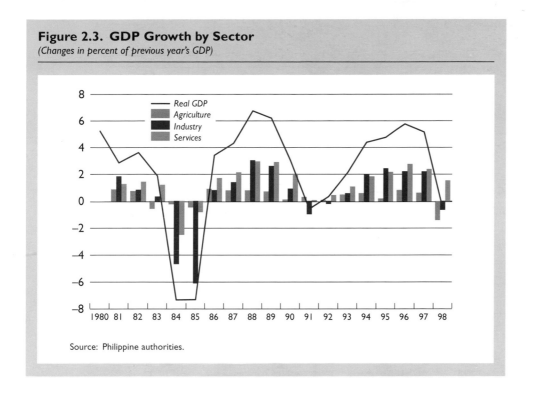

Source: Philippine authorities.

Table 2.4. Structure of Output and Employment
(In percent)

	Shares of Production				Shares of Employment			
	1970	1980	1990	1996	1970	1980	1990	1996
Philippines								
Agriculture	30	25	22	21	54	51	45	43
Industry	32	39	35	32	17	16	15	16
Manufacturing	25	26	25	23	12	11	10	10
Services	39	36	44	47	30	33	40	41
Indonesia								
Agriculture	45	24	19	16	66	56	50	46
Industry	19	42	39	43	10	13	17	14
Manufacturing	10	13	21	25	8	9	12	13
Services	36	34	42	41	24	31	33	39
Malaysia								
Agriculture	29	22	19	13	52	48	31	17
Industry	25	38	40	46	15	18	24	36
Manufacturing	12	21	26	34	8	11	17	27
Services	46	40	41	41	33	35	45	47
Thailand								
Agriculture	26	23	13	11	79	73	67	45
Industry	25	29	37	40	6	8	11	24
Manufacturing	16	22	27	29	4	6	9	15
Services	49	48	50	50	15	20	22	31

Sources: World Bank and International Monetary Fund; Leipziger (1997), Dolan (1993), Hill (1995), Jomo (1990), and Krongkaew (1995).

they encourage increased processing of products before export. Land reform was held back by the vested interests of traditional landowners. During this period, the role of the public sector expanded as public corporations were established, encroaching into more and more areas of economic activity.

The period since 1986 has been marked by a turnaround in the orientation of policies, although policy implementation was hampered by political instability. When the Aquino government took power in 1986, it adopted an ambitious reform agenda that included liberalization of the trade and exchange regimes. The quantitative restrictions on imports were gradually phased out or tariffied, and the tariff structure was simplified and rationalized. A new, more liberal Foreign Investment Act was passed. Many public corporations were privatized. A new program of land reform was also promised as part of the Comprehensive Agricultural Reform Program. Some of the reforms were implemented early on, but others (mainly land reform) were subsequently reversed or watered down. Political instability—there were six coup attempts in the first three years of the Aquino administration—was an impediment to full implementation of the reform program, and a series of shocks to the system (natural disasters, power shortages) contributed to continued macroeconomic imbalances.

The government of Fidel Ramos, which assumed office in 1992, adopted a host of reforms designed to put the economy on a rapid sustainable growth path. During this period, most restrictions on current and capital transactions were lifted and tariff reforms continued (Section V). A new Central Bank Act was passed in 1993, establishing price stability as the key objective of monetary policy and strengthening the legal framework for improved bank supervision. At the same time, the central bank was recapitalized, with the portfolio of nonperforming assets hived off to a separate entity (Sections IV and VI). Marketing monopolies were abolished, and producer price controls were eliminated. Electricity generation and telecommunications were opened to the private sector, foreign participation was allowed in the banking sector, and the domestic shipping and oil sectors were liberalized. A Comprehensive Tax Reform Package was passed in 1998 (see Section III). During this period, the external debt burden was brought down to more manageable levels, helped by debt restructuring (which had begun in the 1980s and was completed in 1994) and prudent fiscal management.

The reforms since 1986 appear to have had a favorable impact on economic performance. Per capita growth has picked up, particularly since 1993. Productivity growth has picked up as well, and the industrial structure is showing signs of dynamism. In

Table 2.5. Economic Growth in the Crisis Countries
(Percent change)

	1996	1997	1998
Philippines	5.7	5.2	−0.5
Indonesia	8.0	4.6	−13.6
Thailand	5.5	−0.4	−8.0
Malaysia	8.6	7.7	−6.7
Korea	6.8	5.0	−5.8

Source: International Monetary Fund, *World Economic Outlook*.

particular, the role of the public sector in the economy has been reduced through fiscal consolidation, the divestment of many public enterprises, and structural reforms such as trade liberalization, financial sector liberalization, and private sector participation in activities that were previously in the public domain (for example, power generation and infrastructure projects). Market incentives have replaced the more direct hand of the government.

Growth Performance During the Asian Crisis

The Philippines has managed to escape the Asian crisis relatively unscathed. In particular, output experienced a slight contraction in 1998, while in the other ASEAN-3 countries and Korea, the decline in output has been severe (Table 2.5). The decline in output in the Philippines was largely a result of adverse weather conditions brought about by El Niño. In 1998, agricultural output fell by more than 6 percent, while nonagricultural output grew by 1 percent. Had weather conditions been normal, the Philippine economy could have avoided a recession. External demand continued to grow during the crisis period, while domestic demand contracted. Domestic investment experienced a large decline, but the drop in domestic demand was muted by continued consumption growth (particularly by the private sector). On the external side, rapid export growth continued, albeit at a slowing pace, while imports contracted reflecting the investment decline (Tables 2.6–2.10).

How is it that the Philippine economy was able to avoid the large declines in output experienced by other crisis countries? The stage of the economic cycle may have played a role in the muted impact of the external shock on the Philippines. At the onset of the Asian crisis, the country was still in the initial stages of an economic boom (as opposed to the most

Table 2.6. Gross National Product by Expenditure and Industrial Origin at Constant 1985 Prices
(Annual percentage changes)

	1993	1994	1995	1996	1997	1998
GNP by expenditure						
Consumption	3.3	3.9	4.0	4.6	4.7	3.3
Private	3.0	3.7	3.8	4.6	5.0	3.5
Government	6.2	6.1	5.6	4.1	1.6	0.8
Gross domestic investment	7.9	8.7	3.5	12.5	11.7	−17.1
Fixed investment	8.7	7.5	4.7	12.0	11.5	−10.7
Construction	10.6	3.7	7.9	15.9	14.6	−3.8
Durable equipment	8.1	11.4	2.2	9.6	9.2	−18.4
Breeding stock and orchard development	1.9	2.6	3.9	6.0	8.5	0.2
Change in stocks	−30.7	94.1	−44.1	45.5	24.5	−351.6
Domestic demand	4.2	4.9	3.7	6.4	6.3	−1.6
Net exports[1]	−2.5	0.5	−2.8	−2.3	−0.2	1.7
Exports of goods and nonfactor services	6.2	19.8	12.0	15.4	17.5	−10.4
Imports of goods and nonfactor services	11.5	14.5	16.0	16.7	14.4	−11.4
GNP by industrial origin						
Agriculture, fishery, and forestry	2.1	2.6	0.9	3.8	2.9	−6.6
Industry	1.6	5.8	6.7	6.4	6.1	−1.7
Mining and quarrying	0.7	−7.0	−6.8	1.3	1.7	1.8
Manufacturing	0.7	5.0	6.8	5.6	4.2	−1.1
Construction	5.7	8.9	6.5	10.9	16.2	−8.1
Electricity, gas, and water	2.9	13.9	13.0	7.5	4.8	4.4
Services	2.5	4.2	5.0	6.4	5.5	3.5
Transportation, communication, and storage	2.6	4.2	5.8	7.4	8.2	6.4
Trade	2.5	4.0	5.6	5.5	5.9	2.4
Finance and housing	2.0	4.0	4.9	8.3	8.0	3.0
Other private and government services	2.8	4.8	4.1	5.4	4.0	3.7
Gross domestic product	2.1	4.4	4.7	5.8	5.2	−0.5
Net factor income from abroad[1]	0.04	1.38	0.35	2.28	0.35	0.6
Gross national product	2.1	5.3	4.9	7.2	5.3	0.1

Source: Data provided by the Philippine authorities.
[1]Contribution to real GNP growth.

heavily affected crisis countries, which had experienced rapid growth for much longer periods). While there existed elements of a bubble economy (two years of rapid economic growth, with a boom in real estate and construction supported by large capital inflows and rapid bank lending), the expansion was still in its early stages, and the adjustment to the reversal of capital flows was not as painful as for the other countries.

Furthermore, the reforms carried out since 1986 helped to improve the resilience of the economy. The increased market orientation of the economy and institutional strengthening made domestic systems more robust. In particular, reforms of the financial sector and trade liberalization seem to have played an important role.

- The reforms have strengthened the structure of the economy and the financial system, building greater resilience against shocks. The experience of the external debt crisis in the 1980s triggered the associated domestic financial crisis and measures to open up the banking system to more competition (including from abroad), creation of a new and independent central bank (Bangko Sentral), and improved banking supervision and prudential regulations. As a result, the banking system was better able to handle subsequent shocks.
- The winding down of government interference in business decisions triggered further reform and changed the behavior of the private sector. In particular, the backlash against "crony

Table 2.7. Gross National Product by Expenditure and Industrial Origin at Current Market Prices

(In billions of pesos)

	1993	1994	1995	1996	1997	1998
GNP by expenditure						
Consumption	1,272	1,442	1,629	1,855	2,082	2,335
Private	1,123	1,259	1,412	1,595	1,762	1,980
Government	149	183	217	260	320	355
Gross domestic investment	354	407	428	522	602	541
Fixed investment	351	400	423	509	593	562
Construction	149	165	184	231	270	270
Durable equipment	177	208	210	245	285	253
Breeding stock and orchard development	25	27	30	33	38	39
Change in stocks	3	7	5	13	9	−20
Domestic demand	1,625	1,849	2,057	2,376	2,684	2,876
Net exports	−125	−107	−149	−191	−251	−100
Export of goods and nonfactor services	462	573	693	880	1,188	1,478
Imports of goods and nonfactor services	587	679	842	1,071	1,439	1,578
Statistical discrepancy[1]	−26	−49	−2	−14	−12	−109
Gross domestic product	1,474	1,693	1,906	2,172	2,421	2,667
Net factor income from abroad	26	43	53	89	102	127
Gross national product	1,500	1,736	1,959	2,261	2,523	2,794
GNP by industrial origin						
Agriculture, fishery, and forestry	319	373	412	448	453	450
Industry	482	551	611	697	780	841
Mining and quarrying	17	17	17	17	17	20
Manufacturing	350	394	438	495	540	583
Construction	79	95	107	128	156	160
Electricity, gas, and water	36	45	49	57	66	78
Services	674	770	883	1,027	1,189	1,376
Transportation, communication, and storage	78	83	89	101	119	140
Trade	208	231	262	295	317	361
Financing and housing	157	182	209	245	282	320
Finance	59	67	78	96	114	130
Dwellings and real estate	99	114	130	148	168	189
Other	231	274	323	386	470	556
Private services	127	147	169	199	234	281
Government services	104	127	154	187	237	275
Gross domestic product	1,474	1,693	1,906	2,172	2,421	2,667
Net factor income from abroad	26	43	53	89	102	127
Gross national product	1,500	1,736	1,959	2,261	2,523	2,794

Source: Data provided by the Philippine authorities.
[1]GDP by industrial origin minus domestic demand and net exports.

capitalism" and the Bangko Sentral's virtually complete retreat from directed lending activities avoided much of the inefficiencies in financial intermediation experienced in other crisis economies. The business environment became increasingly market-oriented as the reforms took hold. As a result, the stronger elements of the private sector have been able to better withstand difficult economic conditions.

• Trade liberalization exposed domestic manufacturers to more competition, forcing them to learn to operate successfully in international markets. A favorable impact of trade liberalization on Philippine growth is suggested by the discussion below.

Table 2.8. Gross Value Added in Manufacturing by Industry Group

	(In billions of pesos at current prices)						(In percent change at constant prices)					
	1993	1994	1995	1996	1997	1998	1993	1994	1995	1996	1997	1998
Food	140.7	164.2	176.2	209.6	221.7	246.3	−1.6	5.5	2.8	6.6	0.8	3.1
Beverage	15.7	17.9	20.7	23.3	26.2	28.4	−6.7	6.0	6.1	7.8	8.5	−0.3
Tobacco	9.1	10.1	10.6	11.6	12.8	13.5	−3.6	3.8	−0.7	8.0	5.9	−4.2
Textiles	10.5	10.0	11.2	11.2	11.1	11.9	−0.7	−7.4	6.3	−2.0	−3.2	−3.8
Footwear and clothing	25.2	27.1	30.4	29.6	31.5	36.5	7.1	5.5	8.1	−8.8	2.7	3.7
Wood and cork products	6.8	5.6	5.8	5.8	6.4	6.5	6.7	−19.4	2.5	−3.7	6.7	−6.3
Furniture and fixtures	5.2	5.9	6.9	7.1	8.2	8.9	−3.8	6.9	11.3	2.0	11.8	−0.1
Paper and paper products	2.9	3.2	3.9	3.9	3.8	4.4	−8.4	4.3	19.4	−2.5	−5.5	6.6
Publishing and printing	4.5	5.0	5.5	6.0	6.6	6.7	−6.2	4.6	6.3	1.3	3.8	−4.3
Leather and leather products	0.2	0.2	0.3	0.3	0.4	0.4	−2.7	1.4	15.0	13.0	12.6	4.7
Rubber products	3.8	3.8	4.4	4.3	4.0	3.8	−13.7	−4.2	11.8	−8.2	−8.2	−11.4
Chemicals and chemical products	28.9	31.2	35.7	39.2	44.8	49.1	3.3	1.3	8.1	5.8	7.3	−0.4
Petroleum and coal products	33.9	34.5	36.9	40.8	42.8	41.9	−0.7	4.7	7.8	8.8	1.2	−5.7
Nonmetallic mineral products	11.7	14.1	17.1	19.6	22.8	20.6	9.8	10.7	14.1	7.5	12.6	−16.5
Basic metals	9.2	10.0	13.4	13.6	13.8	13.3	7.2	3.9	26.8	−3.9	−1.5	−10.3
Metal products	8.7	9.0	9.8	11.3	11.0	10.2	1.6	−1.1	5.0	10.8	−4.3	−12.6
Machinery (except electrical)	3.9	4.3	5.1	6.0	6.9	7.1	4.0	7.0	17.3	15.3	13.5	−5.8
Electrical machinery	16.0	22.7	28.1	33.7	45.6	53.0	14.9	22.7	13.5	14.7	31.1	6.5
Transportation equipment	5.1	6.1	7.2	8.0	7.4	5.4	21.8	7.8	16.6	1.4	−11.1	−34
Miscellaneous manufactures	7.3	8.9	9.3	10.5	12.7	15.2	8.9	13.3	2.2	6.4	13.2	9.6
Gross value added in manufacturing	349.6	393.8	438.2	495.4	540.3	583.1	0.7	5.0	6.8	5.6	4.2	−1.1

Source: Data provided by the Philippine authorities.

Sources of Growth in the 1990s

Trade Liberalization and Growth

The positive impact of trade liberalization on growth has been well documented in the empirical literature (see, for instance, Vamvakidis (1999)). Both cross-country and time-series studies generally show that open economies grow faster and have higher investment shares on average. These results are robust to the choice of a large variety of openness measures, such as trade shares, tariff and nontariff barriers, and indices of trade distortion. Further evidence, noted above, indicates that many of the economies that followed import-substitution policies performed badly during the 1980s and 1990s. Theoretical growth studies have provided the foundations for these empirical findings, arguing that openness influences growth through more investment and technological progress.

From the late 1980s, the market-oriented reforms are reflected in changes in Philippine trade shares. Figure 2.4 shows that the exports-to-GDP ratio increased fairly consistently during the 1980s, with the trend accelerating in the 1990s. The imports-to-GDP ratio shows a similar pattern with the trend starting to accelerate in the late 1980s.

Statistical tests confirm that 1989 to 1992 was marked by a significant change in the behavior of ex-port shares. To determine formally if the structure of trade has changed during the recent decade, we follow a method—developed in Ben-David and Papell (1997, 1998) and described in Appendix 2.1—that determines when structural change in a variable has occurred by estimating the year of a break in the trend of the variable. (Note that the year of the break is not predetermined, but estimated through time-series regressions.) Application of this method to export and import data for 1960–97 yields the following results.

- Estimates show that there has been a change in the trend of these variables: the hypothesis of "no break" can be rejected at the 5 percent significance level for both variables.
- As shown in Table 2.11, the break year for the export share is estimated to be 1992; the export share averaged 20 percent before 1992, and nearly doubled in the period thereafter. The break year of the import share is estimated to be 1989, also with a near-doubling of the import share from its average of 21 percent before 1989.[5]

---

[5]Sachs and Warner (1995) suggest that the Philippines has been an open economy since 1988. Ben-David and Papell (1997) estimated the trend break years as 1982 using the export share and 1979 using the import share. However, the end-point of their sample did not permit 1989 or 1992 to be considered as trend breaks (as explained in Appendix 2.1).

Table 2.9. Production by Major Crops
(Area in thousands of hectares; yield in metric tons per hectare; and production in thousands of metric tons)

	1993	1994	1995	1996	1997	1998
Palay rice						
Area under cultivation	3,282	3,651	3,759	3,951	3,842	3,170
Yield	2.9	2.9	2.8	2.9	2.9	2.7
Production	9,434	10,538	10,541	11,284	11,269	8,555
Wholesale price (peso per kg.)	10.78	12.11	15.07	17.38	16.89	17.39
Corn						
Area under cultivation	3,149	3,006	2,692	2,736	2,726	2,354
Yield	1.5	1.5	1.5	1.5	1.6	1.7
Production	4,798	4,519	4,128	4,151	4,332	3,823
Wholesale price (peso per kg.)						
Yellow	5.60	6.20	7.40	7.68	7.64	8.32
White	5.03	5.94	7.12	7.93	7.06	7.13
Fruit and nuts						
Production	8,695	8,892	8,981	9,287	…	…
Coconut products						
Area under cultivation	3,075	3,083	3,064	3,149	3,314	…
Yield	3.7	3.6	4.0	3.6	3.6	…
Copra price (peso per kg.)	5.0	6.8	7.3	9.2	8.1	11.3
Production (copra equivalent)	2,097	2,074	2,255	2,104	2,231	1,942
Domestic use	2,516	2,490	2,706	2,651	…	…
Export (quantity in thousands of metric tons)						
Copra	27	24	31	3.0	7.0	3.6
Coconut oil	859	848	1,340	793	1,080	1,177
Desiccated coconut	93	75	73	70	77	72
Centrifugal sugar						
Area under cultivation	384	402	302	396	352	…
Farmgate price (peso per kg.)	7.9	9.5	14.0	13.6	12.0	14.9

Source: Data provided by the Philippine authorities.

Table 2.10. Investment and Saving
(In percent of GNP)

	1993	1994	1995	1996	1997	1998
Gross domestic investment	23.6	23.5	21.8	23.1	23.8	19.3
Public	5.7	4.8	4.5	4.4	5.0	4.8
Private	17.9	18.7	17.3	18.7	18.8	14.5
Gross national saving	18.1	19.0	17.5	18.5	18.8	21.1
Public	4.4	3.1	3.1	4.5	4.3	1.5
Private	13.7	15.9	14.4	14.0	14.4	19.6
Foreign saving	5.5	4.5	4.3	4.6	5.1	−1.9
Public saving-investment gap	−1.3	−1.7	−1.4	0.0	−0.7	−3.3
Private saving-investment gap	−4.2	−2.8	−2.9	−4.6	−4.4	5.2

Source: Data provided by the Philippine authorities.

Figure 2.4. Exports and Imports
(In percent of GDP)

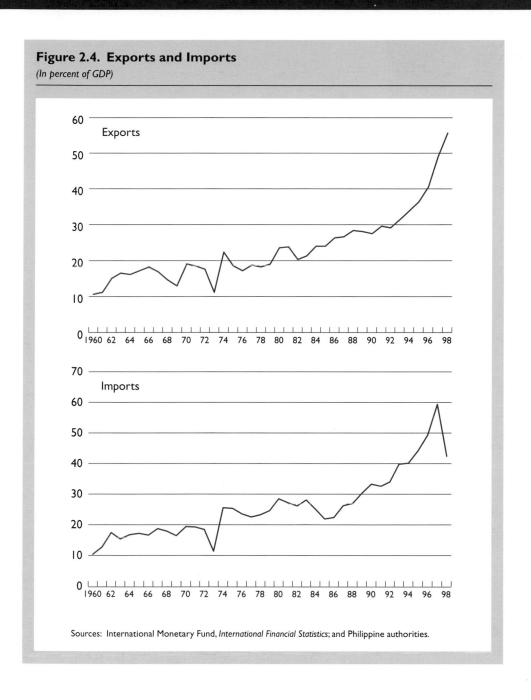

Sources: International Monetary Fund, *International Financial Statistics*; and Philippine authorities.

The estimates above show a structural change in trade patterns at a time when economic performance also improved significantly. While this provides suggestive evidence, a more formal investigation of the impact of trade liberalization on growth has to control for other variables that also influence growth. This is attempted below.

Evidence from Panel Regressions

This part of the section provides estimates of the impact of various determinants—policies and struc-tural factors—on Philippine economic growth. The estimates are based on panel (that is, cross-country, time-series) regressions, and thus provide an estimate of the *average* impact of a particular determinant on growth.[6] These estimated average impacts can be used to shed light on (1) why the Philippines, historically, has done worse than other country groups, particularly in East Asia, and (2) which

---

[6]The methodology follows Fischer (1993) and Barro and Sala-i-Martin (1995).

Table 2.11. Structural Breaks in Trade Shares, 1960–97

Measure of Trade Share	Year of Structural Break	Trade Shares: Pre- and Postliberalization	
		Average value before structural break	Average value after structural break
Exports/GDP	1992	20	38
Imports/GDP	1989	21	40

Source: International Monetary Fund staff estimates.

elements account for the recent improvement in performance.[7]

Slower growth in real per capita GDP in the Philippines relative to other country groups mirrors the behavior of the likely growth determinants. Table 2.12 presents average values over 1970–95 of the growth determinants for the Philippines, and for the groups of developing countries (countries with GDP per capita less than 5,000 in 1995, measured in 1987 U.S. dollars), developed countries, and East Asia (excluding Japan). Comparing the Philippines with the other country groups leads to the following conclusions.

- The Philippine economy remains less open than the other country groups, despite recent liberalization. A variety of trade variables are used to test for the robustness of this conclusion, since trade measures are not always highly correlated with each other.[8] All indicators show that the Philippines, despite the trade reforms in the 1990s and the large increase of the trade share, is less open than all other country groups, and especially compared with the rest of East Asia.
- The investment share of the Philippines is similar to that of other country groups but lower than in the rest of East Asia. This is true both of domestic investment and FDI. However, while

_____

[7]Since the effect of different elements may vary for different countries, the estimates provide an order of magnitude, rather than a precise measure of the impact of a particular policy on growth in the Philippines.

[8]Four variables are chosen, based on the availability of data and their inclusion in earlier studies: the trade share (PPP-adjusted), the import duty ratio, the export duty ratio, and an openness index constructed by Sachs and Warner (1995). The latter is equal to the number of years a country has been "open" in 1970–95.

Table 2.12. Country Comparisons of the Determinants of Growth

	Philippines		Developing Countries		Developed Countries		East Asia	
	1970–95	1995	1970–95	1995	1970–95	1995	1970–95	1995
Real dollar GDP per capita	600	614	1,118	1,172	11,745	14,376	2,640	4,821
Real GDP per capita growth	0.9	2.4	1.2	1.7	2.2	2.2	5.7	7.0
Openness								
Trade/GDP(PPP-adjusted)	12.1	19.9	21.4	23.3	72.8	77.3	70	95.8
Trade/GDP	52.8	80.5	72.0	79.0	93.3	90.7	113.5	148.0
Import duty ratio	14.9	14.8	15.1	12.5	5.1	1.7	6.7	4.4
Export duty ratio	1.7	0.0	4.3	1.1	0.4	0.0	2.9	0.3
Investment shares								
Investment/GDP	24.3	22.2	23.6	24	22.9	21.2	29.6	35.8
Net FDI/GDP	0.7	2.0	1.3	3.0	1.2	2.0	2.5	4.3
Other determinants								
Capital market openness	2.0	2.0	1.8	2.7	5.6	7.9	4.2	5.4
CPI inflation	14.0	8.1	68.8	21.7	9.9	3.1	8.4	7.3
Government consumption/GDP	9.5	11.4	16.0	14.6	17.3	18.0	10.4	9.5
Age dependency ratio	80.9	72.1	81.2	76.0	58.0	52.7	66.3	53.0
School enrollment ratio, primary	96.6	100	76.8	83.8	93.0	93.2	95.2	94.3
School enrollment ratio, secondary	65.6	79.3	40.5	49.4	81.7	101.5	50.5	61.0

Sources: Data are from *World Development Indicators*, with the exception of the capital market openness measure.

the average share of net FDI to GDP was relatively small on average, it has increased considerably in recent years (reaching the ratio in developed economies in 1995). In addition, the savings-to-GDP ratio has been relatively low in the Philippines (21 percent on average in 1970–95, compared with 26 percent in developed countries and 30 percent in East Asia). Higher savings, especially domestic savings, would be necessary to finance a higher rate of investment.

- Capital markets in the Philippines are less open than in developed countries and in the rest of East Asia, as measured by an index of free capital mobility (as well as the average share of net FDI to GDP, as noted earlier). The index—constructed by Gwartney and Lawson (1996) using data from the IMF's *Annual Report on Exchange Arrangements and Exchange Restrictions*—measures both the freedom of foreigners to invest within the country and the freedom of citizens to invest abroad. The higher the value of the index, the freer are capital transactions with foreigners. Measured on a scale of 1 to 10, the Philippines averaged 2, compared with 4 for East Asia and 5.6 for developed economies.
- Inflation has been lower, on average, in the Philippines than in other developing countries.
- The share of government consumption in GDP is lower in the Philippines than in other country groups. Empirical studies have found that government consumption can reduce growth if it crowds out private sector investment; if it increases rent-seeking behavior; and if it distorts market incentives (in contrast, government investment can promote economic growth if it improves infrastructure).
- The age-dependency ratio of the Philippines is comparable to the average in developing countries, but considerably higher than the average in developed countries and in the rest of East Asia.
- With respect to school enrollment ratios, the Philippines is ahead of all other country groups for primary schooling, and behind only the developed countries group for secondary schooling.

Panel regression analysis indicates that greater openness and higher investment shares (including FDI) have a significant influence on growth—which may explain the recent pickup in Philippine performance. The results also indicate that a low inflation environment is conducive to growth. The methodology and estimates are described in Appendix 2.2; the main findings are as follows.

- *Impact of trade liberalization.* The estimates indicate that, on average, opening to international trade leads to faster growth. Based on these estimates, trade liberalization since the 1980s is estimated to have contributed between 0.2 percentage points and 0.7 percentage points to Philippine growth. These estimates should be considered as a lower limit of the impact of trade on growth, since they measure only the direct impact. Trade may also influence growth indirectly through other growth determinants. For example, Levine and Renelt (1992) and Vamvakidis (1999) have shown that open economies invest more than closed economies, and through this effect grow faster.[9]
- *Impact of investment shares.* Higher domestic investment also contributes to faster growth. The Philippine investment share has been quite volatile, and in 1995, was below the historical average. The estimates suggest that an increase of the Philippine investment share from 22 percent to 25 percent would contribute to faster growth of 0.6 percent.

  Foreign direct investment has a positive and statistically significant impact on growth.[10] The Philippine FDI-to-GDP ratio increased from –0.4 percent in 1970 to 2 percent in 1995. The estimates imply that this increase should be correlated with faster growth by about 0.8 percent. If it had reached the average level in the rest of East Asia (4.3 percent in 1995) growth would have been higher by 1.5 percentage points.
- *Impact of other variables.* The coefficient for inflation is always statistically significant, but small, suggesting that episodes of high inflation have a negative impact on growth.

  The regressions indicate the existence of conditional convergence, since the coefficient of the initial GDP per capita is always negative (though not always statistically significant).

  The estimates of the free-capital-mobility variable are not significant in any of the specifications, and therefore, the impact of financial openness on growth could not be established empirically.

  The age-dependency ratio, the ratio of government consumption, and the schooling variables do not have a statistically significant impact, after controlling for differences in the other independent variables. However, these variables are significant in cross-country regressions.

---

[9]Since growth regressions control for differences in investment shares, the estimate of the trade variables will not measure this effect.

[10]Borensztein, De Gregorio, and Lee (1998) find that FDI contributes to economic growth only when the host country has a minimum threshold stock of human capital.

Box 2.1. Estimates of Potential Output for the Philippines, 2000–05

Estimates of potential output are a useful input into policymaking. For example, potential output growth provides a guideline for medium-term growth projections. Potential output growth is also used in estimating a cyclically neutral budget balance, which provides a measure for the actual fiscal stance (expansionary or contractionary, relative to a base year) and fiscal impulse (change in fiscal stance between two periods). Finally, estimates of the output gap—generated from potential and actual output—can be used to gauge inflationary pressures in the economy.

The methods used to derive estimates of potential output for the Philippines are:

Production function approach. This method assumes that economies' production functions can be approximated by the Cobb-Douglas technology with two factors—capital and labor. Assumptions about growth in these two factors are used to derive the series for potential output.

Hodrick-Prescott (HP) filter. This is a statistical method that removes short-run fluctuations and leaves

Estimates of Potential Output Growth for the Philippines: Average, 2000–05	
Production function approach	3.5
Hodrick-Prescott (HP) filter	3.8
Growth accounting approach	4.8

behind a series whose smoothness is determined by a parameter choice.

Growth accounting approach. This method is based on the panel regressions described in the main text. The estimate of potential output is derived on the basis of the coefficient estimates and assumptions about how a deepening of assumed reform efforts will translate into values for the independent variables.

Medium-Term Growth Outlook

The findings mentioned earlier suggest that sustained growth is contingent on continuing with the outward-oriented and market-driven policies adopted since 1986. In particular, the following elements would improve the medium-term growth outlook: (1) continued trade liberalization; (2) raising saving and investment rates, including FDI; (3) maintaining a low-inflation environment; and (4) improved allocation of resources across sectors. Each of these developments would, in turn, require a deepening of reforms, as described below (and in subsequent sections). Under this scenario, potential output growth in the Philippines could rise close to 5 percent for 2000–05 (see Box 2.1).

- *Continued trade liberalization.* The regression results suggest that openness is critical for growth. As noted earlier, despite recent progress, the Philippines is still less open than other country groups; consequently, further trade liberalization is essential. In addition, the experience of other countries suggests that continued growth benefits from trade liberalization require a shift to the provision of broad-based incentives (rather than a "picking-winners" approach), and complementary investments in infrastructure.[11]
- *Higher investment (including FDI).* The regression results indicate strong association between

investment shares and GDP growth. The Philippines' investment share lags behind that of East Asia (though the crisis has emphasized the need to pay attention to *quality* of investment, not just quantity).

Attracting FDI will require continued liberalization and improvements in "governance." An attractive investment climate includes "economic security" (enforcement of contracts; stable legal and tax regime; and reliability of basic economic services).

Raising domestic savings is critical to finance the higher investment rates while limiting the dependence on foreign savings and the resulting vulnerability to capital flow reversals (Figure 2.5).

- *Low inflation.* The regressions results indicate that episodes of high inflation are detrimental to growth. In recent years, the Philippines has been able to avoid high inflation. Continuing this will require prudent monetary policies and a return to fiscal consolidation following the temporary widening of the fiscal deficit during the crisis.
- *Improved allocation of resources across sectors.* As noted earlier, a shift in the pattern of production and employment from agriculture to manufacturing and services would raise growth rates as resources are shifted toward more productive areas of activity. Improving agricultural performance would facilitate this shift (as discussed in Section VII).

---

[11]See Krueger (1998).

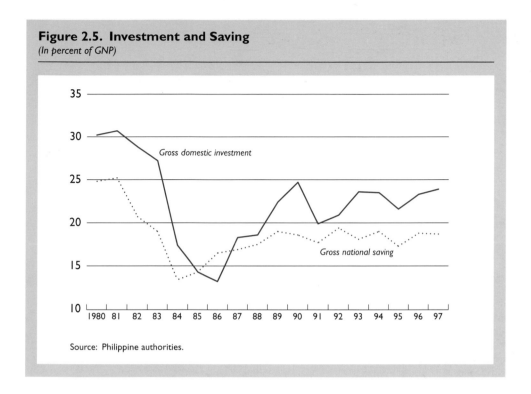

Figure 2.5. Investment and Saving
(In percent of GNP)

Source: Philippine authorities.

Appendix 2.1. Trade Liberalization in the Philippines: Results from "Trend-Break" Tests

The first step is to determine whether the variable of interest follows a unit root process. If the variable does *not* contain a unit root, the test consists of estimating the equation:

$$x = \alpha + \beta DU_t + \gamma t + \partial DT_t + \sum_{i=1}^{n} c_i x_{t-i} + \varepsilon_t,$$

where x is (for example) the ratio of exports to GDP, t is time, DU_t is equal to 1 if $t > T_{br}$, where T_{br} is the break year and 0 otherwise, DT_t is equal to $t - T_{br}$ if $t > T_{br}$ and 0 otherwise, and x_{t-i} is the value of x lagged i times.

If x follows a unit root process, a test in first differences improves power (Vogelsang (1997)). In this case, x has no trend, and structural break is a break in the mean of the change of x. The estimated model is the following:

$$\Delta x_t = \alpha + \beta DU_t + \sum_{i=1}^{n} c_i \Delta x_{t-i} + \varepsilon_t.$$

The number of lags in the regression is determined—following the methodology in Campbell and Perron (1991) and Ng and Perron (1995)—by initially estimating with a maximum number of lags and sequentially dropping one lag until the first significant lag is found. If no lag is significant, the esti-

mated model does not include any lags. Following Ben-David and Papell (1997 and 1998), the maximum number of lags is 8, and the test is conducted for the 10 percent significance level.

The data set is for 1960–97, but the estimation trimming is five years. Hence, the regression is estimated sequentially for each year in 1965–92 (1965 $< T_{br} < 1992$). The value of T_{br}, which maximizes the F-value for testing the hypothesis $\beta = 0$, is the year of the structural break. If no DU_t is found to be statistically significant, then x does not have a structural break. If x follows a unit root and the first model is estimated, the appropriate critical values are taken from Vogelsang (1997). If x does not follow a unit root, the standard F statistic for the hypothesis $\beta = 0$ can be used.

This methodology can detect only one structural break. If the variable in question has more than one structural break, this methodology will detect the larger break (if the breaks do not offset each other), but not any other structural breaks. This is a drawback, but it should be more of a problem with longer time series than the ones used here.

Appendix 2.2. Impact of Trade Liberalization on Growth

The regressions are estimated using a random effects estimator for a panel of all countries with avail-

Table 2A1. Results of Panel Growth Regressions

	(1)	(2)	(3)	(4)	(5)	(6)	(7)
Real dollar GDP per capita	−0.90	−0.29	−0.80	−0.54	−0.38	−0.26	−1.13
	(−2.59)	(−1.11)	(−2.39)	(−1.46)	(−1.01)	(−0.85)	(−2.94)
Net FDI/GDP	0.34	0.28	0.25	0.29	0.56	0.46	0.30
	(2.78)	(3.01)	(2.28)	(1.56)	(4.13)	(3.40)	(1.56)
GDP	0.20	—	0.25	0.01	−0.04	—	0.31
	(0.19)		(1.44)	(0.06)	(−0.22)		(1.74)
Investment/GDP	0.16	0.21	0.18	0.20	0.21	0.20	0.17
	(4.93)	(7.68)	(5.93)	(4.59)	(6.51)	(6.32)	(3.68)
Age dependency ratio	−0.03	0.02	−0.01	−0.03	−0.01	0.02	−0.06
	(−1.35)	(1.23)	(−0.30)	(−1.65)	(−0.27)	(0.90)	(−2.80)
Government consumption/GDP	−0.06	−0.09	−0.04	−0.06	−0.03	−0.05	−0.06
	(−1.30)	(−2.09)	(−0.88)	(−1.15)	(−0.66)	(−1.11)	(−1.12)
CPI inflation	−0.1E−2	−0.1E−2	−0.1E−2	−0.1E−2	−0.1E−2	−0.1E−2	−0.1E−2
	(−3.30)	(−3.75)	(−3.80)	(−3.94)	(−3.58)	(−3.86)	(−4.02)
School enrollment ratio, primary	0.00	−0.01	−0.01	−0.02	−0.01	0.00	−0.01
	(−0.04)	(−0.74)	(−0.36)	(−1.60)	(−0.83)	(−0.31)	(−0.61)
School enrollment ratio, secondary	0.02	0.01	0.00	0.01	0.02	0.00	−0.02
	(1.00)	(0.69)	(0.23)	(0.64)	(1.14)	(0.17)	(−0.94)
Trade/GDP	0.01	...	0.01	0.02	...	...	0.06
	(2.04)		(1.80)	(3.97)			(3.89)
Openness	...	0.10	0.10	...	...	0.10	...
		(2.98)	(2.77)			(2.84)	
Import duty ratio	...	...	...	−0.07	...	...	−0.05
				(−1.76)			(−1.43)
Export duty ratio	...	...	...	0.06	...	...	0.05
				(1.03)			(1.08)
Free capital mobility	...	...	...	—	−0.01	−0.04	0.06
					(−0.18)	(−0.47)	(0.71)
R−squared	0.49	0.62	0.60	0.74	0.53	0.60	0.76
Countries	93	86	83	60	82	77	54
Observations	235	245	207	130	241	224	120

Sources: Data are from *World Development Indicators*, with the exception of capital market and trade openness.

Note: The above estimates are from random-effects panel data regressions. The data are five-year averages for 1970–95. All regressions have GDP per capita growth as the dependent variable. The regressions that comprise the trade share include, in addition, the log of GDP to control for country-size differences.

able data (54 to 93 countries, depending on the independent variables in the regression), with each data point being a five-year average over 1970–95. Since the sample is a panel (that is, it includes both cross-country and time-series variations), the estimated impacts will be smaller than in the more commonly used cross-country regressions,[12] because most of the growth determinants vary considerably across countries, but to a much smaller extent through time. However, these panel regression estimates will be more reliable for projecting the impact of *changes* in policies on growth.

As discussed in the main text, the trade liberalization since the 1980s is estimated to have contributed between 0.2 percentage points and 0.7 percentage points to Philippine growth.

- The numerical estimates of the trade share imply that an increase of this share by 10 per-

---

[12]Growth regressions are usually estimated using a cross section of countries, for 5- or 10- or even 20-year averages. The sample would be too small and variation too little to estimate a growth regression using annual data for only one country.

cent is correlated with faster growth by 0.1 percent to 0.6 percent annually (0.3 percent on average), depending on the specification. The trade share of the Philippines (PPP-adjusted) was equal to 14.2 in 1980 (there are no available data for the PPP-adjusted trade share before 1980) and has increased to 19.9 in 1995.[13] The estimate of the trade share implies that this increase by 5.7 percentage points is expected to be correlated with an increase of GDP growth by 0.2 percentage points during the same period. If the trade share of the Philippines had reached the level of the average trade share in developed economies in 1995 (which was 77.3), growth would have been higher by 1.7 percentage points, and 2.3 percentage points higher if the trade share had reached the average level in the rest of East Asia (equal to 95.8).

- The openness index estimates imply that a year of openness leads to faster growth by 0.1 percent. Since the Philippines has been open since 1988, it is expected that the growth contribution of openness should have been 0.7 percentage points.

- The import duty coefficient is significant at the 10-percent level in only one of the two specifications (and only when the trade share is included in the regression). A possible reason is that the import duty is just a proxy, often not precise, of the weighted average tariff rate. The average estimate of the import duty is –0.06. This estimate implies that a reduction of the import duty ratio by 10 percent is correlated with faster growth by 0.6 percentage points. The Philippine import duty ratio has remained almost the same during 1970–95. As Table 2.12 shows, it was equal to 14.8 in 1995. If it had reached the average level in the rest of East Asia, equal to 4.4 in 1995, growth would have been higher by 0.6 percentage points on average, and if it reached the average level in developed countries, equal to 1.7 in 1995, growth would have been higher by 0.8 percentage points.

References

Barro, Robert J., and Xavier Sala-i-Martin, 1995, *Economic Growth* (New York: McGraw-Hill).

Ben-David, Dan, and David H. Papell, 1997, "Structural Change and International Trade," Discussion Paper No. 1568 (London: Centre for Economic Policy Research).

———, 1998, "Slowdowns and Meltdowns: Postwar Growth Evidence from 74 Countries," *Review of Economics and Statistics*, pp. 561–71.

Benhabib, Jess, and Mark M. Spiegel, 1994, "The Role of Human Capital in Economic Development: Evidence from Cross-Country Data," *Journal of Monetary Economics*, Vol. 34, pp. 143–73.

Borensztein, Eduardo, Jose De Gregorio, and Jong-Wha Lee, 1998, "How Does Foreign Direct Investment Affect Economic Growth?" *Journal of International Economics*, Vol. 45, pp. 115–35.

Campbell, John Y., and Pierre Perron, 1991, "Pitfalls and Opportunities: What Macroeconomists Should Know About Unit Roots," *NBER Macroeconomics Annual* (Cambridge, Massachusetts: National Bureau of Economic Research).

Collins, Susan M., and Barry P. Bosworth, 1996, "Economic Growth in East Asia: Accumulation Versus Assimilation," *Brookings Papers on Economic Activity: 2*, Brookings Institution, pp. 135–91.

Dickey, David A., and Wayne A. Fuller, 1981, "Likelihood Ratio Statistics for Autoregressive Time Series with a Unit Root," *Econometrica*, Vol. 49, No. 4 (July).

Dolan, Richard E., ed. 1993, *Philippines: A Country Study* (Washington: Library of Congress).

Fischer, Stanley, 1993, "The Role of Macroeconomic Factors in Growth," *Journal of Monetary Economics*, Vol. 32 (December), pp. 485–512.

Gwartney, James D., and Robert A. Lawson, 1996, *Economic Freedom of the World* (Vancouver: Fraser Institute).

Heston, Alan, and Robert Summers, 1991, "The Penn World Table (Mark 5): An Expanded Set of International Comparisons, 1950–98," *Quarterly Journal of Economics*, Vol. 106 (May), pp. 327–68 (Mark 5.6 released in January 1995).

Hill, Hal, 1995, *The Indonesian Economy Since 1966* (Cambridge, U.K.: Cambridge University Press).

International Monetary Fund, various issues, *International Financial Statistics* database (Washington).

———, 1998, *World Economic Outlook* (Washington, October).

Jomo, Kwame Sundaram, 1990, *Growth and Structural Change in the Malaysian Economy* (London: Macmillan).

Krongkaew, Medhi, ed., 1995, *Thailand's Industrialization and Its Consequences* (Houndmills, Basingstoke, Hants: Macmillan).

Krueger, Anne, 1998, "Why Trade Liberalization Is Good for Growth," *The Economic Journal*, Vol. 108 (September), pp. 1513–22.

Krugman, Paul, 1994, "Myth of Asia's Miracle," *Foreign Affairs*, Vol. 73 (Nov.–Dec.), pp. 62–78.

Leipziger, Danny, ed., 1997, *Lessons from East Asia* (Ann Arbor: University of Michigan Press).

Levine, Ross, and David Renelt, 1992, "A Sensitivity Analysis of Cross-Country Growth Regressions," *American Economic Review*, Vol. 82 (September), pp. 942–63.

Ng, Serena, and Pierre Perron, 1995, "Unit Root Tests in ARMA Models with Data Dependent Methods for the Selection of the Truncation Lag," *Journal of the American Statistical Association*, Vol. 90, pp. 268–81.

---

[13]Philippine trade over GDP has increased considerably—more than the PPP-adjusted share, as Table 2A1 shows.

Perron, Pierre, 1994, *Further Evidence on Breaking Trend Functions in Macroeconomic Variables* (mimeo, University of Montreal).

Sachs, Jeffrey, and Andrew Warner, 1995, "Economic Reform and the Process of Global Integration," *Brooking Papers on Economic Activity: 1,* Brookings Institution, pp.1–118.

Sachs, Jeffrey, and others, 1998, "Promotion of Broad-Based Economic Growth in the Philippines," a NEDA/UNDP publication.

Sarel, Michael, 1996, "Growth in East Asia: What We Can and What We Cannot Infer From It," *Economic Issues 1;* draws on material originally contained in IMF Working Paper 95/98 (Washington: International Monetary Fund).

———, 1997, "Growth and Productivity in ASEAN Countries," IMF Working Paper 97/97 (Washington: International Monetary Fund).

Vamvakidis, Athanasios, 1999, "Regional Trade Agreements Versus Broad Liberalization: Which Path Leads to Faster Growth? Time Series Evidence," *IMF Staff Papers,* International Monetary Fund, Vol. 46 (March), pp. 42–68.

Vogelsang, Timothy, 1997, "Wald-Type Tests for Detecting Shifts in the Trend Function of a Dynamic Time Series," *Econometric Theory,* Vol. 13, pp. 818–49.

World Bank, 1999, *World Development Indicators* (CD-Rom) (Washington).

Young, Alwyn, 1992, "Tale of Two Cities: Factor Accumulation and Technical Change in Hong Kong and Singapore," in *NBER Macroeconomics Annual* (Cambridge: MIT Press).

———, 1995, "Tyranny of Numbers: Confronting the Statistical Realities of the East Asian Growth Experience," *Quarterly Journal of Economics,* Vol. 110 (August), pp. 641–80.

III Public Finance: Sustainable Fiscal Adjustment

Kristina Kostial and Victoria Summers

Since the early 1990s, there has been a significant improvement in the Philippines' fiscal accounts. The consolidated public sector balance moved from deficits in the range of one-half of 1 percent of GNP to 2 percent of GNP at the beginning of the 1990s to a balanced position in 1996. This reflected not only a substantial reduction in the deficit of the monitored government-owned and -controlled corporations and a strong consolidation in the national government balance, but also an improvement in the position of other public sector entities. Since 1997, fiscal balances have moved back into higher deficits, as fiscal policy turned expansionary in support of domestic demand mainly by accommodating the revenue losses associated with the crisis-related slowdown of growth.

This section describes Philippine fiscal developments in recent years and outlines the reform agenda to ensure medium-term fiscal sustainability. It describes the evolution of the tax system and changes in the level and composition of government expenditures; and developments in public sector entities outside of the national government. It then analyzes the response of fiscal policy to the challenges posed by the Asian crisis, and evaluates the sustainability of Philippine fiscal policy. The last part presents the remaining reform agenda.

The performance of fiscal policy can be assessed along many interrelated dimensions. Tanzi, Chu, and Gupta (1999) provide general considerations that should guide such an evaluation:

- *Quality of the tax system.* Does fiscal policy rest on a fair, efficient, and transparent system of taxation (ideally, a system of easily administered taxes, moderate tax rates, and a minimum number of exemptions)?
- *Level and composition of public expenditures.* Are the aggregate level of expenditures and the composition of expenditures appropriate to the government's objectives with respect to growth and equity?[1] How well has policy been geared toward curtailment of unproductive public expenditures?

- *Fiscal stance.* How well has fiscal policy responded to changing economic circumstances, in particular to the sharp changes as a result of the Asian crisis?
- *Fiscal sustainability.* Could current fiscal policies be maintained into the (indefinite) future without leading the government into insolvency?

Applying these considerations to the conduct of Philippine fiscal policy, the main conclusions of the section are the following:

- *Tax policy.* Major tax reforms since 1986 have been beneficial in increasing the progressivity of taxes, lessening distortions, and simplifying the tax system. However, tax incentives continue to erode the tax base and administration remains weak, resulting in an inadequate revenue yield and weak buoyancy (positive cyclical response) of the tax system.
- *Expenditure policy.* Continued weaknesses in the tax effort and substantial debt service payments have constrained policy choices, particularly by limiting much-needed outlays for infrastructure and social sectors (health and education). Some unproductive expenditures have been scaled down (for example, military expenditures), but others have not, including the cost of an overstaffed civil service and an inefficient intergovernmental transfer system.
- *Fiscal stance.* Policymakers responded appropriately to the regional financial crisis by allowing fiscal deficits to widen in line with the slowing economy. However, faster progress with tax administration reform may have prevented the need for expenditure cuts in 1998, and allowed the provision of a larger expenditure stimulus.
- *Fiscal sustainability.* Indicators of sustainability have improved considerably in recent years. Nevertheless, a review of prospective fiscal developments suggests that the fiscal situation remains vulnerable. Strong economic growth and continued progress in key fiscal reform areas are needed to keep government on a debt sustainable path over the medium-term.

---

[1]The impact of fiscal policy on equity is discussed in Section VII.

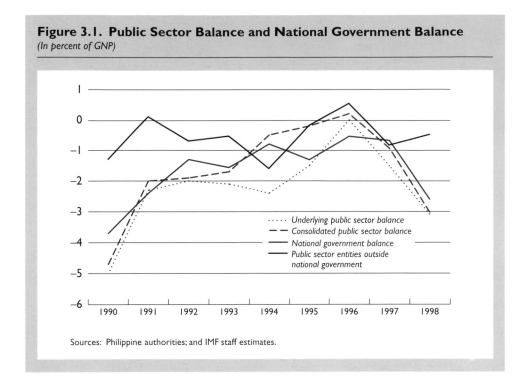

Figure 3.1. Public Sector Balance and National Government Balance
(In percent of GNP)

····· Underlying public sector balance
– – Consolidated public sector balance
—— National government balance
—— Public sector entities outside
national government

Sources: Philippine authorities; and IMF staff estimates.

Fiscal Developments During the 1990s

The consolidated public sector deficit declined sharply during 1990–96 (Figure 3.1). Although some of this improvement was due to nonrecurrent elements such as receipts from the privatization of government assets, the underlying consolidated public sector deficit (which excludes privatization receipts) also improved substantially. Three-fifths of the improvement in the underlying consolidated public sector deficit occurred in 1991. Since then, improvement has been less rapid, and has resulted largely from favorable interest rate developments and from lower expenditure rather than strengthened revenue effort. Fiscal deficits widened in 1997–98, mainly as a result of the slowdown in economic activity associated with the Asian crisis (Tables 3.1–3.8).

The improvement in the consolidated public sector deficit has to a large extent been driven by improvements in the balance of the national government, which went from a large deficit to an almost balanced position in 1996 and 1997. Supported by strong gains in revenues at the beginning of the 1990s, the national government deficit narrowed from about 2 percent of GNP in 1991 to 0.3 percent of GNP and 0.1 percent of GNP in 1996 and 1997, respectively, while the expenditure ratio remained roughly the same. Since then, the national government deficit has widened due to the adverse impact of the Asian crisis mainly on the revenue side. An increase in tax rev-

enues between 1991 and 1998 was more than offset by declines in nontax revenues (excluding privatization). At the same time, noninterest current expenditure increased by about 1.5 percent of GNP, due to a sharp increase in the wage bill and transfers to local government units. In contrast, operation and maintenance outlays and capital expenditures were compressed in an effort to limit the overall deficit.

Other public sector entities also improved their financial position in the 1990s, with aggregate deficits declining to below 1 percent of GNP since 1995. An important element in this regard was the decision of the government in 1996 to discontinue its intervention in the petroleum market via the Oil Price Stabilization Fund. However, in recent years, growing surpluses of the social security institutions, local government units, and government financial institutions have masked a deteriorating position of government-owned and -controlled corporations, in particular, the National Power Corporation.

Reflecting these developments, the public debt-to-GNP ratio declined until 1997, but has picked up since then. Total gross liabilities of the public sector,[2]

___

[2]Defined as domestic and foreign gross liabilities of the national government, the central bank, Central Bank-Board of Liquidation, government financial institutions, the Oil Price Stabilization Fund, all government-owned and -controlled corporations, and the Bangko Sentral ng Pilipinas; this is a broader definition than employed in the Staff Report Tables.

Table 3.1. Consolidated Public Sector Balance

	1993	1994	1995	1996	1997	1998
	(In billions of pesos)					
Consolidated public sector balance	−25.9	−8.7	−4.1	4.6	−23.3	−84.3
Monitored public sector borrowing requirement	−55.8	−7.5	−16.7	−12.4	−40.3	−116.4
National government balance	−21.9	0.0	11.1	6.3	1.6	−50.0
Central Bank-Board of Liquidation net income	−15.1	−8.1	−20.0	−13.8	−25.7	−26.4
Monitored corporations' balance	−25.6	−9.7	−1.3	−11.2	−17.9	−41.7
Oil Price Stabilization Fund balance	−7.9	2.6	−9.2	4.8	−0.8	0.7
Adjustments for intrapublic sector borrowing requirement transfers	14.7	7.6	2.8	1.5	2.5	0.9
Borrowing requirement of remaining public sector	29.9	−1.2	12.6	17.0	17.0	32.1
Surplus of government financial institutions	6.1	3.1	5.0	8.4	4.4	5.4
Net income of Bangko Sentral ng Pilipinas	−1.0	5.3	3.6	−2.3	2.2	7.2
Local government	5.8	4.6	2.0	3.0	4.2	2.0
Social security	11.7	−12.0	0.0	8.5	3.9	17.7
Adjustment for transfers within the public sector	7.2	−2.2	2.0	−0.6	2.3	−0.3
	(In percent of GNP)					
Consolidated public sector balance	−1.7	−0.5	−0.2	0.2	−0.9	−3.0
Monitored public sector borrowing requirement	−3.7	−0.4	−0.9	−0.5	−1.6	−4.2
National government balance	−1.5	0.9	0.6	0.3	0.1	−1.8
Monitored corporations' balance[1]	−1.7	−0.6	−0.1	−0.5	−0.7	−1.5
Underlying consolidated public sector balance	−2.1	−2.4	−1.5	−0.1	−1.5	−3.1
Memorandum item						
GNP (in billions of pesos)	1,500	1,736	1,959	2,261	2,523	2,794

Sources: Data provided by the Philippine authorities; and IMF staff estimates.

[1]For 1998, includes outlays for an infrastructure project of the National Power Corporation, which is not shown in Table 3.7.

as a ratio to GNP, fell from about 110 percent in 1990 to about 90 percent in 1997, but increased to more than 100 percent in 1998. For the national government, the debt-to-GNP ratio fell from 70 percent in 1990 to 51 percent in 1996, before rising to about 60 percent in 1998. As a result of the still high level of outstanding debt, interest still constitutes a significant share of national government expenditure.

Despite the reforms of the 1990s, particularly tax reforms, a number of public sector issues remain to be addressed. In the national government budget, a stronger revenue effort is needed by improving tax administration and curbing fiscal incentives. On the expenditure side, the rapidly rising wage bill and allotments to local government units will need to be contained through civil service reform and a restructuring of intergovernmental fiscal relations. Outside the national government, the most pressing issue is the restructuring and privatization of the National Power Corporation.

Trends in National Government Revenues and Expenditures During the 1990s

There has been substantial consolidation in the national government fiscal accounts in the early 1990s, although part of it was reversed over the past two years. The main issues in the national government budget are weak tax administration, the wide range of tax incentives, intergovernmental fiscal relations, and civil service reform.

Revenues

Historically, tax collection in the Philippines has failed to harness its full potential. Although the revenue effort has been similar to that in Indonesia and Thailand, it has been lower than in Korea and Malaysia (Table 3.9). As discussed below, revenue generation has suffered from weak tax administration

Table 3.2. Operations of the National Government
(In billions of pesos)

	1993	1994	1995	1996	1997	1998
Revenue and grants	**260.4**	**348.9**	**374.6**	**431.7**	**493.4**	**472.7**
Tax revenue	230.2	271.3	310.5	367.9	412.2	416.6
Domestic	147.5	189.0	212.6	263.0	317.0	340.2
Income and profits	74.8	91.9	111.2	136.4	164.2	183.9
Excise	30.3	39.6	38.5	48.4	63.0	60.9
Sales tax/license[1]	33.5	36.5	46.3	59.3	67.7	67.9
Other domestic taxes	9.0	21.1	16.5	19.0	22.1	27.6
International trade taxes	82.7	82.3	98.0	104.9	95.2	76.4
Import duties and taxes[2]	82.0	81.6	97.6	104.6	94.8	76.0
Others[3]	0.7	0.7	0.4	0.3	0.4	0.4
Nontax revenue	30.2	77.6	64.1	63.8	81.2	56.1
Domestic	28.2	76.8	63.1	63.3	79.5	55.7
Other offices	21.1	26.5	25.4	35.1	47.8	42.5
Sequestered assets	0.1	15.3	1.3	0.3	2.7	1.22
Sales of assets	1.6	14.6	21.6	5.4	6.7	0.5
Interest on central bank deposits	4.8	5.5	1.2	0.8	0.5	0.5
Central Bank-Board of Liquidators interest, rebate, and dividend	...	12.7	13.4	21.3	21.5	10.1
Interest from nonfinancial government corporations	0.6	2.2	0.3	0.5	0.2	0.8
Enhanced Structural Adjustment Facility	0.5	0.0	0.0	0.0	0.0	0.0
Foreign grants	1.5	0.7	1.0	0.6	1.7	0.4
Domestic grants	0.0	0.0	0.0	0.0	0.0	0.0
Expenditure	**282.3**	**348.8**	**378.7**	**439.3**	**502.9**	**544.2**
Current expenditure	226.6	296.4	305.8	363.6	403.7	456.1
Personnel services	78.7	92.7	109.1	135.4	172.8	198.5
Maintenance and operations	34.6	46.8	47.0	48.7	51.9	64.4
Interest payments	76.5	108.1	101.1	111.6	110.6	131.5
Domestic	56.2	88.8	79.2	94.1	91.0	105.2
Of which: Central Bank-Board of Liquidators restructuring external	...	29.0	28.4	35.1	32.6	31.7
Foreign	20.3	19.3	21.9	17.5	19.6	26.3
Subsidies[4]	9.1	11.4	7.2	22.6	12.0	4.9
Of which: tax expenditures	3.9	4.4	3.6	6.7	6.7	0.2
Allotments to local government units	27.8	37.4	41.4	45.3	56.4	56.9
Capital expenditure and net lending	55.7	52.4	72.9	75.7	99.2	88.0
Capital expenditures	44.8	43.4	64.5	69.6	93.6	86.5
Infrastructure and other capital outlays	37.8	33.6	52.7	57.5	79.1	71.3
Transfers to local government units	6.9	9.8	11.8	12.1	14.5	15.1
Equity and net lending	9.4	9.0	8.4	3.2	3.0	1.6
Comprehensive Agriculture Reform Program land acquisition and credit	1.5	0.0	0.0	2.9	2.6	0.5
Deficit (–)	**(21.9)**	**0.1**	**(4.1)**	**(7.6)**	**(9.5)**	**(71.5)**
Excluding central bank restructuring	**(21.9)**	**16.3**	**11.1**	**6.3**	**1.6**	**(50.0)**
Financing	21.9	(16.3)	(11.1)	(6.3)	(1.6)	50.0
Foreign (net)	12.9	(11.6)	(13.3)	(5.9)	(6.8)	12.4
Domestic (net)	9.0	(4.7)	2.3	(0.4)	5.2	37.6

Sources: Data provided by the Philippine authorities; and IMF staff estimates.
[1]Including domestic VAT.
[2]Including VAT on imports.
[3]Including travel tax.
[4]Including transfer to the Oil Price Stabilization Fund and tax expenditures.

Table 3.3. National Government Revenues and Grants

	1993	1994	1995	1996	1997	1998
	(In billions of pesos)					
Total revenue and grants	260.4	348.9	374.7	431.7	493.4	472.7
Tax revenue	230.2	271.3	310.5	367.9	412.2	416.6
Taxes on net income and profits	74.8	91.9	111.2	136.4	164.2	183.9
Taxes on domestic production and consumption	63.7	76.0	84.8	107.7	130.7	128.7
Sales and business taxes	33.5	36.5	46.3	59.3	67.7	67.9
Of which: VAT	22.8	25.5	28.8	40.9	47.3	47.5
Excises[1]	30.3	39.6	38.5	48.4	63.0	60.9
Tobacco products	10.3	11.7	13.8	15.0	15.9	17.1
Alcoholic beverages	8.2	9.7	10.1	11.1	13.4	14.3
Petroleum products	8.7	10.6	10.1	16.1	29.3	27.1
Taxes on international trade and transactions	82.7	82.3	98.0	104.9	95.2	76.4
Import duties and import taxes	82.0	81.6	97.6	104.6	94.8	76.0
Others[2]	0.7	0.7	0.4	0.3	0.4	0.4
Other domestic taxes[3]	9.0	21.1	16.5	19.0	22.1	27.6
Nontax revenue[4]	30.2	77.6	64.1	63.8	81.2	56.1
	(In percent of total revenues)					
Total revenue and grants	100.0	100.0	100.0	100.0	100.0	100.0
Tax revenue	88.4	77.8	82.9	85.2	83.5	88.1
Taxes on net income and profits	28.7	26.3	29.7	31.6	33.3	38.9
Taxes on domestic production and consumption	24.5	21.8	22.6	24.9	26.5	27.2
Sales and business taxes	12.9	10.5	12.4	13.7	13.7	14.4
Of which: VAT	8.8	7.3	7.7	9.5	9.6	10.0
Excises[1]	11.6	11.3	10.3	11.2	12.8	12.9
Tobacco products	4.0	3.4	3.7	3.5	3.2	3.6
Alcoholic beverages	3.1	2.8	2.7	2.6	2.7	3.0
Petroleum products	3.3	3.0	2.7	3.7	5.9	5.7
Taxes on international trade and transactions	31.8	23.6	26.2	24.3	19.3	16.2
Import duties and import taxes	31.5	23.4	26.0	24.2	19.2	16.1
Others[2]	0.3	0.2	0.1	0.1	0.1	0.1
Other domestic taxes[3]	3.5	6.0	4.4	4.4	4.5	5.8
Nontax revenue[4]	11.6	22.2	17.1	14.8	16.5	11.9
	(In percent of GNP)					
Total revenue and grants	17.4	20.1	19.1	19.1	19.6	16.9
Tax revenue	15.3	15.6	15.9	16.3	16.3	14.9
Taxes on net income and profits	5.0	5.3	5.7	6.0	6.5	6.6
Taxes on domestic production and consumption	4.2	4.4	4.3	4.8	5.2	4.6
Sales and business taxes	2.2	2.1	2.4	2.6	2.7	2.4
Of which: VAT	1.8	2.0	1.5	1.8	1.9	1.7
Excises[1]	2.0	2.3	2.0	2.1	2.5	2.2
Tobacco products	0.7	0.7	0.7	0.7	0.6	0.6
Alcoholic beverages	0.5	0.6	0.5	0.5	0.5	0.5
Petroleum products	0.6	0.6	0.5	0.7	1.2	1.0
Taxes on international trade and transactions	5.5	4.7	5.0	4.6	3.8	2.7
Import duties and import taxes	5.5	4.7	5.0	4.6	3.8	2.7
Others[2]	0.0	0.0	0.0	0.0	0.0	0.0
Other domestic taxes[3]	0.6	1.2	0.8	0.8	0.9	1.0
Nontax revenue[4]	2.0	4.5	3.3	2.8	3.2	2.0

Source: Data provided by the Philippine authorities.
[1]Data on the components of excise duties are based on Bureau of Internal Revenue collections, which differ slightly from the records of the Treasury.
[2]Foreign exchange tax and travel tax.
[3]Including property taxes.
[4]Including grants and Economic Support Fund and central bank restructuring.

Table 3.4. National Government Expenditures and Net Lending

	1993	1994	1995	1996	1997	1998
	(In billions of pesos)					
Total expenditure and net lending	282.3	348.8	378.7	439.3	502.9	544.2
Current expenditure	226.6	296.4	305.8	363.6	403.7	456.1
Personnel services	78.7	92.7	109.1	135.4	172.8	198.5
Maintenance and other operational expenses	34.6	46.8	47.0	65.4	58.0	63.4
Interest payments	76.5	108.1	101.1	111.6	110.6	131.5
Allotments to local government units	27.8	37.4	41.4	45.3	56.4	56.9
Subsidies	9.1	11.5	7.2	5.9	5.9	5.9
Capital expenditure	44.8	43.4	64.5	69.6	93.6	86.5
Infrastructure and other capital outlays	37.9	33.6	52.7	57.5	79.1	71.3
Transfers to local government units	6.9	9.8	11.8	12.1	14.5	15.1
Equity and net lending	10.9	9.0	8.4	6.1	5.6	1.6
Equity[1]	6.8	3.1	4.6	4.9	4.2	1.3
Loans less repayments	4.2	5.9	3.8	1.2	1.4	0.3
	(In percent of total expenditure and net lending)					
Total expenditure and net lending	100.0	100.0	100.0	100.0	100.0	100.0
Current expenditure	80.3	85.0	80.7	82.8	80.3	83.8
Personnel services	27.9	26.6	28.8	30.8	34.4	36.5
Maintenance and other operational expenses	12.3	13.4	12.4	14.9	11.5	11.6
Interest payments	27.1	31.0	26.7	25.4	22.0	24.2
Allotments to local government units	9.8	10.7	10.9	10.3	11.2	10.5
Subsidies	3.2	3.3	1.9	1.3	1.2	1.1
Capital expenditure	15.9	12.4	17.0	15.8	18.6	15.9
Infrastructure and other capital outlays	13.4	9.6	13.9	13.1	15.7	13.1
Transfers to local government units	2.4	2.8	3.1	2.8	2.9	2.8
Equity and net lending	3.9	2.6	2.2	1.4	1.1	0.3
Equity[1]	2.4	0.9	1.2	1.1	0.8	0.2
Loans less repayments	1.5	1.7	1.0	0.3	0.3	0.1
	(In percent of GNP)					
Total expenditure and net lending	18.8	20.1	19.2	19.4	19.9	19.5
Current expenditure	15.1	17.1	15.5	16.1	16.0	16.3
Personnel services	5.2	5.3	5.5	6.0	6.8	7.1
Maintenance and other operational expenses	2.3	2.7	2.4	2.9	2.3	2.3
Interest payments	5.1	6.2	5.1	4.9	4.4	4.7
Allotments to local government units	1.9	2.2	2.1	2.0	2.2	2.0
Subsidies	0.6	0.7	0.4	0.3	0.2	0.2
Capital expenditure	3.0	2.5	3.3	3.1	3.7	3.1
Infrastructure and other capital outlays	2.5	1.9	2.7	2.5	3.1	2.6
Transfers to local government units	0.5	0.6	0.6	0.5	0.6	0.5
Equity and net lending	0.7	0.5	0.4	0.3	0.2	0.1
Equity[1]	0.5	0.2	0.2	0.2	0.2	0.0
Loans less repayments	0.3	0.3	0.2	0.1	0.1	0.0

Source: Data provided by the Philippine authorities.
[1]Including Comprehensive Agriculture Reform Program land and acquisition and credit.

and the provision of fiscal incentives. Because of low collections from direct taxes (mostly caused by underperformance of the enterprise profit tax due to the extensive use of tax holidays), the Philippines has had to rely more on indirect taxes, particularly import duties.

Philippine revenue policy has aimed at reducing the reliance on international trade taxes while bolstering domestic tax revenue. Mainly because of reductions in

the effective import tariff, revenue of the Bureau of Customs has fallen from more than 5 percent of GNP in the early 1990s to 4 percent of GNP in 1997, and 3 percent of GNP in 1998. At the same time, major tax reforms have yielded an increase in the domestic tax collections by 3 percent of GNP over 1991–98.

Since 1986, tax reform has been an ongoing concern (Appendix 3.1 describes the tax system in

Table 3.5. Operations of Social Security Institutions[1]
(In billions of pesos)

	1993	1994	1995	1996	1997	1998
Revenues	43.7	45.8	49.1	54.2	63.6	84.6
Contributions[2]	23.7	26.5	31.5	34.7	36.5	57.8
Of which: national government[3]	4.6	3.5	5.4	4.8	2.8	13.3
Other revenues	20.1	19.2	17.6	19.5	27.1	26.8
Of which: national government securities	12.2	12.4	9.2	7.9	9.0	12.8
Expenditures	39.2	50.5	50.7	52.7	64.0	80.3
Social security benefits	21.3	24.5	26.3	29.0	30.7	40.2
Operating and other expenditures	3.5	11.0	6.3	7.8	6.8	12.1
Net lending	14.3	15.0	18.1	15.9	26.5	28.0
Of which: national government	7.1	−7.2	1.6	6.9	4.3	13.5
Surplus/deficit	4.6	−4.8	−1.6	1.6	−0.5	4.2
Surplus/deficit before net lending to national government	11.7	−12.0	0.0	8.5	3.8	17.7

Source: Data provided by the Philippine authorities.

[1]Social Security System and Government Service Insurance System, including Philippine Health Insurance Corporation starting in 1997.

[2]By employees and employers.

[3]National government's contribution, as employer, to the Government Service Insurance System.

the Philippines). The two major phases of tax reforms have been the 1986 tax reform package and a comprehensive set of reforms started in 1994 (including the Comprehensive Tax Reform Package of 1996–97). The 1986 reforms included changes in the individual and corporate income tax, the adoption of a VAT, and abolition of most export duties. Starting in 1994, the government embarked on a comprehensive set of reforms that included expansion of the VAT, rationalization of excise and oil product taxes, and major amendments to income tax legislation (Box 3.1).

Table 3.6. Local Government's Budgetary Operations
(In billions of pesos)

	1993	1994	1995	1996	1997[1]	1998[1]
Revenue	44.3	57.6	66.9	75.4	96.7	106.9
Local source revenue	16.3	21.7	26.1	28.7	37.4	46.7
Property taxes	4.9	4.2	7.3	9.9	10.4	12.8
Business taxes	5.3	8.8	8.4	8.7	12.5	15.8
Nontax revenue	6.1	8.7	10.4	10.1	14.5	18.1
Grants and aid	28.0	35.9	40.8	46.7	59.3	60.2
Statutory allotments	27.5	35.2	40.1	45.9	58.5	59.5
Special aid from national government	0.5	0.7	0.7	0.8	0.8	0.7
Expenditure	38.5	53.0	64.9	72.4	92.5	104.9
Current	34.1	46.1	56.5	64.1	83.0	92.0
Of which: economic development	5.3	7.4	9.1	9.7	11.6	14.2
Capital outlays	4.4	6.9	8.4	8.3	9.5	12.9
Surplus/deficit	5.8	4.6	2.0	3.0	4.2	2.0

Source: Data provided by the Philippine authorities.

[1]Preliminary actual.

Table 3.7. Statement of Financial Operations of Major Monitored Public Corporations[1]

(In billions of pesos)

	1993	1994	1995	1996	1997	1998
Total receipts	112.3	107.2	89.2	113.7	117.8	147.0
Operating receipts	102.4	69.2	73.4	96.9	105.6	133.4
Sales of goods and services	97.9	64.2	69.9	92.0	101.8	129.9
Current subsidies	4.5	4.9	3.5	4.9	3.8	3.6
Other	9.9	38.0	15.8	16.8	12.2	13.6
Current expenditures	96.4	74.8	68.1	93.3	99.9	141.0
Operating expenditures	73.0	37.2	40.1	57.9	70.3	108.6
Of which: wages and salaries	4.8	5.5	6.8	8.1	9.5	8.2
Other	23.3	37.7	28.0	35.4	29.6	32.4
Of which: interest payments	11.1	12.1	14.2	12.2	12.9	19.1
Tax payments to the national government	8.6	11.1	6.4	4.5	3.0	3.2
Interest on national government advances	0.5	0.6	0.0	0.9	1.5	0.7
Dividend payments	0.6	11.1	0.5	10.5	4.7	1.3
Capital expenditures	41.6	42.0	22.3	31.6	35.8	44.0
Acquisition of fixed capital assets	33.9	39.5	23.8	26.9	30.5	31.3
Change in inventories	1.1	1.5	0.5	2.8	3.2	10.5
Other	6.6	1.0	−2.0	2.0	2.1	2.2
Internal cash generation	16.0	32.3	21.1	20.4	17.8	6.0
Financing requirement	25.6	9.7	1.3	11.2	17.9	38.0
External financing (net)	21.9	15.4	4.5	16.1	12.3	16.8
Domestic financing (net)	3.8	−5.7	−3.2	−4.9	5.7	21.2
National government equity[2]	5.6	1.5	0.5	1.2	0.1	0.6
National government net lending[2]	1.5	1.9	0.8	−0.4	0.3	0.5
Domestic bank credits (net)	1.4	0.8	−3.7	−3.4	−1.1	12.5
Other domestic financing (net)	−4.8	−9.9	−0.9	−2.3	6.3	7.6

Source: Data provided by the Philippine authorities.
[1]The Metro Manila Transit Corporation is included until its privatization in 1994.
[2]Taken from corporations' accounts; may differ from national government accounts.

While these reforms have produced a more structurally sound tax system, the improvement in collections intended under the Comprehensive Tax Reform Package has not materialized to the extent expected. In particular, the VAT expansion has failed to yield the envisaged revenue gains, with the ratio of domestically collected VAT to GNP falling from 2.1 percent of GNP in 1994 to 1.7 percent of GNP in 1998. While part of this can be attributed to the recent slowdown in economic activity, it is likely that weak administration and failure to rein in tax incentives have also contributed.[3]

Rationalization of tax incentives is an important unfinished item of the reform agenda (Box 3.2). Despite the government's original plans, the final Comprehensive Tax Reform Package legislation did not address the tax incentives problem. Key areas for reform include abolishing tax holidays, rationalizing the granting of incentives under the Investment Priorities Plan, limiting the use of tax credits (which are vulnerable to fraud), and reducing the number of specific laws that render tax administration difficult. Rationalization of incentives and phasing out of tax holidays could result in a substantial, but unquantifiable gain in revenues.[4]

Improving tax administration is also critical. In recent years, both the Bureau of Customs and the Bureau of Internal Revenue have made progress in modernizing their operational procedures—building new computer and information systems and restructuring their organizations. While customs adminis-

---

[3]In addition, the full positive impact of the income tax changes were not realized in 1998, the first year of enactment, due to delays in implementation of some provisions.

[4]The government is in the process of reviewing the fiscal incentive system with a view to rationalizing it.

Table 3.8. Functional Classification of National Government Expenditures[1]

	1993	1994	1995	1996	1997	1998
	(In billions of pesos)					
General public services	40.4	56.1	60.8	76.4	87.8	97.5
Defense[2]	20.4	21.6	25.5	29.9	27.7	28.8
Economic services	75.9	84.8	94.7	101.6	125.0	111.6
Agriculture and agrarian reform	12.6	15.4	17.1	22.6	29.7	18.7
Natural resources	3.4	4.0	4.6	5.3	9.1	6.0
Trade and industry	2.5	5.0	5.9	4.2	4.7	3.2
Power and energy	6.6	5.8	3.2	1.1	1.5	0.9
Water resource development and flood control	9.6	3.4	3.6	2.6	6.3	4.2
Transportation and communications	23.2	33.5	37.9	41.4	45.9	44.3
Others	18.0	17.7	22.4	24.4	27.8	34.3
Social services	71.0	72.2	92.6	118.6	150.5	174.6
Education, culture, and manpower development	39.9	42.4	57.1	72.1	90	104.3
Health, nutrition, population control	7.2	7.4	7.8	10.9	13.4	13.5
Social security, labor, and employment	8.4	4.6	6.4	9.7	19.2	20.7
Housing and community development	1.4	1.2	3.1	5.0	2.3	1.6
Other	14.1	16.6	18.2	20.8	25.7	34.6
Total	207.7	234.7	273.6	326.5	390.9	412.4
	(In percent of GNP)					
General public services	2.7	3.2	3.1	3.4	3.5	3.5
Defense[2]	1.4	1.2	1.3	1.3	1.1	1.0
Economic services	5.1	4.9	4.8	4.5	5.0	4.0
Social services	4.7	4.2	4.7	5.2	6.0	6.2
	(In percent of total)					
General public services	19.5	23.9	22.2	23.4	22.5	23.6
Defense[2]	9.8	9.2	9.3	9.2	7.1	7.0
Economic services	36.5	36.1	34.7	31.1	32.0	27.0
Social services	34.2	30.8	33.8	36.3	38.5	42.3

Source: Data provided by the Philippine authorities.
[1]Net of interest payments and net lending.
[2]Derived by applying functional classification of obligation expenditures to cash disbursement.

tration improved notably, the Bureau of Internal Revenue remains plagued by major deficiencies, including corruption, lack of large taxpayer control, inadequate audit programs, and weak enforcement. The Bureau of Internal Revenue is currently in the process of reassessing its reform strategy.

Expenditures

In addition to the weak revenue effort, sizable interest and wage bills have constrained the Philippines' room for maneuver on the expenditure side (Table 3.10). As a result, capital outlays in the Philippines have been substantially lower than in most other Asian countries. The broad composition of national government expenditures has remained unchanged in the 1990s, with current expenditures of about 16 percent of GNP, and capital expenditures of about 3 percent of GNP. While expenditures show hardly any cyclical response, the composition of current spending has changed markedly in recent years as lower outlays on interest, operations and maintenance, and subsidies were offset by higher allotments to local government units and a ballooning wage bill. The temporary hike in the interest bill in 1998 owing to the regional crisis was countered by restraints in capital outlays.

Transfers to local government units have become a rapidly growing burden on the national government budget. The 1991 Local Government Code,

Table 3.9. Revenue Generation and Structure in the Asian-5
(In percent of GDP, 1990–96 average)

	Philippines	Indonesia	Korea	Malaysia	Thailand
Tax revenues	15.6	15.8	16.6	20.4	16.7
Taxes on income, profits, and capital gains	5.3	9.3	5.9	9.2	5.2
Of which: corporate income tax	2.1	4.9	2.4	6.8	3.0
Social security contributions	0.0	0.0	1.3	0.3	0.2
Taxes on payroll and work force	0.0	0.0	0.0	0.0	0.0
Taxes on property	0.0	0.3	0.4	0.1	0.4
Domestic taxes on goods and services	4.8	5.0	6.3	6.0	7.5
Taxes on international trade and transactions	4.8	0.9	1.4	3.9	3.3
Other taxes	0.6	0.1	1.2	0.9	0.0
Nontax revenues	2.7	1.9	2.6	6.8	2.0
Total revenues	18.3	17.7	19.2	27.2	18.6

Source: International Monetary Fund, *Government Finance Statistics Yearbook.*

which restructured intergovernmental finances (see below), requires the national government to transfer a specific proportion of domestic tax revenue to local government units.[5] Due to its design, transfers to local government units tripled to almost 3 percent of GNP in 1998, and are expected to increase further in the coming years.

While civil service reform has been on the agenda for over a decade, actual progress has been slow. A program to "streamline the bureaucracy" was launched in 1994 to rationalize the compensation structure for the civil service while reducing personnel, so as to maintain the overall wage bill at the 1995 level of 5.6 percent of GNP. While substantial wage increases have been granted to all employees, the size of the civil service has not been sufficiently reduced nor have the wages of senior officials been increased adequately. As a result, the national government wage bill has increased by almost 2 percent of GNP since 1994 to 7.1 percent of GNP in 1998 (Figure 3.2).[6]

Capital spending in the 1990s has been insufficient to greatly reduce the backlog of decades of

---

[5]The national government transfers to local government units 40 percent of domestic revenue of the third preceding year (including 8 percent that is earmarked for capital outlays of local government units).

[6]Following adoption of the 1991 Local Government Code, there was a small drop in national government employment that was reversed in later years.

Table 3.10. Expenditure Structure in the Asian-5
(In percent of GDP, 1990–96 average)

	Philippines	Indonesia	Korea	Malaysia	Thailand
Current expenditure	16.5	8.7	14.4	20.9	11.0
Wage bill	5.6	2.6	2.2	7.9	5.0
Purchase of goods and services	2.8	1.7	3.1	4.3	3.9
Interest bill	5.8	1.8	0.6	4.3	0.9
Subsidies and transfers	2.3	2.7	8.4	5.1	1.2
Capital expenditure	2.7	7.7	2.8	5.1	4.4
Net lending	0.4	0.4	2.2	0.3	0.2
Total expenditure	19.5	16.9	19.4	26.3	15.6

Source: International Monetary Fund, *Government Finance Statistics Yearbook.*

Figure 3.2. National Government Wage Bill and Public Sector Employment

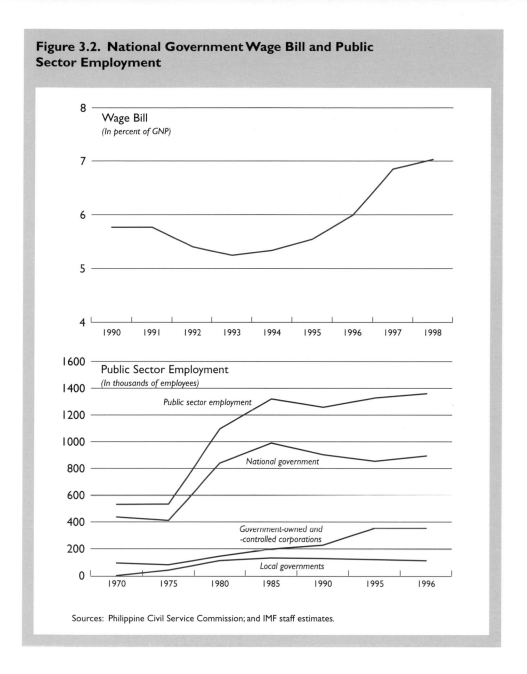

Sources: Philippine Civil Service Commission; and IMF staff estimates.

underinvestment in infrastructure. Despite a relatively high road intensity compared with other East Asian countries, road standards and maintenance are inadequate, and only 20 percent of the road network is paved. Also ports and the rail system suffer from lack of maintenance, and supply of clean and safe water for urban as well as rural residents is insufficient. While the government has tried to encourage private sector participation through build-operate transfer arrangements, private sector involvement in infrastructure has been limited.

Accommodated by a reduction in the interest bill, national government expenditure has been reallo-

cated toward social and general public services (Figure 3.3).[7] However, this development reflects mainly an increase in the wage bill (as discussed above), and has not led to an improvement in the provision of basic education and health care services, as discussed in Section VII.

Military spending in the Philippines has been low during the 1990s, but could rise substantially in the future (Box 3.3).

---

[7]This breakdown includes national government transfers to local government units, but does not cover total local government unit spending.

Box 3.1. Tax Reforms Since 1994

In 1994, the government launched a reform program designed to correct the long-standing problem of low tax collection by expanding the tax base. Much of this ambitious program has been realized with the important exception of tax incentive rationalization. However, despite intentions to raise the tax revenue ratio, particularly for consumption taxes, the reform has turned out broadly revenue neutral.

- The first phase of the program was a *reform of the VAT* system, bringing a significant number of services, previously not taxed, into the system. This law was passed in 1994, though its implementation was delayed until 1996 as a result of a legal challenge to its constitutionality.[1] The effect on revenue has been disappointing as the collection of VAT on domestic consumption fell from 2.1 percent of GNP in 1994 to 1.7 percent of GNP in 1998.
- The second phase of the reform, referred to as the Comprehensive Tax Reform Package, covered income and excise taxes, rationalization of tax incentives, and statutory changes to tax administration.

Excise tax reform was enacted effective at the end of 1996. This legislation rationalized excise taxation on alcohol and tobacco products, in part by levying specific rather than ad valorem taxes to reduce tax evasion. As a result, excise tax revenue jumped by one-half of 1 percent of GNP to 2.5 percent of GNP in 1997; however, with the adverse effect of the Asian crisis on the sale of gasoline, excise tax revenue fell to 2.2 percent of GNP in 1998.

---

[1]Notably, the expanded VAT included within its base value added in financial intermediation services. Such services are universally exempt in existing VAT systems because of measurement difficulties in the credit/invoice VAT. The implementation of this portion of the expanded VAT has been repeatedly postponed and has not yet come into effect.

Also during 1996, *oil product taxation* was rationalized, with a substantial reduction in import tariffs, which was partly offset by the introduction of petroleum excises.

Income tax reform was passed in December 1997. Ultimately, the net revenue gain from the overall income tax package in the form enacted was small.

Major amendments to the *individual income tax* included changes in the rate structure, bringing the top marginal rate into line with the corporate tax rate (currently at 33 percent, but scheduled to be reduced to 32 percent in 2000 and thereafter), and increases in the level of personal exemptions. (The provisions of the individual tax reform, while structurally sound, were anticipated to result in a revenue reduction of approximately ₱8 billion annually; however, a wage increase offset this revenue loss such that revenues from the individual income tax increased slightly). The package included the reimposition of a tax on corporate dividends through final withholding at a 6 percent rate, increasing to 10 percent by 2000.

Important structural improvements were made to the *corporate income tax,* including most notably a gradual rate reduction to 32 percent in 2000; the enactment of a fringe benefits tax; adoption of a net operating loss carry forward; disallowance of tax benefits of interest arbitrage; taxation of interest paid to residents from foreign currency deposit accounts; and the adoption of a corporate alternative minimum tax (although not in the preferred form of a tax on net assets, as originally proposed by the government, but rather as a tax on gross receipts less cost of goods sold).

The Comprehensive Tax Reform Package also included various provisions designed to increase administrative efficiency and reduce the scope for fraud and abuse.

Other Public Sector Entities

After large deficits in the 1980s, the fiscal position of other public sector entities improved substantially in the 1990s. Besides the national government, the consolidated public sector encompasses the following entities:

- Local government units;[8]
- Government-owned and -controlled corporations;
- Oil Price Stabilization Fund—abolished in 1996;
- Central Bank-Board of Liquidators;
- The old Central Bank of the Philippines, replaced in 1993 by the Bangko Sentral ng Pilipinas;

---

[8]Comprising 78 provinces, 81 cities, 1,526 municipalities, and more than 40,000 villages.

- Social security institutions; and
- Government financial institutions.

Their consolidated balance (excluding the national government) has been in the range of small surpluses (in 1991 and 1996) and deficits below 1.5 percent of GNP. Future reform efforts need to focus on intergovernmental fiscal relationships and the financial position of government-owned and -controlled corporations, in particular the National Power Corporation.

Local Government Units

The 1991 Local Government Code reformed the governance structure in the Philippines by transferring more powers to local government units. Along with this reform, many former national government

Box 3.2. Tax Incentives

Philippine law includes a vast array of investment tax incentives of all types, granted by the Board of Investment, special economic zones, the Philippine Economic Zone Authority, and specific laws. Tentative estimates of the revenue loss due to these incentives point to an order of magnitude of at least 1 percent of GNP.

Board of Investment

As originally enacted in 1987, the Omnibus Investments Code provides a number of tax incentives for Board of Investment registered enterprises, including income tax holidays, customs duties exemptions, and export tax credits. Board of Investment registration may be given to firms in export-oriented industries, "catalytic industries" (that is, certain sectors of manufacture and agriculture/forestry), industries undergoing adjustment (for example, textiles), support activities (that is, infrastructure, telecommunications, transportation), and "mandatory inclusions" (for example, minerals, iron, and steel). The scope is broad—it is estimated that approximately one-third of all imports of capital equipment is by Board of Investment registered enterprises.

Investment priorities plan. Under the Omnibus Investment Code of 1987, an annual plan must be drawn up by the Board of Investment and approved by the president. This plan covers priority areas that receive tax and other incentives, and is viewed as a prime vehicle of industrial policy.

Income tax holidays. Board of Investment registered firms are eligible for income tax holidays lasting up to eight years. If tax holidays were to be abolished, this would most likely apply only to newly registered firms, as contracts with already registered firms would need to be grandfathered.

Tax credits. These are benefits designed to offset the adverse incentives of Board of Investment duty exemptions for using imported capital equipment rather than domestically manufactured equipment. Board of In-

vestment enterprises are entitled to credits in the amount of the differential between the 3 percent minimum tariff (or the rate of zero, whichever applies) and the standard tariff rate that would have applied to domestic capital, which they purchase, had it been imported.

Special Economic Zones and Philippine Economic Zone Authority

Enterprises located in the former Clark and Subic bases (the "special economic zones") are entitled to similar tax holidays and duty exemptions as those for the Board of Investment firms, but on a permanent basis. In addition, there are extremely broad provisions for retail duty-free shopping in these zones, extending not only to international travelers upon their return or departure from the Philippines, but to residents of the zones and even residents near the zones. The Philippine Economic Zone Authority (one of the monitored government-owned and -controlled corporations) administers numerous export processing zones that grant tax benefits to eligible firms; these zones have been multiplying rapidly.

Other Laws

Export Development Act of 1994. The Export Development Act allows for various incentives to encourage the growth of export industries.

Agriculture and Fisheries Modernization Act of 1997. This bill exempts from customs duty all imports (not just for capital) used for agriculture; implementing rules and regulations still need to be adopted, but—if interpreted liberally—the implementation of this bill could result in a revenue loss of up to 0.8 percent of GNP.

In addition to the above laws, there exist a plethora of special laws for certain industries (for example, the Iron and Steel Industry Act and Mining Act), many of which fall under the supervision of the Department of Trade and Industry.

---

expenditure responsibilities (in the areas of agriculture, environment and natural resources, health, infrastructure and maintenance, and social welfare) were devolved to local government units, which have become the main provider of the social safety net. To finance the increased local government unit spending, the code has guaranteed transfers from the national government and granted fiscal autonomy to local government units, including local taxing powers and the right to borrow.

Decentralization has more than doubled the size of local government unit budgets. Substantial transfers from the national government, but also improved internal revenue generation, have enabled

local government units to increase their expenditures from 1.5 percent of GNP in 1990 to almost 4 percent of GNP in 1998, while running small surpluses in the range of 0.1–0.4 percent of GNP (Figure 3.4).

However, implementation of the Local Government Code has revealed some structural weaknesses.

- While the code has empowered local government units with many new responsibilities, it has left the existing administrative structures largely intact. As a result, many local government units are not equipped with the necessary organization and implementation capacity to

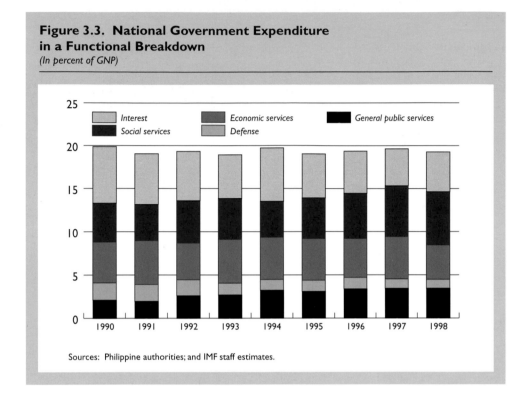

Figure 3.3. National Government Expenditure in a Functional Breakdown
(In percent of GNP)

Sources: Philippine authorities; and IMF staff estimates.

discharge the mandate they received. At the same time, transparency and monitoring of local government units is weak as there are no unified accounting and reporting rules.

- The transfer arrangements are not providing incentives to local government units to increase their tax effort and have created an overdependence of some local government units on the al-

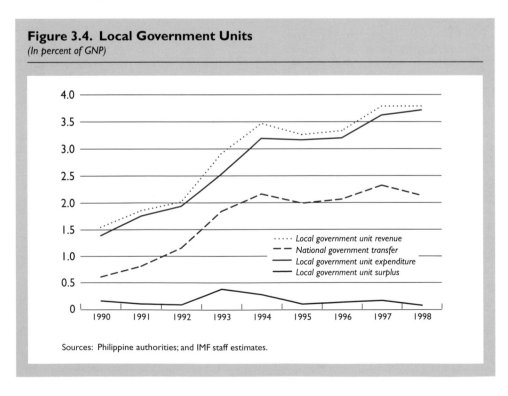

Figure 3.4. Local Government Units
(In percent of GNP)

Sources: Philippine authorities; and IMF staff estimates.

lotments from the national government (some provinces and municipalities now get more than 95 percent of their income from the national government allotment). Also, local government unit revenue collection appears to be inefficient, with the costs of tax collections estimated to range from 30 percent of revenue collected to more than 100 percent.

- Coordination between different levels of government is deficient, and some expenditure responsibilities have not yet been completely devolved, resulting in duplication or inadequate delivery of services. This shortcoming has been exacerbated by the distribution formula, which does not ensure a minimum quality of goods and services provided by local government units.[9]
- While only few local government units have tapped capital markets so far, there is a risk of moral hazard from implicit guarantees from the national government.[10]

Government-Owned and -Controlled Corporations[11]

After a short period of consolidation through the mid-1990s, government-owned and -controlled corporation balances have deteriorated in recent years. Privatization in 1994 and 1995 reduced the size of the government-owned and -controlled corporation sector by roughly 30 percent. Since then, a rise in current spending of the remaining government-owned and -controlled corporations has led to a gradual increase in the consolidated government-owned and -controlled corporations' deficit (Figure 3.5). Principally responsible for this deterioration have been the National Power Corporation and the National Food Authority.

After major progress in the mid-1990s, privatization has leveled off in recent years. In 1986, the Committee on Privatization (to oversee the privatization program) and the Asset Privatization Trust (to deal with the marketing aspect of privatization) were

---

[9]The distribution formula is based on population, land area, class of local government, but not on the cost of devolved functions, the capacity to raise own revenues, or an equalization of needs across jurisdiction.

[10]Local government unit borrowing is not managed within the overall public debt management.

[11]The government-owned and -controlled corporations consist of 13 holding companies, namely the National Power Corporation, Philippine National Oil Corporation, Metropolitan Water and Sewerage System, National Irrigation Administration, National Development Company, Light Rail Transit Authority, National Electrification Authority, National Housing Authority, National Food Authority, Philippine Economic Zone Authority, Philippine National Rail, Local Water Utilities Administration, and Philippine National Port Authority. Metro Manila Transit Corporation was included in the list of government-owned and -controlled corporations until its privatization in 1994.

Box 3.3. Military Expenditures: Developments in the 1990s and Outlook

Military spending in the 1990s has been below the Asian average. Direct military spending has been cut by one-half in 1990–98 to about 1 percent of GNP in 1998, while military spending including outlays for health, education, social security, and housing has been about 1.5 percent of GNP.[1] Currently, about 70 percent of the Department of National Defense's budget is allocated to cover salaries, contributions to a pension fund, as well as direct pension benefits. While roughly 20 percent of the budget is used for operation and maintenance, capital outlays amount only to about 10 percent.

Military spending may increase substantially in the future. The implementation of the Armed Forces of the Philippines Modernization Act (enacted in 1995) will boost military spending as it appropriated an amount of ₱165 billion for the modernization of the Armed Forces of the Philippines over 15 years. The Armed Forces of the Philippines modernization will be financed through an extrabudgetary fund, which has been endowed with ₱30 billion from privatization receipts, but has not yet become operational.

Military Spending
(In percent of GDP)

	1993	1995	1996	1997	1998
Philippines	1.4	1.6	1.5	1.6	1.4
Developing Asian countries	2.0	1.8	1.7	1.7	1.7

Sources: International Monetary Fund, *World Economic Outlook*; and Philippine authorities.

---

[1]Data from other sources (U.S. Arms Control and Disarmament Agency, Stockholm International Peace Research Institute, and Institute for International Strategic Studies) indicate that military spending was in the range of 1.4–2.8 percent of GDP for 1992–96. The variance can be explained by different definitions employed to measure military spending. However, most sources report a declining trend in military spending.

---

created. After a slow start, the privatization process gained strong momentum in the mid-1990s with the sale of Petron and the National Steel Company. In light of the slow pace of privatization in recent years, the mandate of the privatization agencies has been extended until December 1999.

Since the power crisis of the early 1990s, the National Power Corporation has been incurring sizable

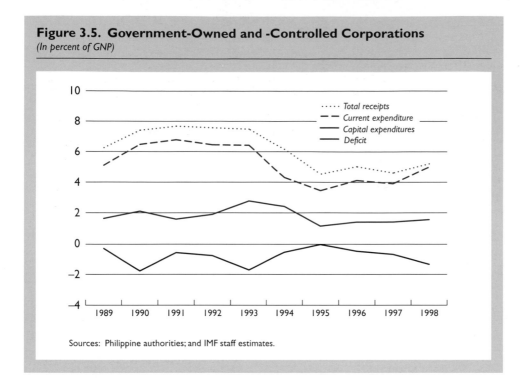

Figure 3.5. Government-Owned and -Controlled Corporations
(In percent of GNP)

Legend:
- Total receipts
- Current expenditure
- Capital expenditures
- Deficit

Sources: Philippine authorities; and IMF staff estimates.

deficits. The National Power Corporation entered the 1990s in a fragile position as it had financed its 1980 expansions by extensive external borrowings (Box 3.4). Its position was further weakened by the power crisis at the beginning of the 1990s. Part of the government's response involved the signing of contracts with Independent Power Producers that locked the National Power Corporation into power purchases on relatively expensive terms for the next decades. Bolstered by fast growing sales, the National Power Corporation's position improved temporarily in the mid-1990s, but it has deteriorated sharply in recent years, reflecting depressed power sales as a result of the economic slowdown and delays in the implementation of tariff increases. Plans for reform of the power sector and privatization of the National Power Corporation have been held up by delays in passing enabling legislation (the Omnibus Electricity Bill).

The National Food Authority's financial position has been somewhat volatile due to its principal mandate to stabilize the domestic market for rice.[12] The National Food Authority was created 27 years ago, with a temporary mandate, until the agricultural sector develops sufficiently. To date, it continues to handle procurement, marketing, and distribution of grains, and its interventions have been costly at

times. In addition to its regulatory and supervisory function, the National Food Authority is involved in providing a limited social safety net to the poorest 10 percent of the population in some regions (by distributing vouchers to poor families, with the help of nongovernmental organizations, for buying fortified rice at a subsidized price). With support from the Asian Development Bank, the government intends to liberalize the grain market in the near future.

Oil Price Stabilization Fund

The government ceased to intervene in the oil market by deregulating the sector in 1996 and subsequently abolishing the Oil Price Stabilization Fund. The Oil Price Stabilization Fund was set up in 1984 to shield consumers from fluctuations in world oil prices and the exchange rate, but delays in price increases led to the accumulation of large deficits in the Oil Price Stabilization Fund. Since deregulation (completed in early 1998), prices for petroleum products are allowed to move freely, and the Oil Price Stabilization Fund has discontinued its operations.

The Central Bank

With the liquidation of the old central bank, a new central bank—Bangko Sentral ng Pilipinas—and a fund to liquidate the old central bank's debt (Central Bank-Board of Liquidators) were created in 1993. The old central bank had been running deficits in the

---

[12]For example, this mandate explains the substantial deficit of 0.4 percent of GNP in 1998 to finance rice emergency stocks in preparation for potential crop damage by La Niña.

Box 3.4. Electricity Sector and National Power Corporation

The National Power Corporation is the largest government-owned and -controlled corporation in the Philippines. It is the only seller of electricity in the wholesale market and has a monopoly in transmission. Distribution is handled by the private sector.

Background

- During the 1980s, the National Power Corporation's substantial expansion was covered almost exclusively by external borrowings guaranteed by the national government (in part because electricity tariffs were not adjusted in a timely manner).
- At the beginning of the 1990s, the Philippines faced severe shortages of electricity, brought on by neglect of maintenance and inadequate capital investment in the late 1980s. The power crisis was alleviated by large and expensive emergency investment projects in new capacity, financed by external borrowing (and some build-operate-transfer arrangements). In addition, the National Power Corporation signed contracts with Independent Power Producers, which locked the National Power Corporation into expensive power purchase agreements for the next several decades.

Main Problems in the 1990s

- The National Power Corporation's debt-to-equity ratio increased from 1.6 in 1993 to 4.2 in 1997, reflecting high operating expenses, increased financing charges, and currency depreciation.
- The arrangements with Independent Power Producers are lucrative to the Independent Power Producers

and expensive for the National Power Corporation. For example, in the wake of the Asian crisis, power sales were depressed, but since the National Power Corporation has minimum off-take agreements with Independent Power Producers, it has had to buy power for which demand did not exist.
- The National Power Corporation's room for increasing its tariffs is limited, as Philippine end-user tariffs are the highest in Asia outside Japan, reflecting not only the National Power Corporation's costs, but also inefficiencies in the distribution sector that are mainly handled by rural electric cooperatives.[1]

Reforms

Plans for reform of the power sector and privatization of the National Power Corporation hinge on passage of the reform program of the Omnibus Power Restructuring Bill currently before congress. Under the reform program, the National Power Corporation's monopoly in power generation would cease. The generating assets would be grouped into several generating companies that would be privatized, and power generation would be private sector-dominated. Open access transmission and distribution systems would be established to support competitive markets in electricity.

---

[1]While East Asian countries' distribution losses were about 13 percent in 1992–95, Philippines' distribution losses were higher by 3 percent. Moreover, the average collection efficiency of the distribution sector is only about 90 percent.

---

range of 1–2 percent of GNP. The Central Bank-Board of Liquidators assumed the (entirely external) debt of the old central bank and—to service the principal and interest on its liabilities—was endowed with government securities for ₱220 billion and mandated to receive a certain share of Bangko Sentral ng Pilipinas' profits. In 1994–98, the Central Bank-Board of Liquidators has had annual deficits of about 1 percent of GNP, and the Bangko Sentral ng Pilipinas has achieved moderate profits in most years.

Social Security Institutions

Reflecting sizable increases in their membership while the number of beneficiaries has been lagging, the social security institutions have been running substantial surpluses.[13] With the exception of 1994, when

the social security institutions invested in shares of Meralco (the Manila Electric Company), the aggregated balance of the social security institutions has been in surplus. After a decline in the surplus in the mid-1990s owing to an increase in benefits, the surplus increased in 1998, reflecting, inter alia, an increase in membership and contribution rates.

However, the financial viability of the social security institutions system is a matter of concern at present levels of benefits and returns. The social security institutions' capacity to pay may be undermined by sizable lending at below-market interest rates to their members and the government and in-house management that is not independent from political interference. This could result in a cut in future pension benefits or the need to raise membership contributions.

Government Financial Institutions

After taking action to improve their lending practices and financial controls in the 1980s, the government financial institutions have been producing profits. The government financial institutions comprise the

---

[13]There are three payroll tax-funded social security institutions with about 20 million members. Public employees are covered under the Government Service Insurance System. Private sector employees have to enroll at the Philippine Health Insurance Corporation and the Social Security System.

Development Bank of the Philippines, Phil Guarantee (recently renamed TIDCORP), and the Land Bank. The aggregated balance of the government financial institutions has been in surplus, hovering about 0.3 percent of GNP in the 1990s. The Development Bank of the Philippines is slated for privatization.

Fiscal Response to the Asian Crisis, 1997–99

The overall fiscal response to the Asian crisis was broadly appropriate, although better tax administration might have prevented the need for expenditure cuts. With monetary policy geared toward stabilizing the peso, fiscal policy took up the task of supporting domestic demand (Box 3.5). The extent of fiscal relaxation reflected the more modest economic slowdown compared with other crisis countries, as well as constraints imposed by the high level of public debt, and concerns over adverse market reaction to a higher deficit. In implementing fiscal policy, better tax collection would have helped shield critical expenditures from cuts, particularly on social priorities and infrastructure.

To examine further the policy response to the crisis, fiscal developments in 1997–98 are decomposed into those caused by economic elements and policy elements, respectively. The analysis decomposes changes in the fiscal balances into:

- endogenous changes owing to economic elements, which are further broken down into three main components: growth and imports, exchange rate, and interest rate;
- changes induced by policy measures, defined to include both active and passive discretionary policy measures;[14] and
- residual changes that cannot be accounted for by either of these elements.

The decomposition highlights the following developments (Table 3.11).

- In 1997, the fiscal deficit widened slightly relative to the previous year, although economic elements worked in the direction of shrinking the deficit.

    Among the *economic elements,* a lower domestic interest bill was the dominant influence on the fiscal outcome.

The major *policy measures* in 1997 were a substantial increase in the wage bill (by 0.9 percent of GNP) and somewhat higher capital expenditure, partly offset by the elimination of the transfer to the Oil Price Stabilization Fund.

- In 1998, the fiscal deficit widened further by almost 2 percentage points of GNP (relative to 1997), with the widening of the deficit owing to changes in economic elements partially contained by policy measures.

    Three *economic ingredients* (income growth, interest rates, and change in the mix of dutiable imports) contributed to a widening of the fiscal balance. The predominant ingredient was the slowdown in growth and the change in the mix of imports, which affected tax revenues by more than 1.5 percent of GNP.

    The *policy measures* were almost entirely on the expenditure side, as outlays were compressed to contain the effect of economic ingredients on the fiscal balance.

Fiscal Sustainability and Medium-Term Outlook

As a minimum policy requirement, fiscal policy should not lead to a situation in which the public debt-to-GNP ratio is increasing continuously. Historical data can be analyzed to determine whether Philippine fiscal policies so far have been sustainable. A medium-term projection can be used to take into account prospective developments that could have a significant bearing on the future sustainability of fiscal policies.

Although there are risks to fiscal sustainability, historical indicators and the medium-term outlook both suggest "sustainable" public debt dynamics. Historical indicators point to a substantial improvement in the national government position.[15] While some developments pose a threat to fiscal sustainability (for example, the system of intergovernmental fiscal finances and the recent increase in the wage bill), the medium-term fiscal outlook appears sustainable provided the government follows through with reforms.

Key indicators of sustainability—fiscal balances and debt-to-GNP ratios—have improved in recent years. However, with a shift to more expansionary fiscal policies in response to the Asian crisis, there has been some deterioration in 1998.

- *Overall balances.* The reduction in the consolidated public sector deficit as well as in the national government budget deficit in the 1990s have resulted in an improvement in fiscal

---

[14]Active policy refers to discrete and well-defined policy measures taken by the authorities, usually in the form of nominal changes in spending or revenue measures. Passive policy refers to not adjusting nominal expenditures as income changes. It should be noted that some judgment is involved in assigning changes in the fiscal balance to one of the categories. Any form of policy inaction can be viewed as a deliberate policy action in favor of the status quo—a problem that is particularly acute in the area of expenditure policy.

[15]Econometric analyses (unit root tests), however, cannot fully rule out nonsustainability of total gross liabilities of the public sector.

Table 3.11. Changes in National Government Fiscal Balances
(Relative to previous year; in percent of GNP)

	1996	1997	1998
Expenditures	19.2	19.9	19.5
Change in expenditure		0.7	−0.5
Cyclical change		0.1	1.2
Change in exchange rate		0.4	1.1
Change in domestic interest costs (including Central Bank-Board of Liquidators)		−0.3	0.2
Other		0.7	−1.7
Identifiable policy changes[1]		0.8	−1.6
Of which: personnel costs (wage adjustment)		0.9	0.3
Allotments to local governments		0.2	−0.2
Transfers to Oil Price Stabilization Fund		−0.4	0.0
Other		−0.1	−0.1
Revenues	18.6	19.2	16.9
Change in revenue		0.6	−2.3
Cyclical change		0.4	−1.2
Income decline/increase		0.4	−1.2
Change in exchange rate		0.3	0.6
Change in mix of dutiable imports		−0.3	−0.6
Other		0.1	−1.1
Identifiable policy changes		−0.1	−0.2
Other[2]		0.2	−0.9
Balance	−0.6	−0.7	−2.6
Change in balance		−0.2	−1.9
Due to cyclical factors		0.4	−2.4
Other		−0.5	0.5
		−0.9	1.4
Identifiable policy changes		0.4	−0.8
Memorandum item			
Nominal GNP (in billions of pesos)	2,261	2,523	2,794

Sources: Data provided by the Philippine authorities; and IMF staff estimates.
[1]Including changes to maintain a constant expenditure/GNP ratio.
[2]Includes change in the effectiveness of tax administration and Central Bank-Board of Liquidators' operations.

sustainability during the 1990s (see section on fiscal developments). In response to the Asian crisis, however, both the national government as well as the consolidated balance deteriorated significantly.

- *Sustainable primary deficit.* The national government budget has registered primary surpluses throughout the 1990s. Moreover, after a period of unsustainable fiscal policies at the time of the debt crisis in the 1980s, the national government's primary balance has been more contractionary than a "sustainable primary balance," with the exception of the crisis year 1998. In Figure 3.6, fiscal sustainability *fs* is measured by comparing the actual primary deficit *pdᵃ* with the sustainable primary deficit *pdˢ*:[16]

$$fs = pd^a - pd^s$$
$$= pd^a - (g - r)d - (g - r^* - c)d^*, \qquad (1)$$

where g is real domestic growth, r real domestic and foreign interest rates, c the rate of real exchange rate depreciation, and d the domestic and foreign debt ratios to GNP.[17] A positive sign indicates that the primary deficit exceeds the sustainable level, resulting in an increase in the debt-to-GNP ratio, while a negative sign implies a decline in the ratio.[18]

---

[16]Defined as the deficit level that could be financed without adding to the debt burden and without resorting to monetary financing.

[17]The character "*" indicates foreign debt and foreign interest payments. This formula does not include a seignorage component, since it is assumed that most of Bangko Sentral ng Pilipinas' profits are transferred to the government.

[18]Alternative fiscal sustainability measures (such as the constant net worth deficit (Buiter (1985)), the primary gap (Blanchard (1990)), and the medium-term tax gap (Blanchard (1990)) are not taken into account, as they are based on a smaller information set of macroeconomic variables.

Box 3.5. Fiscal Stance, 1997–99

Following several years of fiscal consolidation, 1997–98 witnessed a shift to a more expansionary fiscal policy.

- Although the fiscal program for 1997 had envisaged a further deficit reduction, a sizable revenue shortfall resulted in a widening of the deficit, implying a fiscal stimulus of 0.6 percent of GNP. The revenue shortfall reflected mainly administrative slippages in revenue collection, as economic growth was not seriously affected by the regional crisis until 1998; delays in implementing the Comprehensive Tax Reform Package also played a role.
- While the initial program for 1998 aimed at returning gradually to the earlier consolidation path by reversing the policy slippages in 1997, it was modified to accommodate a significant increase in the fiscal deficit to take into account the effects of lower growth and somewhat higher social spending. As a result, fiscal policy imparted a stimulus of 1.2 percent of GNP, reflecting a sharp fall in revenues that was only partly offset by expenditure restraint.

The original program for 1999 had foreseen a return to fiscal consolidation assuming the recovery was well established by then. As prospects for recovery remained uncertain, however, the government decided not to withdraw fiscal stimulus, while medium-term considerations prevented provision of additional stimulus. Thus, the fiscal program was revised to keep a broadly unchanged fiscal stance, with a further fall in revenue offset by expenditure savings.

Fiscal Balances
(In percent of GNP)

	1996	1997	1998	1999
	Actual	Actual	Actual	Projection
Underlying consolidated public sector balance[1]	0.0	−1.5	−3.1	−3.2
National government balance[2]	−0.6	−0.7	−2.6	−2.7
Primary balance[3]	4.1	3.6	2.1	1.6
Neutral national government balance[4]	−2.3	−2.0	−2.7	−2.9
Fiscal stance[5]	−1.7	−1.2	−0.1	−0.1
Fiscal impulse[6]	−0.6	0.6	1.2	0.0
Of which: Revenue	−0.7	−0.1	2.2	0.3
Expenditure	0.1	0.7	−1.0	−0.3
Memorandum items				
Real GDP growth (in percent)	5.7	5.2	−0.5	2.2
Potential GDP growth (in percent)	4.3	4.3	3.0	3.0

Sources: Philippine authorities; and IMF staff estimates.

Note: A caveat needs to be added to this kind of analysis. The analysis is based on the assumption of recurrent cycles around potential output, contrasting the actual fiscal balance with a measure of the cyclically adjusted balance or neutral balance. However, when there are large adjustments including possibly persistent changes in economic conditions (for example, in the exchange rate) and structural changes in the economy, the assumption of a recovery back toward the original equilibrium may be less valid.

[1]Consolidated public sector minus privatization receipts of the national government and government-owned and -controlled corporations.

[2]Includes the net deficit of the Central Bank Board of Liquidators and excludes privatization receipts.

[3]The primary balance is defined as the national government balance excluding interest payments.

[4]Describes a fiscal policy that is neither procyclical nor countercyclical (neutral revenue is defined as the revenue ratio in the base year 1991, when actual output is assumed to have been equal to potential, multiplied by actual GNP; neutral expenditure is the expenditure ratio in the base year, multiplied by potential GNP in the current year).

[5]Defined as the difference between the actual and the neutral fiscal balance. A positive fiscal stance represents an expansionary fiscal policy relative to the base year, while a negative fiscal stance represents a contractionary fiscal policy relative to the base year.

[6]Defined as the change in the fiscal stance between succeeding years. Positive fiscal impulse stems either from a revenue impulse, a situation in which actual revenues grow more slowly than neutral revenues, or one in which actual expenditures grow more rapidly than neutral expenditures, or both.

- *Level of public indebtedness.* After a steep rise in the 1980s, national government debt has been on a declining trend from a peak near 90 percent of GNP in 1986 to about 60 percent at end-1990. A similar picture emerges for gross liabilities of the public sector ("public debt" in

Figure 3.6. Sustainability of National Government Primary Balances
(In percent of GNP)

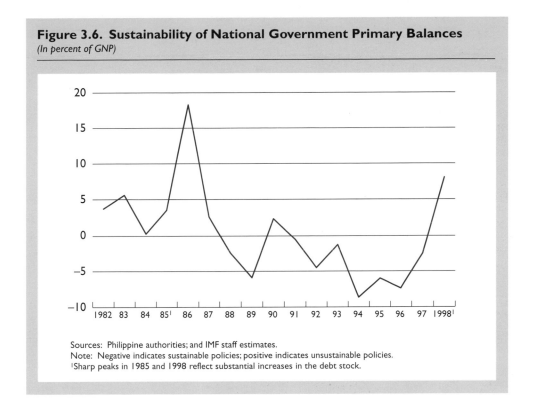

Sources: Philippine authorities; and IMF staff estimates.
Note: Negative indicates sustainable policies; positive indicates unsustainable policies.
¹Sharp peaks in 1985 and 1998 reflect substantial increases in the debt stock.

the following) (Figure 3.7). The peak in the debt stocks in the mid-1980s, with public debt reaching almost 150 percent of GNP, coincides with the debt crisis, when the government had to assume guaranteed private sector obligations in the context of debt rescheduling.

A number of prospective fiscal developments could pose a risk for sustainability. Pressure for more expansionary fiscal policies might arise on both the revenue and expenditure sides, including intergovernmental finances. Moreover, the national government's finances may be adversely affected, as it has to take over contingent liabilities of some sectors (such as the National Power Corporation).

National Government Revenues

- A significant part of the fiscal adjustment in the 1990s was based on nonrecurrent receipts from privatization—a development that is not likely to be repeated in the medium term.
- Planned changes to the tax system are likely to have a substantial impact on revenues. To bolster revenues, the losses from continued trade liberalization need to be offset by gains from curbing tax incentives (in contrast with continued pressures to expand such incentives).
- Weak tax administration remains a major risk.

National Government Expenditures

- The rapidly increasing wage bill threatens future consolidation.
- Weaknesses in intergovernmental finances also endanger fiscal consolidation. In particular, continually rising national government transfers to local government units (partly caused by the present transfer formula) would raise the fiscal deficit unless national government expenditures are devolved at the same time. In addition, as local government units have the right to borrow, there is a risk of weakening fiscal discipline unless appropriate debt management and control procedures are in place.

Other Public Sector Entities

- It is possible that the government may have to assume some liabilities of other sectors as part of their restructuring. These sectors include the banking sector, the energy sector, and other sectors with public enterprise involvement. Even if the government intends ultimately to privatize many of the government-owned and -controlled corporations, it may need first to "clean up" their balance sheets.

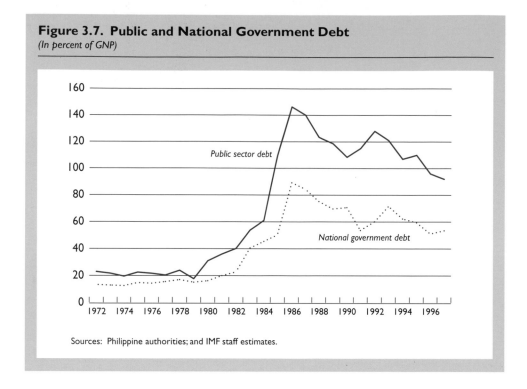

Figure 3.7. Public and National Government Debt
(In percent of GNP)

Sources: Philippine authorities; and IMF staff estimates.

- While a comprehensive assessment of the financial position of the social security institutions is not available, some current features of the system might endanger actuarial solvency.
- The continued intervention in the grain market is financially risky, and may result in a drain on the budget. Owing to the unpredictable nature of the National Food Authority's operations, its intervention adds volatility to the consolidated balance.

Under an illustrative medium-term scenario—which assumes that many of the areas of vulnerability discussed above are addressed satisfactorily—the public sector debt stock declines from 73 percent of GNP in 1998 to about 60 percent of GNP in 2010, despite the assumption of debt from other sectors. The illustrative scenario (detailed assumptions and results are presented in Appendix 3.2) assumes that the national government takes over part of the liabilities and implements reforms in the banking and energy sectors and other sectors with public enterprise involvement. Despite the consequent increase in the interest bill, the improvement in the revenue ratio and the reduction in the wage bill assumed under the scenario are sufficient to permit a decline in the debt-to-GNP ratio. Even if medium-term real GNP growth turned out to be somewhat weaker than the assumed 5 percent, fiscal policies would remain sustainable—albeit, of course, with a slower reduction of the debt stock.

Remaining Reform Agenda

Further public sector reforms are essential to support sustainable rapid growth. The following summarizes the key items on the reform agenda considered in the Medium-Term Philippine Development Plan, 1999–2004:

- *A strengthened revenue effort under a less distortionary and more efficient tax system.* Tax administration needs to be strengthened to ensure sufficient revenues, transparency, and uniform treatment of taxpayers. Strategic priorities are better control of large taxpayers and adequate enforcement procedures.

  Fiscal incentives should be streamlined and substantially reduced. This will help raise the revenue ratio, make the tax system less distortionary, and reduce discretion in tax administration.
- *More growth-oriented expenditure.* Further reform of intergovernmental finances will be key to sustained fiscal consolidation. To avoid duplication of responsibilities and rationalize expenditures, the scope of devolved services should be reviewed with a view to improving efficiency and quality of services. The revenue-sharing formula should be revised to encourage the mobilization of local revenues and ensure regional equity, and the credit policy framework should include appropriate incentives for prudent local government unit borrowing decisions.

The structure and size of the civil service need to be rationalized.

- *Reforms in other public sector entities.* The reforms should focus, in particular, on the National Power Corporation, whose financial position is not sustainable. Deregulation of the electricity market, and reform and privatization of the National Power Corporation should proceed swiftly after passage of the Omnibus Electricity Bill.

The National Food Authority's intervention in the grain market should be phased out gradually. Increasing private sector participation in the rice market should be allowed, and rice should be sold at cost-recovery prices.

Appendix 3.1. Summary of the Tax System
(As of December 31, 1999)

Taxes	Nature of Tax	Special Rules, Exemptions, Allowances, and Deductions	General Rates
National taxes (Presidential Decree No. 1158, the "National Internal Revenue Code," as amended by Presidential Decree No. 1994, Executive Order No. 273, and Republic Act No. 8424, "The Tax Reform Act of 1997")			
1. Profit taxes			
1.1. Individual income tax	Resident citizens are taxable on worldwide income. Nonresident citizens, including overseas contract workers, and resident and nonresident aliens are taxable only on Philippine source income. In the cases of resident citizens, nonresident citizens, resident aliens, and nonresident aliens engaged in a trade or business in the Philippines, income subject to tax is in general taxed under the schedule in the far right column. Philippine source income of nonresident aliens not engaged in a trade or business is subject to tax at the flat rate of 25%. (Capital gains on sales of untraded shares and on real estate are treated the same as for residents. Special rules apply to income of alien individuals employed by regional or area headquarters of multinational corporations and offshore banking units.) Decedents' estates and trusts are subject to income tax on their income, subject to the same rules as for individuals. Income distributed currently is deducted. Estates and trusts are subject to a ₱20,000 exemption. Gross income includes all income from whatever source derived, unless specifically exempted.	*Exceptions—treatment of certain passive income:* Interest, royalties, dividends, and prizes are taxed on a scheduler basis through final withholding in the case of all citizens, resident aliens, and nonresident aliens engaged in a trade or business, as follows: Interest, prizes, and royalties 20% Interest on deposits in foreign currency deposit system 7½% Interest on long-term deposits held more than five years Exempt Royalties on books and literary works 10% Dividends 6% 1/1/98; 8% 1/1/99; 10% 1/1/00 Net capital gains on shares not traded on the stock exchange are subject to final tax at the rate of 5% if the net gain is ₱100,000 or less, and 10% if more than ₱100,000 in the year. Capital gains from the disposition of real estate are subject to a final tax of 6% of the gross sales price. (Gain realized on sale of a principal residence may be deferred if the proceeds are reinvested in a new principal residence, not more than once every 10 years.) *Exemptions, allowances, and deductions from gross income included in the calculation of taxable income:* *Personal exemption:* Single individual ₱20,000 Head of family ₱25,000 Married individual ₱32,000 Each dependent up to 4 ₱8,000	Rate schedule **Annual taxable income — Marginal rate** *(Thousands of pesos)* Not over ₱10 — 5% More than ₱10 but not exceeding ₱30 — ₱500 + 10% of excess over ₱10 More than ₱30 but not exceeding ₱70 — ₱2,500 + 15% of excess over ₱30 More than ₱70 but not exceeding ₱140 — ₱3,500 + 20% of excess over ₱70 More than ₱140 but not exceeding ₱250 — ₱22,500 + 25% of excess over ₱140 More than ₱250 but not exceeding ₱500 — ₱50,000 + 30% of excess over ₱250 More than ₱500 — ₱125,000 + 34% of excess over ₱500 in 1998 Effective January 1, 1999, the top marginal rate shall be 33%, and effective January 1, 2000, the top marginal rate shall be 32%.

Appendix 3.1 *(continued)*

Taxes	Nature of Tax	Special Rules, Exemptions, Allowances, and Deductions	General Rates
1.1. Individual income tax *(concluded)*	*Filing:* Universal filing, except for individuals whose gross income does not exceed their personal exemptions; whose only income is passive income subject to final withholding; or whose income is compensation derived from a single employer, which does not exceed ₱60,000, and which was properly withheld by the employer. *Estimated tax:* Quarterly estimated tax payments are required for both self-employed individuals and corporations.	*Exclusions (most significant):* Life insurance proceeds; gifts and bequests; compensation for injuries and sickness; retirement benefits; certain prizes and awards; certain 13th month pay; social security contributions; gains from the sale of bonds and certificates of indebtedness with maturity in excess of five years; gains on redemptions of mutual fund shares; fringe benefits—see next section. *Deductions:* No deductions for expenses of earning income are permitted to statutory employees other than limited health care insurance premiums. In lieu of the following, individuals may elect a standard deduction amount. Otherwise, deductions include all ordinary and necessary expenses incurred in the conduct of a trade or business, including losses (with three-year carryforward and capital loss limitation), taxes, bad debts, interest paid (subject to reduction by 39% (38% beginning 1/1/00) of the interest income subject to final withholding tax), depreciation and depletion, charitable contributions, and pension contributions.	
1.2. Tax on the profits of enterprises	The same definition of gross income and deductions applies to corporations as to individuals—the income tax is unified. Rules detailed here regarding depreciation, fringe benefits, and the foreign tax credit would apply to individuals as well as to corporations. Resident foreign corporations are subject to the same rules as domestic corporations, with the addition of a branch profits tax of 15% on profits remitted. Regional operating headquarters are subject to tax at 10% of taxable income. Nonresident foreign corporations are subject to tax of 34% (reducing to 32%) of gross income from Philippine sources, with special rules for interest and dividends. Special rules apply to insurance companies. Extensive income tax holidays have been previously granted under the auspices of the Board of Investment.	*Intercorporate dividends:* exempt. *Depreciation:* Rules are prescribed by regulation, and may include the straight line method; declining balance method; sum of the year's digit method. *Fringe benefits tax:* A final tax of 34% (declining to 32%) of the grossed-up monetary value of fringe benefits furnished to employees (other than rank and file employees), including (but not limited to) housing, expense accounts, vehicles, household servants, interest on below-market loans, membership fees and dues, expenses for foreign travel, vacation expenses, educational assistance (including to dependents), life or health insurance in excess of what the law allows. Pension contributions to plans and de minimis benefits are excluded. *Foreign tax credit:* Credit available to citizens and domestic corporations for income tax paid or incurred to any foreign country, subject to a per country limitation rule.	Effective January 1, 1998, tax rate is 34% of taxable income; January 1, 1999, rate is 33%; January 1, 2000, rate is 32%. (Effective January 1, 2000, and subject to certain general economic conditions being satisfied (e.g., tax effort of 20%), the president may permit corporations to be taxed at the rate of 15% on gross income less cost of goods sold.) Nonprofit educational institutions and hospitals are subject to tax of 10% of taxable income. Passive income is subject to tax under the same rules as applicable to individuals, described above. Corporate minimum tax: 2% of gross income less cost of goods sold, beginning in fourth year of operation of the business. Excess over the regular tax may be carried forward and credited against the income tax for three succeeding years.

Appendix 3.1 *(continued)*

Taxes	Nature of Tax	Special Rules, Exemptions, Allowances, and Deductions	General Rates
2. Social security contributions (payroll taxes)			Rates *(as percentage of average monthly income)*:
(a) Pension funds (SSS: R.A. 1161 (Social Security Act); R.A. 8282 (amendments to Social Security Act); GSIS: R.A. 8424)	Government pension funds consist of the GSIS (Government Service Insurance System) and SSS (Social Security System; general populace government pensions for other workers). Employers, including government agencies, withhold applicable tax and make contributions. The funds also provide disability, death, sickness, unemployment, and maternity benefits.	GSIS, SSS, and PHIC contributions are excluded from gross income for purposes of determining the income tax. Benefits received from GSIS under R.A. 8291, including retirement gratuity received by government officials and employees, are tax exempt.	SSS — 8.4% (employer 5.04%; employee 3.36%); for income not exceeding ₱10,000; 1% (employer 1%) for sickness, death, and disability; for income not exceeding ₱1,000 per month. GSIS — 21% (9% employee and 12% employer) for income not exceeding ₱10,000 per month; 14% (2% employee and 12% employer) for income in excess of ₱10,000 per month.
(b) Health insurance R.A. 7875 (National Health Insurance Act)	Health insurance premiums are now paid to the new health care fund (Philippine Health Insurance Corporation (PHIC)), which was separated from the GSIS and SSS in 1998 under a separate new agency.		PHIC — 2.5% (employer 1.25%; employee 1.25%) for income not exceeding ₱3,000 per month.
3. Taxes on goods and services			
3.1. Value-added tax	Credit-invoice VAT through the retail level, imposed on sales, etc., of goods and services and on the import of goods. Threshold of ₱550,000 per year, adjusted by the CPI annually. Persons making otherwise taxable sales whose gross sales are below the threshold are subject to a presumptive tax of 3% of gross quarterly sales or receipts. Under the statute, financial services are subject to the VAT, but the tax has not yet been implemented with respect to financial services. Excess credits carry forward, except for those attributed to capital goods purchases or zero-rated sales. At the taxpayers' option, these may be refunded or credited against other national taxes.	Zero rated: (1) export sales and certain related sales of goods and services; (2) foreign currency denominated sales. Exemptions: various food and nonfood agricultural, marine, and forest products in their original states; fertilizers, seeds, feeds; coal and natural gas and petroleum products subject to excise tax, including raw materials therefore; Import of vessels of more than 5,000 tons and spare parts; personal effects, professional instruments and implements, household effects, etc. imported in connection with settlement; services subject to Percentage Tax (see section 3.2); certain services of agricultural contract growers; medical, hospital, veterinary, and dental services; educational services; sales by artists of their work; services rendered by regional headquarters; sales by various types of cooperatives; sale of real property not primarily held for sale in the course of a trade or business, or of low-cost housing; lease of residential units with monthly rentals not exceeding ₱8,000; sales or imports of books, newspapers, and magazines.	10%.

Appendix 3.1 *(continued)*

Taxes	Nature of Tax	Special Rules, Exemptions, Allowances, and Deductions	General Rates
3.2. Other percentage taxes	Percentage taxes at varying rates are applied to sales of various services, including cars for rent or hire; domestic and international carriers; franchises; international communications services; banks and nonbank financial intermediaries; gross receipts of finance companies; life insurance premiums and agents of foreign insurance companies; amusements of various sorts; and gambling winnings of various sorts. Also applies to sales or exchanges of listed stock (other than by dealers); and to Initial Public Offerings of shares in closely held corporations—these are financial transactions taxes.		*Selected rates:* *International air shipping* — 3% of quarterly *and* gross receipts *Electric, gas, and water utilities* — 2% of gross receipts *Broadcasting (gross receipts less than ₱10 million/year)* — 3% of gross receipts (but may elect VAT instead) *International communications* — 10% of amounts paid for services *Gross receipts of banks and nonbank financial intermediaries as follows:* Interest on lending with maturity less than 2 yrs. — 5% Interest 2–4 yrs. — 3% Interest 4–7 yrs. — 1% Over 7 yrs. — 0% Dividends — 0% Royalties, rentals, other gross inc. — 5% *Amusements* — 15–30% of gross receipts including broadcast rights *Rates:* Sales of listed shares — 0.5% Shares sold through Initial Public Offerings: Up to 25% of total outstanding — 4% 25–33⅓% of outstanding — 2% Over 33⅓% of outstanding — 1%
3.3. Excise taxes	Tax imposed at specific rates; some of the rates depend on retail price.		
3.3.1. Alcohol	Tax imposed at specific rates. Rates vary with net retail price.		*Rates:* *Distilled spirits, per proof liter:* Produced from nipa, coconut, cassava, camote, buri or cane — ₱4–8 Produced from raw materials other than the above — ₱75–300 *Wines, per bottle:* Sparkling wines/champagne — ₱100–300 Wines containing 14 percent of alcohol by volume or less — ₱12 Wines containing more than 14 percent and less than 25 percent of volume — ₱24 Wines containing more than 25 percent of volume are taxed as distilled spirits. *Fermented liquor, per liter* — ₱6.15–2.15
3.3.2. Tobacco	Tax imposed at specific rates. In the case of machine-packed cigarettes, rates vary with net retail price per pack (of 20).		*Cigars:* ₱1 per cigar *Cigarettes packed by hand:* ₱0.40 per pack *Cigarettes packed by machine:* Net retail price per pack — Tax per pack Less than ₱5 — ₱1 ₱5–₱6.50 — ₱5 ₱6.50–₱10.00 — ₱8 More than ₱10 — ₱12

Appendix 3.1 *(continued)*

Taxes	Nature of Tax	Special Rules, Exemptions, Allowances, and Deductions	General Rates
3.3.3. Petroleum products	Specific rates vary with product, per liter of volume capacity.		*Rates by product, per liter of volume:* Lubricating oils ₱4.5 Processed gas ₱5.0 Naphtha, regular gasoline ₱4.8 Leaded premium gasoline ₱5.35 Unleaded premium gasoline ₱4.35 Aviation turbo jet fuel ₱3.67 Kerosene ₱0.6 Diesel fuel ₱1.63 Liquefied petroleum gas ₱0 Bunker fuel oil ₱0.3
3.3.4. Automobiles	Ad valorem rates based on engine displacement. In the case of imported automobiles *not for sale,* tax imposed on base equal to total customs value including duties, plus 10%.		*Rates:* *Engine displacement in cc's* *Gasoline* / *Diesel* / *Rate of tax* up to 1,600 / up to 1,800 / 15% 1,601 to 2,000 / 1,801 to 2,300 / 35% 2,001 to 2,700 / 2,301 to 3,000 / 50% 2,701 or over / 3,001 or over / 100%
3.3.5. Luxuries	Ad valorem rate on jewelry, perfumes, and pleasure vessels and yachts.		20% of wholesale price or import value used by Customs, net of excise and VAT.
4. Documentary stamp taxes	Stamp tax falls upon issuance and transfer of financial instruments, deeds, mortgages, other instruments (but not upon financial derivatives). Tax applies to bonds, stocks, debentures issued in foreign countries if sold or transferred in the Philippines.		*Some rates:* Issuance of debentures and certificates of indebtedness—₱1.50 per ₱200 face value; sales and transfers of shares—₱1.50 per ₱200 par value. Each bank check or order for payment—₱1.50 bonds; loan agreements, deposit substitutes, bills of exchange, government securities—₱0.30 per ₱200 face value.
5. Customs duty (Tariff and Customs Code)			

(a) Import tariffs	Tariffs are being reduced gradually under the reform program.	*Exemptions:* Many import tariff incentives have been granted under Board of Investment programs. There are also various special economic zones, including the former Clark and Subic airbases, in which imports are duty free. The annual investment incentive plans entail tariff exemptions as well.	Effective protection rates:
			Overall weighted average
			  in 1998: 13.2%
			
			Agriculture, fishery,
			  and forestry 14.3%
			  Agriculture 18.8%
			  Fishery 8.2%
			  Forestry 2.7%
			Mining 0.6%
			Manufacturing 13.5%

(b) Export tariffs	None.		
6. Mineral excises	Tax based on gross output (but see metallic minerals).		*Rates:* Coal and coke ₱10 per metric ton Nonmetallic minerals 2% of actual market value Metallic minerals Rates increasing from 1% to 2% of actual market value over six years Indigenous petroleum 3% of fair international market price, first taxable sale after extraction

Appendix 3.1 *(concluded)*

Taxes	Nature of Tax	Special Rules, Exemptions, Allowances, and Deductions	General Rates
7. Estate and donor's taxes 7.1. Estate tax	Net estate of both resident and nonresident decedents is subject to tax. Only that part of the gross estate located in the Philippines is included in the net estate of a nonresident.	*Exemption* for first ₱200,000. *Deductions from gross estate* for: expenses and claims against the estate; property received by bequest or gift within five years of death and previously subject to estate or donor's tax (proportionate phaseout of deduction over five years); bequests from the estate for public use; net share of surviving spouse in conjugal property. *Foreign tax* credit for estate tax imposed by other countries, subject to per country limitation.	Marginal rates of estate tax range from 5%, from ₱200,000 to ₱500,000, up to 20% on the *value of the net estate* in excess of ₱10,000,000.
7.2. Donor's tax	Total net gifts annually made by resident or nonresident persons, direct or indirect, in trust or outright, are subject to tax for the donor.	*Exemption* for the first ₱100,000. *Exemptions* in the case of residents for dowries or gifts made on account of marriage by parents up to ₱10,000; gifts made to the national government or its subdivisions; charitable gifts to accredited organizations. The latter two exemptions also apply to nonresidents. *Foreign tax credit* for donor's taxes imposed by foreign countries.	Marginal rates of donor's tax range from 2% from ₱100,000 to ₱200,000, up to 15% where net gifts exceed ₱10,000,000. Net gifts to "strangers" (those outside specified degrees of relationship) are taxable at 30% regardless of amount.

The actuarial solvency of social security institutions needs to be preserved, including by improving the management of their investment resources and delinking them from political interference. Moreover, the coverage of social security institutions should be extended.

Appendix 3.2. Illustrative Medium-Term Scenario

The illustrative scenario (see Table 3A1) is predicated on the following principal assumptions and reforms:

- Real GNP growth will pick up to 5 percent in the medium term, while inflation will stabilize at 5 percent.
- Government savings rise by 2 percent of GNP over the next 10 years, with capital spending increasing from 3 percent of GNP to 4 percent of GNP.
- Impending reforms of the taxation of the financial sector, the tariff structure, and tax incentives will be revenue neutral. At the same time,

the revenue ratio (excluding Central Bank-Board of Liquidators) will be raised by about 2 percent of GNP over the next five years, to return to the level of 1997.
- The wage bill will be reduced gradually over the next five years from 6.5 percent of GNP in 1999 to 5.6 percent of GNP in 2006.
- The reform of intergovernmental relationships will stabilize national government transfers to local government units at about 4 percent of GNP from 2003 onward.
- As a working assumption, the national government budget will assume long-term debt from other sectors of about 15 percent of GNP.
- The deficit of the government-owned and -controlled corporations will be eliminated gradually over the medium term.
- For presentational simplicity, it is assumed that the national government will take over the debt service for the entire stock of public debt and the financing of the government-owned and -controlled corporation and Central Bank-Board of Liquidators deficits from 2000 onward. The scenario does not take into account any surpluses of the remaining public sector entities (social security institutions, govern-

Table 3A1. Illustrative Medium-Term Fiscal Scenario
(In percent of GNP)

	1998	1999	2000	2001	2002	2003	2004	2005	2006	2007	2008	2009	2010
Public debt	72.9	90.8	80.2	80.5	79.5	78.0	76.2	74.2	72.0	69.5	66.9	64.1	61.3
Foreign	38.5	47.9	41.7	39.0	36.1	33.5	31.1	28.8	26.7	24.8	23.0	21.3	19.8
Domestic	34.5	42.9	38.6	41.6	43.4	44.5	45.1	45.4	45.3	44.7	43.9	42.8	41.5
National government deficit	−1.9	−2.3	−4.3	−3.9	−3.7	−3.5	−3.4	−3.2	−2.9	−2.7	−2.4	−2.3	−2.1
Revenues	16.5	15.8	16.6	16.9	17.2	17.5	17.7	17.9	18.1	18.2	18.3	18.3	18.3
Expenditure	18.3	18.1	20.9	20.8	20.9	21.0	21.1	21.1	21.0	20.9	20.7	20.6	20.4
Of which: interest bill[1]	3.6	3.4	5.5	5.3	5.4	5.4	5.4	5.4	5.3	5.2	5.0	4.9	4.7
Of which: capital expenditure	3.1	3.0	3.4	3.5	3.6	3.7	3.8	3.9	4.0	4.0	4.0	4.0	4.0
Of which: wage bill	7.1	6.4	6.4	6.3	6.1	5.9	5.8	5.7	5.6	5.6	5.6	5.6	5.6
Of which: maintenance	2.3	2.1	2.4	2.5	2.6	2.7	2.7	2.7	2.7	2.7	2.7	2.7	2.7
Government-owned and -controlled corporation deficit	−1.5	−1.1	−0.9	−0.8	−0.7	−0.6	−0.5	−0.4	−0.3	−0.3	−0.2	−0.2	−0.1
Central Bank-Board of Liquidators deficit	−0.9	−0.4	−0.7	−0.6	−0.5	−0.4	−0.4	−0.3	−0.3	−0.2	−0.2	−0.1	−0.1

Source: IMF staff estimates.
[1]Assumes that the national government will service all public sector debt (including Central Bank-Board of Liquidators and government-owned and -controlled corporations) and assume liabilities of 15% of GNP of other sectors.

ment financial institutions, and local government units).

References

Blanchard, Olivier Jean, 1990, "Suggestions for a New Set of Fiscal Indicators," OECD Working Paper No. 79 (Paris: Organization for Economic Cooperation and Development).

Buiter, William H., 1985, "A Guide to Public Sector Debt and Deficits," *Economic Policy,* Vol. 1 (September).

Tanzi, Vito, Ke-young Chu, and Sanjeev Gupta, eds., 1999, *Economic Policy and Equity* (Washington: International Monetary Fund).

IV Monetary and Exchange Rate Policy

Vivek B. Arora

Over the past two decades, the Philippines has been transformed from an economy that performed substantially below its potential to a dynamic emerging-market economy. Most recently, the economy has been able to weather the Asian crisis better than many other countries in the region, and has emerged from the crisis with strengthened institutions and a track record of successful crisis management.

A key feature underlying the transformation and the favorable recent experience has been the evolution of monetary policy institutions and decision making, from a controlled and only partially effective system in the early 1980s to an independent, well-functioning system at the end of the 1990s. In the early 1980s, monetary policy was far from independent and lacked a coherent focus, contributing to a loss of monetary control, spiraling inflation, and a full-blown external payments crisis. At the end of the 1990s, the situation is dramatically different, with an independent, modern central bank that has a clear mandate to control inflation and an established reputation for sound macroeconomic management.

A crucial element underlying the improvement in monetary policy implementation has been the establishment of a new central bank, the Bangko Sentral ng Pilipinas. The old Central Bank of the Philippines became insolvent, largely as a result of its bailing out of domestic banks that had run into financial difficulties during the 1980s, and was closed down in 1993. In the same year, the new Bangko Sentral ng Pilipinas was established with a fresh balance sheet, recapitalized by the national government, and given a clear mandate under the revised Central Bank Act to pursue price stability conducive to sustained growth. Since its establishment, the Bangko Sentral ng Pilipinas has faced new challenges, including a surge in capital inflows (1994–96) and their sharp reversal in the wake of the Asian crisis (1997–98). The Bangko Sentral ng Pilipinas has met these challenges successfully, although at times a certain lack of clarity in the monetary framework has hampered policy implementation (for example, in resolving the tensions between external and domestic targets). Overall, however, monetary policy under the Bangko Sentral ng Pilipinas has consistently been marked by a clear focus on macroeconomic stability.

A signal achievement of the Bangko Sentral ng Pilipinas has been successful monetary management during the Asian crisis. The crisis management strategy centered around the floating of the peso accompanied by a relatively tight interest rate policy. Exchange market intervention was limited to what was needed for building up reserves to programmed levels and for "smoothing" operations (providing liquidity during periods of severe market pressure). Interest rates were used to "lean against the wind" of exchange market pressure—without, however, using interest rates aggressively to defend a particular level of the peso. Nonmarket measures (for example, a volatility band on daily fluctuations) were sometimes used to support the exchange rate when exchange market pressures were especially severe, but their use was only temporary. Since late 1998, with the peso stabilizing and inflation well under control, monetary policy has shifted toward supporting the recovery. Credit growth has remained weak, however, notwithstanding the decline of interest rates below precrisis levels. Reviving credit growth without undermining the hard-won stabilization gains has become an important policy concern.

In the period ahead, the main challenges for the Bangko Sentral ng Pilipinas are to control inflation and sustain confidence in the peso on a lasting basis. Consistent with its legal mandate, the Bangko Sentral ng Pilipinas will need to consolidate its independence in pursuing the goal of price stability. As key requirements to this end, the Bangko Sentral ng Pilipinas needs to maintain a strong financial position and implement monetary policy in a consistent and transparent framework that is well understood by the public.

Early Experience: 1980–93

Crisis, Reforms, and Renewed Pressures

Monetary developments during the 1980s and early 1990s were marked by two "watersheds"—the debt crisis in 1983 and the demise of the old central bank in 1993. Throughout the period, monetary policy was conducted in a difficult environment, characterized by conflicting demands on the central bank as well as political and economic instability. Monetary policy lacked a coherent focus because the central bank had limited autonomy and no clear mandate on the basis of which to resolve these conflicting demands. The central bank was expected to play its traditional monetary role, but in addition was burdened with financing the fiscal deficit, bailing out troubled commercial banks, and channeling resources to priority sectors. The effectiveness of bank supervision was hampered by government interference in the banking system, which also featured large-scale lending by government financial institutions to nonviable borrowers, often at controlled interest rates.[1]

In the early 1980s, a combination of elements contributed to a buildup of financial pressures. The external position weakened as expansionary fiscal policies were financed by accumulation of external debt and monetary policy accommodated rapid credit expansion by domestic banks. The imbalances became unsustainable in the face of a series of external and domestic shocks. In 1983, massive capital flight triggered off a full-blown financial crisis, including default on external debt service and widespread insolvency of domestic banks and enterprises. A deep and protracted recession followed, with four years of economic contraction and aftereffects of the crisis that continued to affect the economy for a decade.[2]

The response to the crisis entailed an important change in the monetary regime, featuring a floating exchange rate system and a shifting of monetary policy implementation away from controls and toward more indirect instruments. After large devaluations in 1983–84, and a sharp rise in inflation, the central bank in 1984 switched to a floating exchange rate system and adopted base money as the chief intermediate monetary target. Interest rate controls and credit ceilings were phased out and replaced by open-market instruments and reserve requirements as main tools of monetary control. The new focus on base money facilitated the restoration of monetary control, and inflation was brought down relatively quickly—albeit in an environment of high real interest rates and contracting economic activity.

The second half of the 1980s saw further progress in improving monetary operations, although the legacy of the crisis continued to weigh heavily on the economy. The period saw important reforms in

bank supervision, development of monetary policy instruments, and major reforms in public enterprises and banks. These reforms were supported by the accession of a new government (led by Corazon Aquino) in 1986 that oversaw an improvement in public governance and a new, market-oriented, and outward-looking approach to economic policies. Commercial banks, however, continued to suffer from weak balance sheets and high intermediation costs (the latter in part resulting from the weak financial position of the central bank), while the unresolved external debt situation cut off the country from foreign credit and, more generally, undermined confidence. As a result, domestic interest rates remained high throughout the period. Toward the end of the decade, fiscal and monetary policies slipped again, partly under the pressure of political instability. While formally floating, the exchange rate of the peso was "managed" to a significant extent during this period (including through moral suasion by the central bank). The rising imbalances were exacerbated by external and domestic shocks, leading to a near-crisis in 1990–91 that again necessitated a sharp adjustment of macroeconomic policies. In the ensuing slowdown of growth, banks' balance sheet problems arose again, triggering renewed emergency assistance by the central bank.

Years of Change: 1993–97

A Reformed Central Bank and New Challenges for Monetary Policy

Starting in 1993, economic policies were given a renewed focus on macroeconomic stability and market-oriented reforms under the new administration of President Fidel Ramos elected the previous year. Political stability was regained and reforms initiated in key sectors, including banking. Macroeconomic policies were focused more clearly on stability—a key measure in this regard being the establishment of a new central bank.

A Reformed Central Bank

The new Bangko Sentral ng Pilipinas was established in 1993 as an independent monetary authority with full administrative autonomy (Box 4.1).[3] With a strengthened balance sheet and the legal autonomy provided to it by the new Central Bank Act, the Bangko Sentral ng Pilipinas was well placed to implement monetary policy effectively and to facilitate

---

[1]On the macroeconomic setting in the 1980s, see Templo (1998) for a brief but lucid summary; and Dohner and Intal (1988) and World Bank (1987) for more detailed discussions.

[2]See World Bank (1987) for a fuller discussion of the episode.

---

[3]The old central bank was declared insolvent and its assets and liabilities transferred to the Central Bank-Board of Liquidators.

Box 4.1. The Bangko Sentral ng Pilipinas

Establishment. The Bangko Sentral ng Pilipinas was established in 1993 to replace the former Central Bank of the Philippines.

The Central Bank of the Philippines suffered extensive losses as a result of its rescues of domestic banks in the 1980s and eventually became insolvent. The bad assets of the Central Bank of the Philippines were taken over by a new body, the Central Bank-Board of Liquidators, and the Bangko Sentral ng Pilipinas was established as the new central bank.

Establishment of the Bangko Sentral ng Pilipinas entailed an extensive restructuring of its administrative setup and operating procedures as well as a recapitalization program. The balance sheet of the Bangko Sentral ng Pilipinas was fortified by new capital from the budget, treasury bills for open-market operations, and a large amount (₱220 billion) of deposits from the national government. In addition, the Bangko Sentral ng Pilipinas was exempted from all taxes for a five-year period. The new Central Bank Charter clarified that the primary objective of monetary policy was to "maintain price stability conducive to the balanced and sustained growth of the economy."[1]

Institutional setting. The policymaking body of the Bangko Sentral ng Pilipinas is the Monetary Board, which is appointed by the President for six-year terms.

The board is a seven-member body, comprising the Governor of the Bangko Sentral ng Pilipinas (as its chairman), a cabinet member, and five members from the private sector. The board decides on an inflation objective after close coordination by the Bangko Sentral ng Pilipinas with other key agencies (including the National Economic Development Authority, the Department of Finance, the Department of Budget Management, and the Bureau of the Treasury) through interagency committees (the Committee on the Philippine Financial Program and the Development Budget Coordinating Committee), and approves a monthly monetary program consistent with the inflation objective.

Intermediate targets. Monetary policy implementation is formally based on quantitative targets for the stock of base money.

Base money targets replaced credit targets in 1984. The switch was intended to place greater emphasis on reducing inflation, which had risen to more than 50 percent. The idea was that by controlling base money, the Bangko Sentral ng Pilipinas would have greater control over broad money, which was closely related to inflation. On account of the uncertainties surrounding money demand, base money targets have typically been raised to allow for unexpected increases in money demand reflected in higher-than-targeted international reserves. Starting in 1994, when capital inflows surged and there was a need to guard against the inflationary risks of cap-

ital inflows, such increases in base money targets have been made only if inflation has been on track.

In late 1995, the Bangko Sentral ng Pilipinas switched to a de facto fixed exchange rate regime, seeking to maintain the peso at a value of ₱26 per $1. The Bangko Sentral ng Pilipinas continued to set base money targets, notwithstanding the currency peg that eliminated scope for an independent monetary policy. The floating of the peso on July 11, 1997, restored the consistency of the monetary and exchange rate framework.

Instruments. The main instruments of monetary policy are open-market operations, reserve requirements, and a "special deposit facility" for banks. On a day-to-day basis, the Bangko Sentral ng Pilipinas adjusts the level of base money through open-market operations, mainly comprising short-term repurchase and reverse repurchase agreements. The interest rates on short-term repurchases and reverse repurchases are the key "policy" interest rates determined by the Bangko Sentral ng Pilipinas. The policy rates form the reference rates around which other short-term interbank rates fluctuate. The Bangko Sentral ng Pilipinas also engages in outright purchases and sales of government securities.

Reserve requirements. The Bangko Sentral ng Pilipinas from time to time adjusts reserve requirements, which consist of a statutory reserve requirement and a liquidity reserve requirement. Reserve requirements apply only to peso deposits (not foreign currency deposits). The statutory reserve requirement is partially remunerated—40 percent of it earns interest, albeit at a below-market rate (of 4 percent, effective July 2, 1999)—while the liquidity reserve requirement, being held in the form of government securities, is remunerated at 100 basis points below the 91-day T-bill rate (a market rate). The statutory reserve requirement, although it has been lowered since the early 1990s (when it was 21–25 percent), remains high relative to other countries. Traditionally, the high statutory reserve requirement reflected the need for central bank financing of the budget and the central bank's weak net income position. The income position has once again become an issue with expiry of the Bangko Sentral ng Pilipinas's five-year tax exempt status in mid-1998 (discussed below). The statutory reserve requirement was reduced from 13 percent in 1997 to 10 percent in 1998. The liquidity reserve requirement, initially only 2 percent, was raised in mid-1997 to 8 percent as part of the effort to tighten policies; during 1999, the liquidity reserve requirement was gradually lowered during January–July.

Special deposit facility. Since December 1998, the Bangko Sentral ng Pilipinas has provided a "special deposit facility" for banks. The facility, which carries a small markup over the 91-day T-bill rate, serves as an alternative to reverse repurchases for withdrawing liquidity from the system and does not incur the documentary stamp tax. While little used at first, since March 1999, the stock of special deposits has increased substantially (to ₱41 billion in early August, compared with reverse repurchases of ₱105 billion).

---

[1]The Bangko Sentral ng Pilipinas was also charged with supervising the financial system, which is discussed in Section VI on the banking sector. This box focuses on the Bangko Sentral ng Pilipinas' role in monetary policy.

Box 4.2. Key Monetary Aggregates and Interest Rates

Measure of money	Definition
Reserve money	Currency plus deposit money banks' reserve deposits.
Base money	Reserve money plus deposit money banks' reserves held as government securities, reserve-eligible securities, and the reserve deficiency.
Broad money (M3)	Narrow money plus quasi money; where narrow money comprises currency plus domestic currency demand deposits, and quasimoney comprises domestic currency time and saving deposits.
M4	M3 plus foreign currency deposits of residents.

Interest rates	Features
RP and RRP rates	Policy rates. Preannounced by the Bangko Sentral ng Pilipinas.
T-bill rates	Market rates. Determined at weekly auction every Monday. The three-month T-bill rate is the bellwether market rate.
Interbank rates	Market rates.
Interbank call loan rate	Short-term interbank rate.
Prime lending rate	Rate charged by banks to prime borrowers. Falls within a margin (currently 1–6 percentage points) above the three-month T-bill rate, the margin being based on an informal agreement of banks with the Bankers' Association of the Philippines.
Deposit rates	Determined by banks.

financial intermediation. Fiscal adjustment and reforms, privatization of government-owned and -controlled corporations, and banking sector reforms also lightened the burden that had been felt by the old central bank. Finally, the Bangko Sentral ng Pilipinas started with a clean balance sheet, with capitalization from the national government.[4]

New Challenges for Monetary Policy

Monetary Framework and the Demand for Money.[5] Monetary policy has responded flexibly, and with a clear focus on macroeconomic stability, to the challenges that have arisen in recent years, although at times the framework of targets and instruments has not been fully clear. As noted, since 1984, monetary policy has been formally based on a floating exchange rate and base money targets in pursuit of an inflation objective. At times, however, the Bangko Sentral ng Pilipinas has appeared to follow multiple objectives—for example, during 1995–97, the peso was de facto pegged to the U.S. dollar while base money targets were retained—which may have complicated the implementation of monetary policy.[6] At the same time, the Bangko Sentral ng Pilipinas has been successful in meeting its overriding objective of a low and stable inflation rate, which it has accomplished principally through use of a monetary targeting framework. In recent years, the exchange rate has been market-determined, with foreign exchange market intervention limited to smoothing sharp fluctuations in the exchange rate.

Monetary policy has been complicated by instability in the demand for money, which has limited the usefulness of monetary targets. Demand for base money has been difficult to predict against the background of unstable broad money demand and significant unforeseen shifts in the money multiplier. The instability of money demand is not surprising given the major dislocations (as well as innovations) experienced by the financial system, other domestic shocks, as well as external shocks in recent years. It should be noted that the Bangko Sentral ng Pilipinas recognizes the instability in money demand and the complications such instability imposes on the monetary targeting framework. In response, the Bangko Sentral ng Pilipinas has tended to act on the side of caution, keeping base money well below its targeted

[4]The national government issued to the Bangko Sentral ng Pilipinas ₱170 billion in treasury bills and ₱50 billion in treasury bonds, together equivalent to about 15 percent of GNP, or 125 percent of base money. These transfers (of ₱220 billion) have been dedicated to servicing the liabilities of the old central bank (handled by the Central Bank-Board of Liquidators). In addition, the national government committed to subscribe fully to the authorized capitalization of the Bangko Sentral ng Pilipinas in the amount of ₱50 billion (of which ₱10 billion has been transferred to date).

[5]Box 4.2 summarizes the key monetary aggregates and interest rates.

[6]See Debelle and Lim (1998) for a discussion.

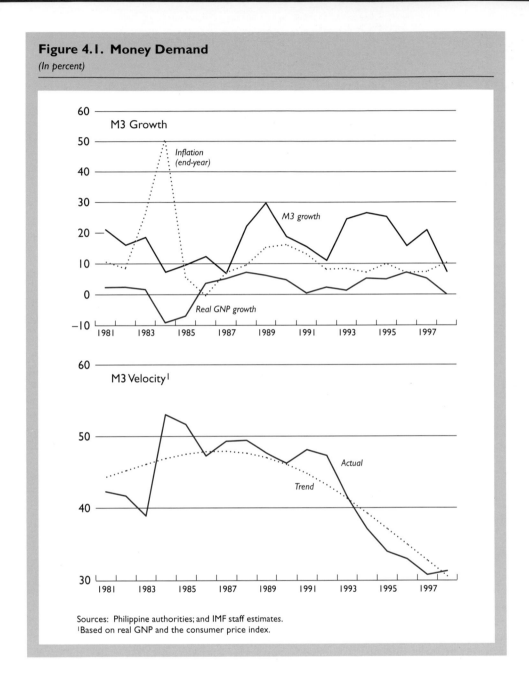

Figure 4.1. Money Demand

(In percent)

M3 Growth

Inflation
(end-year)

M3 growth

Real GNP growth

M3 Velocity¹

Actual

Trend

Sources: Philippine authorities; and IMF staff estimates.
¹Based on real GNP and the consumer price index.

ceilings. In addition, because of the difficulty of predicting money demand, the Bangko Sentral ng Pilipinas has relied on a broader set of indicators to guide monetary policy.

As one would expect for a developing country with a growing economy and increasing financial intermediation, the demand for money in the Philippines has increased significantly over the past two decades. The recurrent macroeconomic cycles and financial crises have, however, created instability and unpredictability in the demand for money in the short term. The income velocity of money has correspond-

ingly shown a trend decline, but has been characterized by marked short-run volatility (Figure 4.1).

The increase in the demand for money has been reflected in a substantial increase in the ratio of money to GNP. The share of the broadest monetary aggregate, M4, in GNP nearly doubled from 31 percent in 1980 to 58 percent in 1998 (Figure 4.2). In part, the increase reflected a growing demand for foreign currency deposits of residents, which increased from close to zero in 1980 to 17 percent of GNP in 1998. But it also reflected growing demand for peso deposits, as M3 increased from below 30

Figure 4.2. Money and Credit

(In percent of GNP)

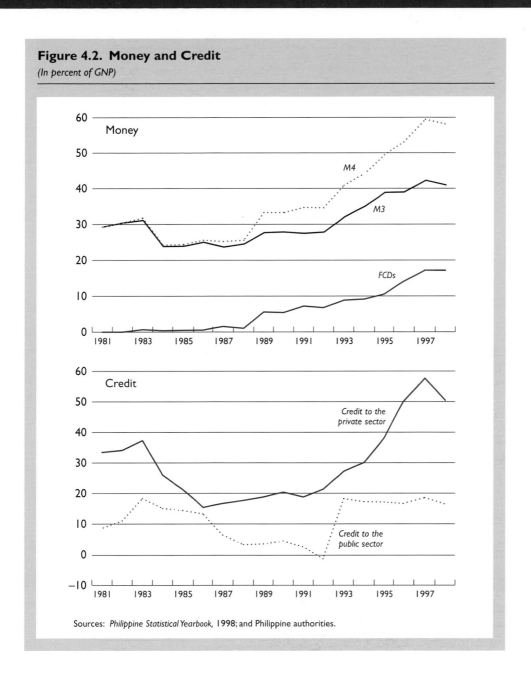

Sources: *Philippine Statistical Yearbook,* 1998; and Philippine authorities.

percent of GNP in 1980 to 41 percent of GNP in 1998. Reserve money, on the other hand, increased only modestly, from 7 percent of GNP in 1980 to 9 percent of GNP in 1998 (see Table 4.1).[7]

The trend decline in the income velocity of money is consistent with the standard pattern for developing countries with ongoing financial deepening.[8] The standard pattern is a U-shaped curve: velocity declines in the early stages of financial development, as growing monetization contributes to an increase in the demand for money; subsequently, velocity increases with increasing financial sophistication, as the growth of money substitutes (for example, credit cards) contributes to a reduction in the demand for

---

[7]The modest increase in reserve money relative to the broader aggregates reflects that the increase in the broader aggregates owed to a growth in savings deposits (associated with development of the banking system) rather than in currency. In part, it also reflects the lowering of reserve requirements on peso deposits over time, as the Bangko Sentral ng Pilipinas has been on a much sounder financial footing than the old central bank, as well as the rise of (nonreservable) foreign currency deposits.

[8]See, for example, Bordo and Jonung (1987).

Table 4.1. Summary of Monetary Accounts

(In billions of pesos)

	1993 Dec.	1994 Dec.	1995 Dec.	1996 Dec.	1997 Mar.	1997 Jun.	1997 Sep.	1997 Dec.	1998 Mar.	1998 Jun.	1998 Sep.	1998 Dec.
Bangko Sentral ng Pilipinas												
Reserve money	171.7	182.4	212.7	243.3	223.8	211.9	218.5	266.5	223.7	205.5	187.3	239.8
Net foreign assets	56.7	91.8	118.4	232.3	249.8	217.6	246.8	211.9	220.1	261.2	271.8	232.7
Net domestic assets	115.0	90.6	94.3	11.0	−26.0	−5.7	−28.3	54.6	3.6	−55.7	−84.5	7.1
Credit to public sector	182.0	151.3	156.0	135.5	62.6	104.5	83.0	151.2	137.7	151.3	127.3	138.9
National government	166.2	139.2	151.8	133.7	60.8	101.6	80.1	148.2	134.7	148.4	124.4	134.7
Assistance to financial institutions	4.2	4.0	3.2	3.2	3.2	4.7	8.9	8.2	15.6	17.8	18.0	18.2
Total rediscounting	7.3	5.3	5.9	6.5	6.1	6.6	6.6	6.6	6.8	6.9	7.7	7.3
Open market instruments[1]	−48.7	−31.5	−23.3	−91.6	−61.0	−82.5	−30.8	12.8	−20.1	−51.9	−80.3	−29.2
Other items net	−29.8	−38.5	−47.5	−42.7	−36.9	−39.0	−96.0	−124.2	−136.5	−179.8	−157.2	−128.1
Monetary survey[2]												
Net foreign assets	104.7	123.6	117.9	69.9	75.1	−10.7	−51.6	−76.9	−66.1	−67.1	0.6	16.5
Net domestic assets	394.8	507.2	668.5	844.0	860.8	966.7	1,076.0	1,251.3	1,222.4	1,240.9	1,143.4	1,202.8
Domestic credit	682.1	821.6	1,084.0	1,507.7	1,499.7	1,618.1	1,777.4	1,922.9	1,853.6	1,899.2	1,872.3	1,868.9
Public	274.1	299.8	335.3	377.2	325.9	356.4	404.0	468.2	451.1	478.5	443.0	459.7
National government, net	216.2	243.5	283.9	322.8	267.1	293.6	322.7	379.6	365.4	381.4	351.8	360.8
Private	408.0	521.7	748.7	1,130.5	1,173.8	1,261.7	1,373.5	1,454.7	1,402.5	1,420.7	1,429.3	1,409.2
Resident FCDUs[3]	−136.2	−158.8	−206.7	−317.6	−336.1	−348.8	−367.7	−433.4	−402.1	−435.0	−489.8	−477.9
Net other items	−151.1	−155.6	−208.8	−346.1	−302.9	−302.5	−333.8	−238.2	−229.1	−223.2	−239.0	−188.1
Total liquidity	499.5	630.8	786.4	913.9	935.8	956.1	1,024.4	1,174.4	1,156.3	1,173.8	1,144.0	1,219.3
M3	480.3	607.6	761.4	881.4	901.8	923.4	987.7	1,066.0	1,057.4	1,082.8	1,065.1	1,144.6
Narrow money	133.9	152.0	184.9	222.0	216.3	224.3	222.7	258.3	241.9	251.2	238.4	281.5
Quasi-money	341.8	451.0	570.3	652.8	678.3	692.3	755.6	795.6	803.4	820.7	818.4	856.9
Deposit substitutes	4.6	4.6	6.2	6.6	7.2	6.8	9.4	12.1	12.1	10.9	8.3	6.1
Other liabilities	19.2	23.2	25.0	32.5	34.0	32.6	36.8	108.4	98.9	91.0	78.9	74.8

Source: Data provided by the Philippine authorities.

[1]Mostly reverse repurchase agreements.

[2]Effective February 1996 Development Bank of the Philippines was reclassified from specialized government bank to commercial bank and hence was included.

[3]Foreign currency deposit units.

money.[9] The process appears still to have some way to go in the Philippines, as the ratio of M3 to GNP, at 41 percent, is low by Asian standards (Table 4.2). The short-run volatility in velocity can be traced to the macroeconomic cycles and financial crises that the Philippine economy has faced. The periods of sharp increases in velocity (mainly the mid-1980s and 1998) were also periods of overheating and/or financial crises (Figure 4.1).

An empirical analysis of the demand for broad money indicates a long-run, equilibrium (cointegrating) relationship between money demand and nominal income (Appendix 4.1). The relationship appears, however, to have become less stable in recent years. The demand for M3 is positively influenced by real income and negatively influenced by ex-

pected inflation. However, it was not possible to find a satisfactory short-run dynamic (error-correction) equation. The failure to find a satisfactory error-correction model implies that the short-run predictability of money demand is low, limiting the usefulness of monetary targeting.

In the 1990s, a pickup in the pace of financial development has been accompanied by an increase in the volatility of money demand. The analysis in Appendix 4.1 indicated structural breaks in the relationship between money demand and its determinants in the mid-1980s and in 1990. This suggests that the (long-run) relationship between broad money and inflation may be becoming less close than previously.

Capital Inflows and Monetary Expansion

During 1994–96, monetary management was complicated by a surge in capital inflows. The monetary

---

[9]See Section VI for a review of the spread of financial intermediation in the Philippines.

Table 4.2. Selected Countries: Broad Money/GDP, 1998

(In percent)

China	131[1]
India	54[1]
Indonesia	58[1]
Korea	175[2]
Malaysia	155[2]
Philippines	41[2]
Thailand	106[3]

Sources: Data provided by the Philippine authorities; and IMF staff estimates.

Note: Ratio for Philippines is relative to GNP.

[1]M2.

[2]M3.

[3]M2A.

policy approach shifted several times, in search of a way to deal with the inflows, resulting in rapid monetary expansion in 1994–95, followed by policy tightening in 1996–97. The exchange rate was allowed to appreciate in 1993–94, but subsequently increasing concern over the exchange rate first led to some stop-go cycles in the monetary stance and then, from late 1995, to a de facto peg to the U.S. dollar. The experience with sterilization was mixed: on the one hand, sterilization was accompanied by higher interest rates, which in turn attracted further inflows and resulted in rising fiscal costs; on the other hand, monetary expansion in 1996 *was* contained by a large contraction in net domestic assets of the Bangko Sentral ng Pilipinas (offsetting the expansion from rising net foreign assets; see Figure 4.3).[10]

In late 1994, a first wave of capital inflows (including remittances) put pressure on base money; the authorities responded by attempting to keep base money within the program ceilings. Their initial policy response to the inflows was to allow the exchange rate to appreciate, while using sterilized intervention to smooth the trend.

As inflation gradually receded, the policy stance was changed, but the change did not prove sustainable. The authorities became concerned that the strong exchange rate might endanger the then-nascent export-led recovery and signal that monetary policy was too tight. Net domestic assets of the Bangko Sentral ng Pilipinas were increased, raising base money well above the program ceiling until the exchange rate stabilized at end-1994 (some 13 per-

cent stronger than its 1993 level). This policy, however, proved not to be sustainable. Reserves began to fall almost immediately. In addition, interest rates declined initially but began to rise sharply as inflationary expectations increased.

Following the experience in 1994, the authorities shifted to a strategy involving elements of inflation targeting. Although they continued to formulate base money targets, policy implementation was to depend on whether inflation was on track (consistent with a projected monthly path).[11] As long as this was the case, the operating target was the net domestic assets of the Bangko Sentral ng Pilipinas. Targeting net domestic assets was intended to allow the Bangko Sentral ng Pilipinas to accommodate unexpected capital inflows, which would likely reflect higher-than-expected demand for money. (Base money targets could be increased for any excess of foreign reserves over the targeted level.) If the Bangko Sentral ng Pilipinas felt, however, that the inflows might be inflationary, they could choose not to intervene and instead allow the exchange rate to appreciate. If inflation turned out higher than targeted, the operating target was base money (as before). In these circumstances, the authorities would respond to unexpected capital inflows either by allowing the exchange rate to appreciate or by sterilized intervention.

The approach was felt to have several important advantages. It established the reduction of inflation as the clear objective of monetary policy. It put less weight on intermediate targets, which may have been sending misleading signals, and more on the final objective (inflation). And it allowed the authorities flexibility in how to respond to capital inflows, depending not on the nature of the underlying shock (difficult to identify), but on its impact on prices.

Performance under this approach was mixed. This was mainly because, in addition to inflation control, monetary policy continued to follow other objectives (such as the level of the exchange rate). Policy cycles emerged under which interest rates were pushed down until foreign reserves began to decline, forcing the monetary stance to be tightened again (Table 4.3). A notable example occurred in early 1995. Soon after the new monetary strategy was adopted, it became clear that money demand was weaker than expected. The authorities responded by keeping the operating targets (base money/net domestic assets) well below projected ceilings. By midyear, the policy had started to generate large capital inflows, and the authorities started to relax the monetary stance. Interest

---

[10]It is difficult with the available data to formally estimate an "offset coefficient," which measures the extent to which the central bank's domestic money operations are undone by capital flows in the reverse direction.

[11]The judgment of whether inflation was on track was on a backward- rather than a forward-looking basis, since it was based on whether inflation in any particular month was higher or lower than projected for that month at the time the monetary targets were formulated.

Figure 4.3. Monetary Impact of Foreign Inflows

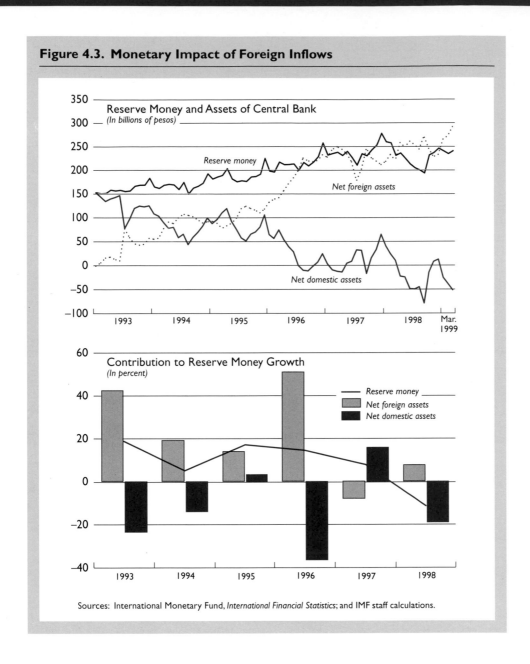

Sources: International Monetary Fund, *International Financial Statistics*; and IMF staff calculations.

rates started to decline, but market confidence fell steadily and culminated in September–November in a speculative attack on the peso.

The overall experience with sterilized intervention also was mixed. On the one hand, sterilization preserved a large interest differential in favor of the peso, while the signals sent by exchange market intervention suggested to market participants that if the exchange rate were to move, it would move only in an upward direction. The result was effectively a one-way bet for speculators, resulting in a flood of additional inflows. At the same time, it is clear that the Bangko Sentral ng Pilipinas, even if unable to stem the inflows through exchange market interven-

tion, did manage to tighten domestic monetary operations sufficiently to prevent a surge in reserve money (Figure 4.3).

Fixed Exchange Rates and an Externally Financed Credit Boom

The period from 1996 to mid-1997 was characterized by a fixed exchange rate and an externally financed credit boom, which placed new pressures on monetary policy. As noted, in late 1995, the Bangko Sentral ng Pilipinas switched to a de facto fixed exchange rate regime, pegging the peso to the U.S. dollar. The action was followed by a period of rapid

Table 4.3. Selected Interest Rates
(In percent)

	1993 Dec.	1994 Dec.	1995 Dec.	1996 Dec.	1997 Mar.	Jun.	Sep.	Dec.	1998 Mar.	Jun.	Sep.	Dec.
					(End of period)							
Manila reference rates												
MRR 60	14.8	9.8	11.4	11.8	11.0	9.9	13.6	17.3	16.8	13.9	13.9	13.7
MRR 90	15.0	8.8	10.3	11.1	10.3	9.6	11.5	14.1	14.7	12.0	12.2	13.4
MRR 180	14.1	9.1	10.4	10.3	8.9	8.4	10.5	12.9	13.7	12.3	12.1	12.4
Average of all maturities	14.7	9.6	11.1	11.7	10.8	9.8	13.4	17.1	16.8	13.9	13.8	13.6
Average lending rate	16.4	13.4	14.6	14.5	13.8	13.2	17.4	20.7	20.9	17.8	17.7	18.1
91-day treasury bill rate	15.9	10.3	12.0	11.6	10.5	10.5	13.9	16.7	15.8	15.0	13.8	13.5
Reverse repurchase (term) rate	0.0	14.0	13.4	11.1	10.5	10.7	13.8	12.5	13.0	14.6	14.2	13.6
Interbank call loan rate	24.1	12.0	14.1	11.2	10.5	13.2	19.6	21.4	13.2	13.3	15.5	14.0
					(Period average)							
Manila reference rates												
MRR 60	9.9	8.6	9.9	11.8	10.6	10.3	15.1	18.1	17.6	14.1	14.1	13.7
MRR 90	13.2	8.9	8.8	11.0	9.4	9.9	12.4	14.8	15.3	12.7	12.6	13.3
MRR 180	12.2	8.4	9.4	10.3	8.4	8.7	11.6	13.4	13.7	11.8	12.0	13.0
Average of all maturities	12.9	8.6	9.8	11.6	10.4	10.2	14.9	17.9	17.4	14.1	14.1	13.6
Average lending rate	14.8	13.4	13.7	14.8	13.7	13.3	18.2	20.4	20.1	16.0	14.6	14.8
91-day treasury bill rate	12.5	12.7	11.7	11.7	9.5	11.0	15.3	17.7	16.597	14.004	13.822	13.43
Reverse repurchase (term) rate	0.0	10.4	12.3	11.1	10.2	10.5	13.9	12.0	16.1	14.5	13.9	13.5
Interbank call loan rate	19.2	10.4	12.1	11.2	10.2	14.4	15.7	13.6	13.3	13.3	15.5	13.9

Source: Data provided by the Philippine authorities.
[1]End-period data refer to the average for the last week of each period.

credit growth, fueled by large-scale external borrowing (much of it short term), a boom in asset prices, and a widening of the external current account deficit. A strong bias in incentives toward borrowing and lending in U.S. dollars rather than in pesos (reserve requirements and taxation were higher for peso transactions, see Table 4.4) contributed to a buildup in foreign exchange exposure and the attendant vulnerabilities.

The rapid expansion in credit was entirely in private sector credit, which grew by 44 percent in 1995 and more than 50 percent in 1996. Credit to the real estate and construction sectors accounted for a large part of the increase, even though their shares still remained relatively modest (at mid-1997, real estate accounted for about 11 percent of outstanding bank loans, and construction for less than 4 percent).[12] A significant part of the increase was financed by for-

eign inflows, with banks' net foreign liabilities and foreign currency deposits rising sharply in 1996. Although banks were subject to overall limits on foreign exchange exposure, they met the limits in part by lending domestically in foreign exchange and by holding forward positions (mostly with exporters). Faced with these developments, the Bangko Sentral ng Pilipinas, starting in 1996, progressively tightened prudential limits (including by placing a limit on the share of real estate loans in a bank's portfolio, and by imposing a liquid-asset cover requirement on foreign currency deposits—see Section VI).

The Crisis and Its Aftermath: 1997–99

In common with other Asian countries, the Philippines came under severe financial pressure in mid-1997. On July 11, a few days after the floating of the Thai baht, the peso was floated, and the focus of monetary policy in the subsequent period was on

---

[12]See, for example, Bangko Sentral ng Pilipinas (1999), Table 31.

Table 4.4. The Bias Against Peso Intermediation

	Peso	Foreign Currency
Statutory reserve requirement	10 percent	None
Liquidity reserve requirement	4 percent	None
Liquid asset requirement on deposits	None	30 percent
Depositors	20 percent tax on interest income	7.5 percent tax on interest income
Banks	33 percent tax on interest income from loans; 20 percent tax on interest income from T-bills and other qualified assets.	10 percent tax on interest income earned on loans to residents; no tax on interest earned on loans to nonresidents.

Source: Data based on information provided by the Philippine authorities.

restoring confidence in the peso and containing inflation. More recently, as the peso has strengthened and inflation remained well under control, attention has shifted toward supporting a recovery in the real economy.

The Crisis Management Strategy

The Bangko Sentral ng Pilipinas has been broadly successful in managing the currency turmoil. It reacted promptly to the onset of the crisis in July 1997, floating the peso and tightening monetary policy through higher interest rates. For about a year, the external position remained vulnerable, and the Bangko Sentral ng Pilipinas used interest rates to "lean against" pressures on the peso—but without raising rates aggressively in an attempt to defend any particular level of the peso.[13] In recent months, interest rates have gradually come down and are now below their precrisis levels. Credit growth has remained weak, however, reflecting weakness in credit demand (consistent with the output gap and uncertainty regarding the strength of the recovery) as well as banks' desire to strengthen their balance sheets.

While the monetary framework has continued to be formally based on base money targets, interest rates have become the driving variable. In implementing monetary policy, the Bangko Sentral ng Pilipinas typically forms a judgment about the appropriate level of policy interest rates based mainly on market signals about underlying monetary conditions (such as the exchange rate and market interest rates). In the period since the crisis, the use of a de facto interest rate target, oriented initially mainly to conditions in the exchange market, was appropriate given the uncertainties about money demand (exacerbated as a result of the crisis). As a result, monetary targets have typically been missed (undershot) by large margins.

While open market operations are the principal monetary policy instrument, the Bangko Sentral ng Pilipinas has also made significant use of reserve requirements. During the height of exchange market pressures in 1997, total reserve requirements (on peso deposits) were raised to 21 percent, comprising an 8 percent "liquidity reserve" (remunerated at close to market rates) and a 13 percent statutory reserve (largely unremunerated—Box 4.1). The use of reserve requirements was partly to effect a rapid tightening of liquidity conditions when necessary (without an up-front rise in Bangko Sentral ng Pilipinas' "headline" policy rates); considerations over the Bangko Sentral ng Pilipinas' net income position have also played a role in the choice of policy instruments (as explained below).

The peso has continued to float, with exchange market intervention limited to what was needed for meeting the reserve targets under the current IMF program and for smoothing operations. Nonmarket intervention measures have sometimes been used to restore orderly market conditions during periods of severe pressure; such measures have typically been used on a temporary basis. One such measure has been a "volatility band" that entailed a suspension of

---

[13]Initially, overnight policy interest rates were raised to about 30 percent (for a relatively short period). Over the following year, rates trended down to the 15 percent range (with inflation in the upper single digits). Whenever there was serious pressure in the exchange market, the Bangko Sentral ng Pilipinas would raise policy interest rates.

Box 4.3. Financial Obligations of the Bangko Sentral ng Pilipinas

Bangko Sentral ng Pilipinas Transfers to the Government

Under the new Central Bank Act (1993), the Bangko Sentral ng Pilipinas is committed to transferring 75 percent of its net profits (net income after tax) to the Central Bank-Board of Liquidators' sinking fund until such time as the Central Bank-Board of Liquidators' liabilities are extinguished. Subsequently, it is envisaged under the act that the Bangko Sentral ng Pilipinas would reduce its transfers to the national government to 50 percent. The government committed itself to transferring an additional ₱50 billion to the Bangko Sentral ng Pilipinas for recapitalization; of this, ₱10 billion has been transferred.

In practice, actual transfers are based on a Memorandum of Agreement between the national government and Bangko Sentral ng Pilipinas that was signed in 1993 as well as on Section 132 of the new Central Bank Act. Under the Memorandum of Agreement, Bangko Sentral ng Pilipinas remits as interest rebate to the national government the excess of net income after taxes over 1 percent of its total assets (domestic and foreign). The balance of net income equivalent to 1 percent of total assets is split between the Central Bank-Board of Liquidators and Bangko Sentral ng Pilipinas: 75 percent of it (called "dividend") is transferred for paying off Central Bank-Board of Liquidators' liabilities; and 25 percent is retained by Bangko Sentral ng Pilipinas for building up capital/reserves as mandated in the new charter. In sum:

(Net income after taxes) minus (1 percent of total assets*)
= Interest rebate to the national government

*75 percent for the Central Bank-Board of Liquidators;
25 percent retained by Bangko Sentral ng Pilipinas.

For example, in 1998, net income after taxes was ₱8.1 billion (accruals basis). Total assets were ₱730 bil-
lion, so 1 percent of total assets were ₱7.3 billion. Interest rebate to the national government was thus ₱0.8 billion (derived as ₱8.1 billion minus ₱7.3 billion). Transfers to the Central Bank-Board of Liquidators were ₱5.5 billion (equal to 75 percent of ₱7.3 billion) and the Bangko Sentral ng Pilipinas retained ₱1.8 billion (equal to 25 percent of ₱7.3 billion).

Taxation of the Bangko Sentral ng Pilipinas

Following its establishment, the Bangko Sentral ng Pilipinas was exempt from taxation for a five-year period, which ended in July 1998. Subsequently, the Bangko Sentral ng Pilipinas has had to pay taxes, including documentary stamp tax, on its open-market operations. In 1998, Bangko Sentral ng Pilipinas paid taxes of ₱8.8 billion to the Bureau of Internal Revenue; in the first half of 1999, Bangko Sentral ng Pilipinas paid ₱3.5 billion to the Bureau of Internal Revenue.

An amendment to the Central Bank Act, seeking to restore tax exemption for the Bangko Sentral ng Pilipinas, among others, was submitted to Congress in January 1999 and remains pending (as of August 1999). A phased elimination of the documentary stamp tax (on secondary issues) is envisaged as part of the ongoing financial sector tax reforms, but this too will take time.

Meanwhile, the Bangko Sentral ng Pilipinas has moved toward less costly forms of monetary operations. Special deposit accounts, which unlike standard reverse repurchases are not subject to the documentary stamp tax, are substantial as noted. In January, the Bangko Sentral ng Pilipinas entered the Multitransactions Interbank Payments System; open-market operations conducted through the Multitransactions Interbank Payments System are paperless and thus also not subject to the documentary stamp tax.

---

foreign exchange trading whenever the exchange rate moved outside a specified range.[14] Another measure has been the use of nondeliverable forward contracts, under which the Bangko Sentral ng Pilipinas provided forward cover to eligible borrowers (for example, companies with unhedged foreign liabilities, selected banks).[15] Despite the recent pressures expe-

rienced from volatile capital flows—first the surge in inflows in 1994–97, then the outflows in 1997–98—the authorities have remained steadfast in their opposition to capital controls.

The Bangko Sentral ng Pilipinas lost its tax-exempt status in July 1998, with the expiration of a five-year transition period granted at its creation in 1993. It has since paid taxes, mainly a documentary stamp tax on open-market operations and tax on income earned from the sale of government securities. In addition, the Bangko Sentral ng Pilipinas has been required since 1993 to transfer part of its earnings to the national government (Box 4.3). A draft bill is pending in congress that would restore the Bangko Sentral ng Pilipinas' tax exemption; at the same time, Bangko Sentral ng Pilipinas' transfers to the government would be increased. Under a

---

[14]The band was initially invoked by the Bankers' Association of the Philippines on July 11, 1997—and entailed a suspension of trading for two hours whenever the rate moved more than 1.5 percent on either side of the opening rate. The band was reintroduced in October 1997, and involved the suspension of trading for half an hour, one hour, and the rest of the day, respectively, whenever the exchange rate moved 2 percent, 3 percent, and 4 percent away from a central rate. The band was lifted in March 1998.

[15]See Section V for a discussion of the use of nondeliverable forward contracts in the Philippines.

proposed financial sector tax reform package, the documentary stamp tax on secondary issues would in any case be eliminated. In the meantime, the Bangko Sentral ng Pilipinas has shifted monetary operations partly to instruments that do not incur tax, such as reserve requirements, a special deposit facility for banks, and paperless open-market operations.

Future Challenges

Looking ahead, continued success of monetary policy will require a consistent and transparent policy framework, appropriate operational arrangements, and independence for the Bangko Sentral ng Pilipinas to use its instruments to achieve its statutory goal of controlling inflation. As the crisis subsides, the Bangko Sentral ng Pilipinas needs to clarify the monetary framework, including the choice of an intermediate target, if any (the alternative being adoption of an inflation-targeting framework). A particular challenge for monetary policy will be managing potentially volatile capital flows—suggesting continuation of the floating exchange rate regime. While a clear and consistent monetary framework is necessary, success on this front will likely require active support from fiscal policies. The Bangko Sentral ng Pilipinas should remain both operationally and financially independent. Independence in this context refers to the Bangko Sentral ng Pilipinas retaining full discretion over the use of its instruments of monetary control, with a view to achieving the inflation objective (set in collaboration with other government agencies). The monetary operations of the Bangko Sentral ng Pilipinas should remain free of taxes, and the government should fulfill its outstanding obligation to complete capitalization of the Bangko Sentral ng Pilipinas, so that income considerations do not influence the choice of monetary instruments. To complement its independence, the Bangko Sentral ng Pilipinas needs to ensure that its actions are transparent and well understood by the public.

Appendix 4.1. Analysis of Demand for Broad Money in the Philippines

The specification of the demand function for money follows the traditional practice of describing real money balances as a function of a scale variable and an opportunity-cost variable. The scale variable is represented by real GNP, to represent real income, and the opportunity-cost variable by expected inflation, to represent the value of the goods that are forgone when money is held instead. The money-demand equation is specified as:

Table 4A1. Augmented Dickey-Fuller Tests for a Unit Root, 1991–98
(Test statistics)[1]

Series[2]	With Trend and Intercept		With Only Intercept	
	Level	First difference	Level	First difference
Broad money, M3 (real)	−1.6*	−5.7**	0.2*	−5.1**
GNP (real)	−2.4*	−17.4**	−0.3*	−16.3**
CPI inflation	−3.8*[3]	−4.8**	−3.6**	−4.9**

Sources: IMF staff calculations, based on data provided by the Philippine authorities.

[1]*: unit root not rejected. **: unit root rejected.

[2]All series are in logarithms. Inflation is measured as the first difference of the log of the CPI.

[3]1 percent level of significance.

$$\frac{M}{P} = \alpha_0 + \alpha_1\left(\frac{Y}{P}\right) + \alpha_2\pi^e + \in. \qquad (1)$$

In the equation, (M/P) and (Y/P) represent the logarithms of real money balances and real GNP, respectively; π^e represents expected inflation (measured as the first difference of the logarithm of the price level (CPI)); and $\in$ represents the error term.[16] The coefficients on real income and inflation would be expected to be positive and negative, respectively.

It is common when estimating money-demand functions to use the methodology of cointegration. An important reason that the methodology is attractive is that a cointegrating relationship among variables can be interpreted as the long-run equilibrium relationship among them. A cointegrating relationship among real money balances, real income, and expected inflation, for example, would indicate that even if these variables experience a shock that drives them out of equilibrium, they will eventually return to the equilibrium relationship.

As a preliminary exercise, in order for it to be legitimate to include the above series together in a regression, it was necessary to test that the time series were of a similar order of integration. Unit-root tests indicated that the variables were integrated of order 1: the levels were nonstationary but their first differences were stationary (Table 4A1). For inflation, this was true only around a trend.

---

[16]The above equation imposes homogeneity of degree one in prices.

Table 4A2. Demand for Money, 1991–98

(Dependent variable: real M3; independent variables: real GNP, expected inflation)

Likelihood ratio (Johansen test)	44.34
Cointegration status	Not rejected
Number of cointegrating equations	One
Estimated coefficients	
(t-statistics in parentheses)	
Long-run coefficients	
Real GNP	3.62 (5.4)
Expected inflation	−0.84 (−2.5)
Error-correction estimates	
Lagged dependent variable	0.18 (1.1)
Real GNP (first difference)	0.12 (0.9)
Expected inflation (first difference)	−0.01 (−2.9)
Error–correction term	−0.02 (−4.3)

Source: IMF staff calculations.

A Johansen cointegration test on equation (1) indicated that a cointegrating relationship could not be rejected (Table 4A2). The number of cointegrating equations was one. The coefficients on real GNP and inflation had the expected signs (positive and negative, respectively) and were significant.[17] The short-run error correction model, however, was not satisfactory: the error correction coefficient, while it had the right sign, was small (0.02). (In addition, the income variable was not significant.) The failure to find a satisfactory error correction model implies that the short-run predictability of monetary developments is poor. This result is consistent with the expected effect of financial liberalization on developments in the monetary aggregates, as well as with the monetary and real shocks that the economy has experienced.

A Chow test was used to test for structural breaks in the relationship and found that a structural break in 1983 and another in 1990 could not be rejected. (The F-statistics were 4.3 and 3.7 respectively, with 2.7 being the critical level.) This coincides with the financial crisis of 1983 in the first instance, and the

acceleration of financial development in the 1990s in the second.

References

Aghevli, Bijan, Mohsin Khan, P.R. Narvekar, and Brock Short, 1979, "Monetary Policy in Selected Asian Countries," *IMF Staff Papers,* International Monetary Fund, Vol. 26 (December), pp. 775–824.

Arora, Vivek, 1996, "The Stability of the Demand for Money in Korea," in *Selected Issues for the 1996 Article IV Consultation with Korea* (Washington: International Monetary Fund).

Bangko Sentral ng Pilipinas, 1999, *Selected Philippine Economic Indicators* (Manila: Bangko Sentral ng Pilipinas, Department of Economic Research, May).

Bordo, Michael, and Lars Jonung, 1987, *The Long-Run Behavior of the Velocity of Money: The International Evidence* (New York: Cambridge University Press).

Central Bank of the Philippines, various years, *Annual Report* (Manila: Central Bank of the Philippines).

Debelle, Guy, and Cheng H. Lim, 1998, "Preliminary Considerations of an Inflation Targeting Framework for the Philippines," IMF Working Paper 98/39 (Washington: International Monetary Fund).

Dohner, Robert, and Ponciano Intal, 1988, "Debt Crisis and Adjustment in the Philippines," in *Developing Country Debt and the World Economy,* ed. by Jeffrey Sachs (Cambridge, Massachusetts: National Bureau of Economic Research).

International Monetary Fund, 1998, *International Financial Statistics, 1998 Yearbook* (Washington: International Monetary Fund).

Kochhar, Kalpana, Prakash Loungani, and Mark Stone, 1998, "Policy Lessons from the East Asian Crisis," IMF Working Paper 98/128 (Washington: International Monetary Fund).

Singson, Gabriel, 1998, "Strategic Issues in Managing Capital Flows: The Experience of the Philippines," speech delivered at the Asian Development Bank (Manila: Bangko Sentral ng Pilipinas web page, www.bsp.gov.ph/ADB98).

Templo, Ofelia, 1998, "Managing Stabilization and Recovery: The Case of the Philippines," paper presented at OECD symposium on Structural Aspects of the East Asian Crisis (Paris: November 16–17, 1998).

Tseng, Wanda, and Robert Corker, 1991, *Financial Liberalization, Money Demand, and Monetary Policy in Asian Countries,* IMF Occasional Paper 84 (Washington: International Monetary Fund).

World Bank, 1987, *Philippines: A Framework for Economic Recovery* (Washington: World Bank).

———, 1999, *Philippines: The Challenge of Economic Recovery* (Washington: World Bank).

---

[17]The coefficient on GNP (3.6) was larger than found in earlier analyses (for example, Aghevli and others (1979) and Tseng and Corker (1991)), which tended to find a coefficient of about 1.5.

V External Sector

Charalambos Christofides

Although the external sector came under heavy pressure during the Asian crisis, it proved less vulnerable than in the most heavily affected countries. The policy response to crises in the mid-1980s and early 1990s, particularly in external debt management and banking policies, helped contain the buildup of imbalances and manage the crisis as it unfolded. Nevertheless, large capital inflows in the mid-1990s nearly overwhelmed the policy framework and led to overvaluation of the peso, a growing current account deficit, and rapidly rising short-term debt. The de facto pegging of the peso to the U.S. dollar in late 1995 exacerbated the vulnerability to short-term capital flow reversals. When the tide turned in 1997, the authorities tried for a few months to defend the peso, but then adapted quickly by floating the peso, tightening financial policies, and accelerating structural reforms. These policies succeeded in stabilizing the external position without the severe disruption experienced in the other crisis countries.

Recent trade developments indicate that a favorable structural change took place in the early 1990s, with exports strongly benefiting from prior investments and regulatory changes. Philippine export market shares increased faster than three of the "Asian-5" (Indonesia, Korea, Malaysia, Philippines, and Thailand), with the exception of Korea's. The change reflects rapidly increasing exports of electronics and electronic components. Although such growth has come partly at the expense of more traditional exports, it has shown the Philippines' capacity to partake fully in one of the most dynamic and competitive export markets in the world.

Developments in the Balance of Payments and External Debt

Background

The Philippine economy experienced major external imbalances over the past two decades. Starting in the early 1980s, the economy slid into a full-blown balance of payments crisis, resulting in default on external debt followed by a severe recession.[1] The crisis was the result of earlier policies favoring an expansion of the public sector, import substitution, and easy credit to the private sector financed through external debt. Although efforts to support exports had started as early as 1970 with the Export Incentives Act,[2] effective protection remained substantial, especially in import substituting sectors. Large public and private investments initiated during this period were heavily dependent on imports and foreign financing, and eventually proved unable to generate the foreign exchange earnings to service the debt. The resulting vulnerability became unsustainable in the face of large external shocks[3] and growing political uncertainty.[4]

From the mid-1980s, reforms produced a gradual improvement in economic performance, but the economy remained vulnerable to a "boom-and-bust" cycle. The period 1986–89 saw a recovery of growth and investment and a return of foreign capital, supported by policy reforms, including a breakup of agricultural monopolies, import liberalization, and tighter debt management. However, import dependence remained high and domestic saving weak, and a strong recovery of growth combined with expansionary fiscal policy resulted in a return of unsustainable current account deficits (peaking at more than 6 percent of GDP in 1990). Thus, a few years of rapid growth were capped by near-exhaustion of reserves, a peso depreciation, and yet another debt rescheduling.

In the early 1990s, reforms accelerated and the economy became more resilient in the face of external shocks. Trade liberalization accelerated, with average nominal tariffs expected to fall below 10 percent by 2000 (from more than 40 percent in 1980,

---

[1]In 1988, debt restructuring agreements were concluded in line with a 1987 Paris Club agreement. In all, almost $13 billion of debt was restructured—about 136 percent of 1988 exports of goods and services.

[2]R.A. No. 5186 offered fiscal exemptions to exporters of both goods and services to stimulate exports of nontraditional manufactures.

[3]Including a jump in world interest rates, recession in the United States, and Latin America in a debt crisis.

[4]Culminating in the assassination of Ninoy Aquino in 1993.

Table 5.1. Balance of Payments[1]
(In millions of U.S. dollars)

	1994	1995	1996	1997	1998
Trade balance	−7,850	−8,944	−11,342	−11,127	−28
(In percent of GNP)	−11.9	−11.7	−12.8	−13.0	0.0
Exports, f.o.b.	13,483	17,447	20,543	25,228	29,496
Imports, f.o.b.	21,333	26,391	31,885	36,355	29,524
Services (net)	3,964	4,765	6,839	5,696	880
Service receipts	10,550	14,374	19,006	22,835	13,917
Remittances/foreign currency deposit withdrawals	5,824	8,696	10,169	11,748	8,363
Other	4,726	5,678	8,837	11,087	5,554
Service payments	6,586	9,609	12,167	17,139	13,037
Interest	1,579	2,179	2,167	2,567	2,516
Other	5,007	7,430	10,000	14,572	10,521
Transfers (net)	936	882	589	1,080	435
Current account	−2,950	−3,297	−3,914	−4,351	1,287
(In percent of GNP)	−4.5	−4.3	−4.4	−5.1	1.9
Financial account	4,096	4,106	8,021	988	72
Foreign investment	1,558	1,609	1,168	762	1,672
Direct investment	1,289	1,361	1,338	1,113	1,592
Portfolio investment	269	248	−170	−351	80
MLT loans and bonds	657	1,454	2,690	4,824	2,850
Inflows	3,713	4,105	6,329	7,724	5,791
Outflows	3,056	2,651	3,639	2,900	2,941
Trading in bonds in secondary market[1]	..	..	...	−676	−1,082
Short-term, trade-related capital	1,002	−56	540	495	−1,521
Commercial banks' National Food Authority (increase −)[2]	674	564	4,211	1,188	−963
Other (including errors and omissions)	205	535	−588	−5,605	−884
Overall balance	1,146	809	4,107	−3,363	1,359
Net international reserves (increase −)	−1,802	−631	−4,107	3,363	−1,359
Bangko Sentral ng Pilipinas (BSP) gross reserves (increase −)	−1,200	−640	−3,983	2,977	−2,038
Fund credit (net)	−219	−336	−323	435	651
Purchases	53	0	0	700	730
Repurchases	−272	−336	−323	−265	−79
Change in other BSP liabilities	−383	345	199	−49	28
Memorandum items					
BSP gross reserves	7,122	7,762	11,745	8,768	10,806
(In months of imports of goods and services)	3.1	2.6	3.2	2.0	3.0
BSP adjusted gross reserves[3]	6,372	6,662	10,445	7,568	9,606
(In months of imports of goods and services)	2.7	2.2	2.8	1.7	2.7
BSP NIR	5,297	5,928	10,035	6,672	8,031
Monitored external debt[4]	37,079	38,553	41,470	50,728	53,509
External debt	37.1	38.6	41.5	50.7	53.5
(In percent of GNP)	56.4	50.6	47.0	59.3	78.3
Debt-service ratio[5]	20.4	16.2	15.5	111.9	12.8
Export volume (percent change)	13.5	16.0	20.1	32.9	19.8
Import volume (percent change)	18.0	13.3	20.9	21.9	−11.3
GNP	65,742	76,180	88,276	85,606	68,326

Sources: Philippine authorities; and IMF staff estimates.

[1]Represents net repurchase of Philippine-issued bonds in secondary markets abroad.

[2]Commercial banks' National Food Authority will differ from the monetary survey due to differences in coverage.

[3]Gross reserves less gold and securities pledged as collateral against short-term liabilities.

[4]Broad measure of external liabilities. In addition to external debt, it includes liabilities of foreign banks operating in the Philippines to their head offices, branches, and agencies, and domestic government securities held by nonresidents as well as some external debt not captured by regular debt statistics.

[5]In percent of exports of goods and services.

Table 5.2. External Indicators

	1993	1994	1995	1996	1997	1998
	(In millions of U.S. dollars; end of period)					
Gross official reserves[1]	4,721	6,372	6,662	10,445	7,568	9,606
(In months of imports of goods and services)	2.5	2.7	2.2	2.8	1.7	2.7
Net international reserves of the central bank	3,496	5,297	5,928	10,035	6,671	8,031
	(In percent of GNP)					
Exports	20.6	20.5	22.9	23.8	29.4	43.2
Imports	31.8	32.5	34.6	37.0	42.4	43.3
Trade balance	−11.2	−11.9	−11.7	−13.1	−13.0	0.0
Current account	−5.5	−4.5	−4.3	−4.6	−5.1	1.9
	(Annual percent change)					
Export volume	13.2	14.0	17.0	20.7	23.1	19.5
Export unit price	2.3	4.0	10.6	−2.4	−7.0	−2.0
Import volume	19.9	18.6	14.5	22.8	16.4	−12.8
Import unit price	1.1	2.2	8.0	−1.6	−6.2	−7.2
Terms of trade	1.2	1.8	2.4	−0.8	−0.9	5.5
Memorandum items						
Peso/dollar exchange rate						
Annual average	27.1	26.4	25.7	26.2	29.5	40.9
End-of-period	27.7	24.4	26.2	26.3	40.0	39.1

Sources: Data provided by the Philippine authorities; and IMF staff estimates.
[1]Adjusted for gold- and security-backed borrowing.

and 27 percent in 1990).[5] In 1991, a new Foreign Investment Act was introduced, which simplified the approval process and allowed foreign ownership of up to 100 percent in many sectors. In 1992, a sweeping exchange liberalization removed current and most capital account restrictions. These reforms strengthened resource allocation in the economy, boosted exports, and were followed by full restoration of the Philippines' access to global capital markets—setting the stage for the Philippines' relatively robust performance during the Asian crisis (Tables 5.1–5.7).

Despite severe early pressures from "contagion," the external position has proved remarkably resilient in the face of the Asian crisis. As for other countries in the region, the crisis first manifested itself in falling equity prices and pressure on the exchange rate, with an acceleration of capital outflows, particularly in the aftermath of the Thai baht devaluation in July 1997. Contagion was evident in the lack of differentiation in the key foreign exchange bond spread indicators, which initially rose to prohibitive levels for all countries affected by the crisis, with little differentiation between borrowers.[6] Compared with the most heavily affected crisis countries, however, capital outflows from the Philippines were less severe, and the hemorrhage of reserves was arrested earlier. Unlike in previous crises, external debt service was not interrupted, and the domestic banking and corporate sectors—while showing signs of stress—were able to withstand severe external shocks better than in the past.

Nevertheless, while the crisis was less severe in the Philippines than in some other countries in the region, it revealed underlying weaknesses that remain to be addressed. The trade deficit had widened to more than 10 percent of GNP by 1997, and the peso was significantly overvalued. While capital flows through the early 1990s consisted mainly of longer-term (including concessional) lending from both multilateral agencies and other bilateral sources,[7] 1995–96 witnessed a jump in short-term

---

[5]Moreover, all but one quantitative restriction have been tariffed.

[6]See Baig and Goldfajn (1998).
[7]See International Monetary Fund (1995).

Table 5.3. Volume, Unit Prices, and Values of Principal Exports
(Unless otherwise indicated, volumes in thousands of metric tons; unit prices in U.S. dollars per ton; and values in millions of U.S. dollars)

	1993	1994	1995	1996	1997	1998 Prelim.
Coconut oil						
Volume	859	849	1,339	793	1,109	1,178
Price	416	560	616	720	607	599
Value	358	475	826	571	673	706
Desiccated coconut						
Volume	93	75	73	70	77	72
Price	897	934	933	1,220	1,152	1,016
Value	84	70	68	85	88	73
Copra meal/cake						
Volume	488	574	756	475	570	540
Price	93	92	88	119	92	65
Value	45	53	67	56	53	35
Sugar						
Volume	324	182	153	318	198	185
Price	314	333	430	429	418	432
Value	102	61	66	136	83	80
Lumber						
Volume (thousands of cubic meters)	89	41	87	146	144	44
Price (US$/cubic meters)	292	236	209	171	178	227
Value	26	10	18	25	26	10
Plywood						
Volume (thousands of cubic meters)	40	10	17	12	14	6
Price (US$/cubic meters)	435	428	341	362	363	333
Value	17	4	6	5	5	2
Copper concentrates						
Volume	334	293	282	159	117	101
Price	327	385	476	329	371	248
Value	109	113	134	52	44	25
Copper metal						
Volume	137	137	120	126	96	102
Price	1,933	1,963	2,843	2,351	2,405	1,737
Value	264	270	341	297	232	178
Gold						
Volume (troy oz.)	151	176	416	202	149	114
Price (US$/troy oz.)	339	370	370	270	330	298
Value	51	65	62	55	49	34
Iron ore						
Volume	3,919	4,666	4,692	4,435	4,718	3,381
Price	16	16	16	16	19	18
Value	62	74	74	70	90	60
Bananas						
Volume	1,153	1,155	1,213	1,253	1,150	1,140
Price	196	186	184	188	188	190
Value	226	215	224	237	217	216
Fish, fresh or preserved (value)	343	379	378	295	291	306
Other nonmanufactured (value)	756	824	934	1,065	1,114	861
Garments (value)	2,272	2,375	2,570	2,423	2,349	2,356
Electronics (value)	3,551	4,984	7,413	9,988	13,052	17,156
Other manufactured (value)	2,906	3,256	3,885	4,684	6,087	6,354
Special transactions and reexports (value)	203	255	381	499	775	1,044
Total exports	11,375	13,483	17,447	20,543	25,228	29,496

Source: Data provided by the Philippine authorities.

Table 5.4. Composition of Imports, 1993–98

	1993	1994	1995	1996	1997	1998 Est.
	(In millions of U.S. dollars)					
Mineral fuels and lubricants	2,016	2,040	2,461	3,008	3,074	2,021
Oil	1,316	1,308	1,931	2,458	2,458	1,433
Volume (millions of barrels)	83	86	117	130	127	114
Price ($/barrel)	16	15	17	19	19	13
Nonfuel imports	15,581	19,293	23,930	28,877	33,281	27,503
Capital goods	5,610	6,868	8,029	10,472	14,369	12,051
Raw materials and intermediate goods	7,855	9,606	12,174	14,058	14,634	11,586
Consumer goods	1,587	2,109	2,784	3,331	3,091	2,621
Special transactions[1]	529	710	943	1,016	1,187	1,245
Total	17,597	21,333	26,391	31,885	36,355	29,524
	(In percent of total)					
Mineral fuels and lubricants	11.5	9.6	9.3	9.4	8.5	6.8
Nonfuel imports	88.5	90.4	90.7	90.6	91.5	93.2
Capital goods	31.9	32.2	30.4	32.8	39.5	40.8
Raw materials and intermediate goods	44.6	45.0	46.1	44.1	40.3	39.2
Consumer goods	9.0	9.9	10.5	10.4	8.5	8.9
Special transactions[1]	3.0	3.3	3.6	3.2	3.3	4.2
Total	100.0	100.0	100.0	100.0	100.0	100.0

Source: Data provided by the Philippine authorities.
[1]Imports on consignment (for export use).

borrowing. Clearly, macroeconomic policies and prudential systems were not fully attuned to the challenges of the Philippines' emerging integration in the globalized capital markets. Assessment of balance of payments developments was seriously hampered by statistical problems related to transactions through foreign currency deposit accounts. The remaining section explores these developments in greater detail.

Recent Developments

The Philippine current account has been marked by large cyclical swings in recent years. The current account deficit widened to more than 5 percent of GNP in 1997, followed by a surplus of 2 percent in 1998. The trade balance shifted even more sharply, from a deficit of more than 13 percent of GNP in 1997 to balance in 1998. This dramatic adjustment reflected the combined effects of weaker growth, peso depreciation, and continued expansion of the most important export market (the United States). Imports contracted sharply (by 19 percent in dollar terms) reflecting lower volumes (13 percent) as well as prices. Part of the improvement in the trade account was offset by weaker services, especially in-

come transfers (which in the Philippines are particularly important given the large number of Philippine workers employed abroad).[8]

Unlike most other crisis countries, the Philippines has benefited from continued strong export growth. Exports volumes rose by 23 percent in 1997 and by 20 percent in 1998. This reflected the fact that Philippine exports go disproportionately to the United States (which continued to grow fast while Asian growth slumped), and have shown evidence of structural improvement, with strong gains in market shares arising mainly from investments in the electronic sector.[9]

Mirroring the current account, the capital account moved from large-scale inflows in 1995–96 to a sizable outflow in 1997. Like other Asian countries, the Philippines experienced a surge of inflows during 1993–96 (averaging about 6 percent of GNP). Net inflows fell to 1 percent in 1997 and were close to zero in 1998, the first full year following the Asian

---

[8]Income transfers were probably affected by rate of return considerations and by income considerations. In peso terms, fewer dollars needed to be exchanged to support a given income transfer following the depreciation of the peso.
[9]Described in Box 5.1.

Table 5.5. Nonmerchandise Trade
(In millions of U.S. dollars)

	1993	1994	1995	1996	1997	1998 Prelim.
Nonmerchandise trade, net	2,507	3,964	4,765	6,800	5,696	887
Earnings	7,497	10,550	14,374	19,006	22,835	13,881
Freight and merchandise insurance	156	185	252	331	391	294
Other transportation	71	54	29	34	36	38
Travel	1,178	973	1,124	1,546	2,341	1,418
Investment income	548	773	1,147	1,753	1,956	1,499
Profits, earnings, and dividends	70	116	344	700	589	302
Interest income	478	657	803	1,053	1,367	1,197
Central bank	219	322	345	476	568	587
Commercial banking system	259	335	458	577	799	610
Government	56	19	24	18	7	12
Nonmerchandise insurance	12	4	54	21	16	16
Personal income	2,276	3,009	3,869	4,306	5,742	4,932
Peso conversions of foreign currency deposits	1,680	2,815	4,827	5,863	6,006	3,410
Commissions and fees	173	207	164	373	260	181
Construction activity	10	6	10	18	27	37
Operating expenses	476	695	673	822	1,214	539
Other services	861	1,810	2,201	3,921	4,901	1,505
Payments	4,990	6,586	9,609	12,206	17,139	12,994
Freight and merchandise insurance	1,176	1,300	1,950	2,285	2,602	1,886
Other transportation	278	181	132	40	113	109
Travel	130	196	422	1,266	1,935	1,950
Investment expense	1,887	1,919	2,671	2,720	3,017	2,919
Profits, earnings, and dividends	326	311	469	470	394	318
Reinvested earnings	43	29	23	44	56	85
Interest expenses	1,518	1,579	2,179	2,206	2,567	2,516
Government	18	15	20	37	49	20
Nonmerchandise insurance	64	77	76	42	68	31
Personal income	13	13	15	57	0	0
Commissions and fees	150	275	340	775	623	551
Construction activity	23	23	65	1,186	511	218
Other services	1,251	2,587	3,918	3,798	8,221	5,310

Source: Data provided by the Philippine authorities.

crisis. Capital inflows included foreign direct investment (which averaged about $1.2 billion during 1993–97 compared with $0.6 billion during the three preceding years), borrowing by commercial banks (with net liabilities up by almost $1 billion a year on average), and medium- and long-term loans (which rose from annual net outflows of $1.1 billion during 1990–92 to inflows of $2.3 billion during 1993–97). Trade-related capital and supplier credits stayed about the same during this period.

The growing capital inflows during 1994–96 raised concerns at the time, and policies (especially monetary and exchange rate policies) were searching for ways to contain their effects (see Section IV). The focus perhaps was too narrowly directed at limiting nominal peso appreciation and/or controlling the monetary impact of the inflows. In hindsight, a more strategic and consistent approach was warranted, especially to forestall the large rise in short-term foreign borrowing in 1995–96. By the same token, it is important to note that a significant part of the capital inflows received by the Philippines during that period were medium- to long-term investments responding to the increase in capital productivity resulting from reforms. In particular, there were large foreign investments in the fast-expanding electronics export sector (see below), which rapidly became the dominant export sector in the Philippines.

During 1997, capital withdrawals started in the equity markets, followed by turnarounds in commercial bank net foreign assets and capital flight. Trade financing and suppliers' credits also declined, al-

Table 5.6. Direction of Trade
(In percent)

	Exports, f.o.b.						Imports, f.o.b.					
	1993	1994	1995	1996	1997	1998 Prelim.	1993	1994	1995	1996	1997	1998 Prelim.
United States	38.4	38.1	35.3	33.9	34.9	34.2	20.0	18.5	18.4	18.5	19.7	21.8
Japan	16.0	15.0	15.7	17.9	16.6	14.3	22.9	24.3	22.6	22.4	20.4	20.4
European Union, of which:	18.2	18.0	18.0	17.9	18.5	20.9	12.8	10.3	10.2	14.0	14.9	11.0
Germany	5.2	4.9	4.0	4.1	4.2	3.5	3.5	3.6	3.5	3.8	3.2	2.9
Netherlands	3.2	3.8	4.6	5.4	6.6	7.9	1.4	1.3	1.2	1.0	1.4	0.8
United Kingdom	4.8	4.7	5.3	4.6	4.3	6.0	2.2	1.8	2.1	1.5	1.5	1.1
France	1.8	1.4	1.2	1.1	0.9	0.9	1.1	1.1	1.2	1.0	3.4	1.7
Middle East, of which:	2.3	1.8	1.3	1.2	0.9	0.8	8.4	7.4	8.5	8.5	7.3	5.9
Saudi Arabia	0.6	0.4	0.4	0.3	0.1	0.1	4.2	4.4	6.2	5.2	2.9	1.9
Kuwait	0.1	0.1	0.1	0.1	0.1	0.0	1.1	0.4	0.1	0.1	0.0	0.1
Iraq	0.0	0.0	0.0	0.0	0.0	0.0	0.0	0.0	0.0	0.0	0.1	0.1
ASEAN, of which:[1]	3.7	5.4	7.9	8.5	7.2	6.7	5.3	4.9	6.0	7.0	7.4	9.2
Indonesia	0.4	0.5	0.7	0.7	0.8	0.4	1.9	1.7	2.2	2.0	1.9	2.0
Malaysia	1.4	1.6	1.8	3.3	2.5	3.9	2.0	2.0	2.2	2.5	2.6	3.2
Singapore	3.3	5.3	5.7	6.0	6.4	6.2	5.6	6.8	5.9	5.5	6.0	5.9
Australia	1.0	1.0	0.8	0.8	0.8	0.6	2.7	2.8	2.8	2.5	2.6	2.3
Hong Kong SAR	4.8	4.8	4.7	4.2	4.6	4.5	5.0	5.2	4.8	4.3	4.3	4.4
Korea	1.9	2.2	2.5	1.8	1.9	1.7	5.1	5.2	5.2	5.2	6.0	7.4
BRO[2]	0.1	0.1	0.1	0.1	0.0	0.0	0.5	0.9	1.3	1.5	1.1	0.6
China	1.5	1.2	1.2	1.6	1.0	1.1	1.0	1.4	2.2	2.1	2.4	4.1
Other	12.0	12.3	12.5	12.1	13.5	15.1	16.3	19.3	18.0	14.0	13.8	12.9
All countries	100.0	100.0	100.0	100.0	100.0	100.0	100.0	100.0	100.0	100.0	100.0	100.0

Source: Data provided by the Philippine authorities.
[1]Association of Southeast Asian Nations.
[2]Baltics, Russia, and other countries of the former Soviet Union.

Table 5.7. International Reserves of the Banking System
(In millions of U.S. dollars; end of period)

	1993	1994	1995	1996	1997	1998
Monetary authorities (net)	3,496	5,297	5,928	10,035	6,672	8,031
Assets	5,922	7,122	7,762	11,745	8,768	10,806
Liabilities	2,426	1,825	1,834	1,710	2,096	2,776
Of which: IMF	1,219	1,064	728	405	889	1,562
Commercial banks (net)[1]	912	238	−1,336	−5,838	−7,415	−6,392
Assets	4,008	5,028	5,170	6,803	6,440	6,432
Liabilities	3,096	4,790	6,506	12,641	13,855	12,824
Banking system	4,408	5,535	4,592	4,197	−743	1,638
Assets	9,930	12,150	12,932	18,548	15,208	17,238
Liabilities	5,522	6,615	8,340	14,351	15,951	15,600

Source: Data provided by the Philippine authorities.
[1]Monetary claims on, and liabilities to, nonresidents.

Box 5.1. Electronics Exports—Rapid Growth

Although growth of electronics exports took off only in 1994, the sector has long historic roots in the Philippines. This was evident in the continuous upgrading of the capabilities of the sector, which started in the 1970s with basic assembly and packaging of components, added assembly and testing technologies in the 1980s, and expanded to the production of complete computer peripherals, module assembly, and component manufacturing in the 1990s. Wafer fabrication and original design is considered as being within the sector's capabilities within the next five years.

Despite the Asian crisis, 38 new electronics companies were registered during 1998 (according to Board of Investment/Philippines Economic Zone Authority data), at a total project cost of ₱15 billion, bringing the total number of companies to 462. Of these, 138 were Philippine (although such companies were relatively small), 133 Japanese, 46 Korean, 39 United States (accounting for about 70 percent of exports), and 20 Taiwanese.

The geographic distribution of electronics exports is well diversified, with 32 percent going to the United States, 22 percent to Europe, 15 percent to other ASEAN countries, 13 percent to Japan, 8 percent to Taiwan Province of China, and 10 percent to other destinations. In terms of employment, the sector contributes about 250,000 jobs in 1998, up from 38,000 in 1985. Employment in the semiconductor subsector has been growing more slowly than in other electronics subsectors, reflecting its relative capital intensity.

Elements contributing to the sector's growth include:

- A high emphasis by local producers on the quality of production, using the latest manufacturing techniques.
- Wages are higher in the Philippines relative to China and Indonesia, but local labor is considered highly skilled, technically proficient, cost competitive, and

Electronics Exports

	Exports (In billions of U.S. dollars)	Growth Rate (In percent)	Share in Total Exports (In percent)
1994	4.9	28	36
1995	7.6	55	43
1996	10.6	40	52
1997	15.0	41	59
1998	19.7	32	67

Source: Semiconductor Industries Association.

well trained. The Philippines has significant numbers of technically trained (engineering and information technology) personnel: with a labor force of 31.2 million, of which 28.3 million are employed; the Philippines had 438,988 enrolled students in 1997–98, and graduated 74,750 students a year (in technical fields). In all, there are 1,345 colleges and universities.

- The strategic location of the Philippines (together with human resources) is often cited as the dominant reason for foreign direct investment.

Domestic value added in electronics exports has almost tripled since the 1980s, increasing to almost 30 percent (25 percent for computers) in 1998, from about 10 percent in the early 1990s. This finding, however, does not apply to all manufacturing processes (for example, packaging is still heavily dependent on imports, especially of wafers).

though largely in tandem with declining import volumes—there is no evidence of significant cuts in trade lines.[10] Likewise, commercial banks' large foreign currency deposit base proved stable throughout the crisis.[11] There was also continued strength in medium- and long-term net inflows, and relatively strong foreign direct investment (which increased from 1997 to 1998).

Faced with the sudden decline in net private capital inflows, the authorities increased public foreign borrowing, including from multilateral[12] and bilateral[13] resources. This policy was part of a strategy to allow an orderly adjustment to the shock in private capital flows while containing the underlying vulnerabilities. The strategy to control vulnerabilities centered on a relatively tight monetary policy, a floating exchange rate (with occasional—and limited—intervention to prevent disorderly market con-

[10]This was in contrast to the experience in the early 1990s, when most trade lines were not rolled over.

[11]The stability of short-term foreign bank lines may be attributable to the fact that Philippine banks in the 1990s have become net depositors in the euro markets, with part of foreign currency deposit unit deposits redeposited abroad.

[12]Mainly the IMF (extension and augmentation of the 1994 Extended Fund Facility, and a new Stand-By Arrangement in March 1998), the World Bank (a Banking Sector Reform Loan in 1998, and additional program loans planned for 1999), and the Asian Development Bank (with loans for the energy sector, capital market, and Metro Manila air quality development).

[13]Most notably from Japan (OECF and JEXIM), and significantly expanded under the "Miyazawa" initiative.

Box 5.2. Nondeliverable Forwards: Their Use in the Philippines

A *nondeliverable forward* is a forward contract without an exchange of principal; instead, only the difference between the contract exchange rate and the spot rate at maturity is settled, in local currency. The nondeliverable forward typically covers the foreign exchange risk (in case of a depreciation; the central bank makes a profit when the currency appreciates) of an underlying foreign loan, the maturity of which tends to match that of the nondeliverable forward. The contract exchange rate is usually determined by the current exchange rate adjusted for the differential between the domestic T-bill rate and the London interbank offered rate.

There is *little conceptual difference* between foreign exchange market intervention through nondeliverable forwards and intervention through forwards. The main exception concerns the accounting treatment of nondeliverable forwards, which makes them less transparent (as they are not reflected in reserves when they are contracted):

• In forward (currency swap) intervention, commercial banks would make a simultaneous spot sale of dollars to the central bank and a forward purchase of dollars from the central bank. The central bank would then sell the dollars in the foreign exchange market. The net effect of these transactions on reserves would be zero (unless reserves were explicitly defined to exclude forward liabilities), but forward liabilities would go up by the full amount of the swap.

• In intervention through nondeliverable forwards, commercial banks are encouraged to borrow abroad,

selling the dollar proceeds in the foreign exchange market. In exchange, they get a nondeliverable forward from the central bank, which assures them of having enough pesos to buy the dollars they will need at the end of the contract. When the loan is unwound, the commercial banks repays the foreign dollar loan.

The Bangko Sentral ng Pilipinas has used *two main types of nondeliverable forwards:*

(1) *Special nondeliverable forwards,* contracted primarily with local branches of foreign banks. Typically, these borrow foreign exchange from their parent banks, at maturities of up to one year. The banks would sell the loan proceeds in the interbank foreign exchange market (thereby supporting the peso). The nondeliverable forward in effect covers the downside foreign exchange risk for the bank, with an upside potential for the Bangko Sentral ng Pilipinas.

(2) The *currency risk protection program,* applied to corporations with unhedged foreign exchange liabilities contracted prior to some cutoff date. The corporation in effect gets a foreign exchange guarantee from a local bank that "off loads" the risk through a nondeliverable forward with the Bangko Sentral ng Pilipinas.

The *stock of nondeliverable forwards* rose to about $1 billion in 1998 (mainly special nondeliverable forwards), following pressures in the foreign exchange market.

ditions),[14] measures to strengthen the banking sector, and better monitoring of short-term debt.[15] The lessons learned from the earlier crises, especially the safeguards put in place to prevent renewed excessive debt accumulation, clearly contributed to the success of this strategy.

While the external position remained vulnerable through the summer of 1998, it has since improved. These developments were in line with global market developments, but domestic elements were also at play. In particular, while there was some market uncertainty following the May 1998 elections about the policies of the future government, confidence improved once the government had set out its policies. Since September 1998, the peso has appreciated significantly and gross usable reserves have risen to

more than 120 percent of short-term debt, up from less than 80 percent in early 1998.

Following the steady decline in the debt/GNP ratio through 1996, the ratio has increased again in recent years, to 76 percent, partly influenced also by the peso depreciation. Debt-reduction operations, prudent fiscal policies, and rapid growth had reduced debt relative to GNP from 65 percent in 1990 to 47 percent in 1996. In addition, a policy of lengthening debt maturities had reduced the debt-service burden (with the debt-service ratio falling from 35 percent in 1990 to about 13 percent in 1996). Mainly because of peso depreciation, the debt-service ratio, however, has remained low at 13 percent in 1998 (Tables 5.8–5.9).

External Competitiveness

During 1993–97, the current account deficit grew to more than 5 percent of GDP, and the peso is estimated to have become overvalued by 10–20 per-

---

[14]Intervention during this period was mainly in the form of nondeliverable forward contracts between the Bangko Sentral ng Pilipinas and market participants. The use of nondeliverable forwards in the Philippines is briefly summarized in Box 5.2.

[15]For a description of efforts to improve external data, see Box 5.3.

Table 5.8. Total External Debt

	1993	1994	1995	1996	1997	1998
			(In millions of U.S. dollars)			
External debt						
Short term	5,035	5,197	5,279	7,207	8,439	7,185
Of which: commercial banks	383	1,156	1,800	3,245	3,611	3,571
Medium and long term	29,188	32,387	33,274	34,668	36,122	39,070
Of which: commercial banks	1,627	2,133	2,440	2,789	3,770	4,208
IMF	1,312	1,139	814	405	872	1,562
Total	35,535	38,723	39,367	42,280	45,433	47,817
Monitored external liabilities[1]						
Short term	...	...	...	...	11,513	10,245
Of which: commercial banks	...	...	...	...	6,693	6,631
Medium and long term	...	...	...	...	38,343	41,702
Of which: commercial banks	...	...	...	...	5,066	5,436
IMF	...	...	...	...	872	1,562
Total	...	...	...	...	50,728	53,509
			(In percent of total external debt)			
External debt						
Short term	14.2	13.4	13.4	17.0	18.6	15.0
Of which: commercial banks	1.1	3.0	4.6	7.7	7.9	7.5
Medium and long term	82.1	83.6	84.5	82.0	79.5	81.7
Of which: commercial banks	4.6	5.5	6.2	6.6	8.3	8.8
IMF	3.7	2.9	2.1	1.0	1.9	3.3
			(In percent of total monitored external liabilities)			
Monitored external liabilities[1]						
Short term	...	...	...	...	22.7	19.1
Of which: commercial banks	...	...	...	...	13.2	12.4
Medium and long term	...	...	...	...	75.6	77.9
Of which: commercial banks	...	...	...	...	10.0	10.2
IMF	...	...	...	...	1.7	2.9
			(In percent of GNP)			
External debt						
Short term	9.1	7.9	6.9	8.4	9.9	10.1
Of which: commercial banks	0.7	1.8	2.4	3.8	4.2	5.0
Medium and long term	52.8	49.3	43.7	40.2	42.2	55.1
Of which: commercial banks	2.9	3.2	3.2	3.2	4.4	5.9
IMF	2.4	1.7	1.1	0.5	1.0	2.2
Total	64.2	58.9	51.7	49.0	53.1	67.5
Monitored external liabilities[1]						
Short term	...	...	...	...	13.5	14.5
Of which: commercial banks	...	...	...	...	7.8	9.4
Medium and long term	...	...	...	...	44.8	58.8
Of which: commercial banks	...	...	...	...	5.9	7.7
IMF	...	...	...	...	1.0	2.2
Total	...	...	...	...	59.3	75.5

Sources: Data provided by the Philippine authorities; and IMF staff estimates.

[1]Monitored external liabilities are defined as external debt plus liabilities of foreign banks in the Philippines to their headquarters, branches, and agencies; some external debt not registered with the central bank; and private capital lease arrangements.

cent. The peso appreciated faster in real effective terms than other Asian currencies, and the current account deficit widened significantly beyond the level consistent with medium-term equilibrium even after accounting for the impact of the economic cycle.

In 1998, the current account turned into a surplus, as output growth fell far below potential and the peso "overshot" to become temporarily undervalued. The exchange rate, however, has appreciated significantly since late 1998, virtually eliminating by mid-1999 all of the estimated undervaluation.

Table 5.9. External Debt Service

	1993	1994	1995	1996	1997	1998
	(In millions of U.S. dollars)					
Debt service before rescheduling and accumulation of arrears	3,594	4,907	5,032	5,026	5,597	5,061
Principal (excluding IMF)	2,012	3,056	2,494	2,541	2,843	2,437
Multilateral	471	566	682	657	633	597
Bilateral	827	1,257	1,385	1,154	1,342	1,125
Banks and financial institutions[1]	540	843	193	200	590	426
Other[2]	174	390	234	530	278	289
IMF repurchase	64	272	359	279	186	108
Interest	1,518	1,579	2,179	2,206	2,568	2,516
Multilateral	633	711	634	593	542	505
Bilateral	642	742	784	634	579	551
Banks and financial institutions	152	32	363	550	707	640
Other	91	94	398	429	740	820
Rescheduling	818	478	0	0	0	0
Paris Club	211	0	0	0	0	0
Commercial banks	607	478	0	0	0	0
Change in arrears	0	178	−178	0	0	0
Debt service after rescheduling and changes in arrears	3,511	4,251	4,854	5,026	5,597	5,061
	(In percent of exports of goods and services)					
Debt-service ratio (including IMF)						
Before rescheduling	22.9	20.4	15.8	12.7	11.9	12.8
Ratio of interest payments (before rescheduling) to GNP	2.7	2.4	2.9	2.5	3.0	3.7

Sources: Data provided by the Philippine authorities; and IMF staff estimates.
[1]Excluding monetary liabilities and debt conversions.
[2]Figures for 1995–97 include some debt-equity and bond-equity conversions, as well as some prepayments.

External Competitiveness Indicators

Because of recent volatility and data limitations, the usual real exchange rate indicators provide little evidence regarding the adequacy of competitiveness at a certain exchange rate. Because there are no direct measures of an "internal" real exchange rate (prices of nontradables relative to those of tradables), the proxy of nonfood prices in the consumer price index relative to the price of food was used (Figure 5.1, top panel). This measure shows sizable real appreciation during the 1990s (some 25 percent from end-1989 to end-1997; 13 percent since end-1995), but is obviously distorted by the larger volatility of food prices.[16]

Other measures of competitiveness, such as the real effective exchange rate index compiled by the IMF, show a much larger appreciation prior to the crisis, followed by sizable depreciation after the float of the peso in mid-1997. Figure 5.1 (bottom panel) shows real appreciation of more than 50 percent from the trough in 1990 to mid-1997, followed by a depreciation of about 30 percent. The problem, then, is to determine an appropriate base period during which the exchange rate was judged to have been in equilibrium. While 1993 has often been cited as a year with broad equilibrium both domestically and in the external accounts, such an assessment inevitably involves a large amount of judgment.

Comparison with the "Asian-4" countries (Figure 5.2) shows that the Philippine peso has been stronger in real effective terms throughout much of the 1990s. That this relative real appreciation was not reversed during the recent crisis is significant and may indicate that fundamental structural change has been at work. A more formal assessment, based on an analysis of the medium-term underlying current account position, is given in Appendix 5.1. Figure 5.3 suggests that the current account in the Philippines responds significantly to movements in the

---

[16]For example, in 1997–98, reflecting the impact of drought on food prices, the ratio continued rising notwithstanding the large depreciation after the float of the peso in mid-1997.

Figure 5.1. Real Exchange Rate Measures[1]

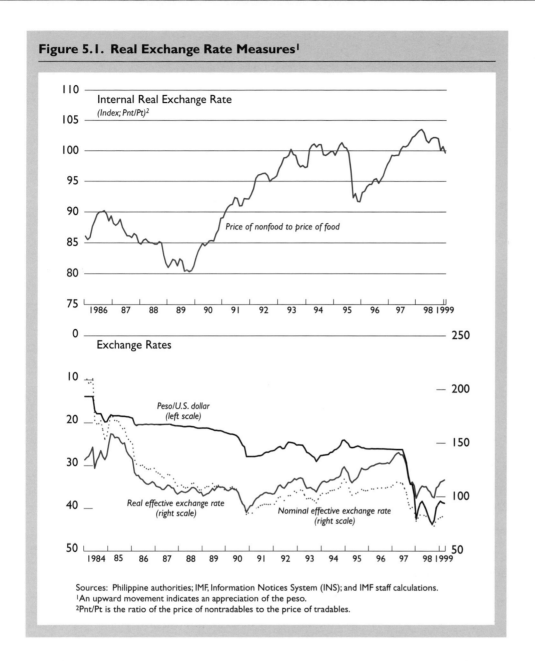

Sources: Philippine authorities; IMF, Information Notices System (INS); and IMF staff calculations.
[1]An upward movement indicates an appreciation of the peso.
[2]Pnt/Pt is the ratio of the price of nontradables to the price of tradables.

real effective exchange rate, a finding confirmed by the econometric estimates in Appendix 5.1.

Exports as Indicators of Competitiveness

Since the early 1990s, the Philippines appears to have experienced a favorable structural improvement in its external trade. Analysis of trade flows can provide useful insights on competitiveness. In particular, structural changes in trade flows and sustained changes in market share can be indicators of shifts in the equilibrium exchange rate. As documented in Section II, econometric analysis confirms a structural break in trade performance around the early 1990s; the ratios of export to import volumes (Figures 5.4 and 5.5) support a similar conclusion.

There has been a significant gain in export market share since 1994, following a decade of relative stagnancy. Figure 5.6 shows that the growth of Philippine export market share has outpaced that of all the other Asian-5 countries, except Korea. This is indicative of a favorable structural shift, in particular since it coincided with real appreciation.

Developments in Export Components

The main driving force behind the recent favorable export performance has been the electronics

Figure 5.2. Asian Exchange Rates[1]

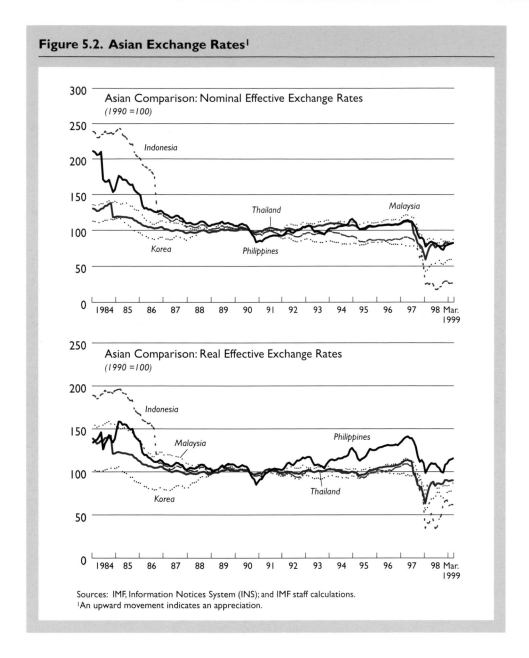

Sources: IMF, Information Notices System (INS); and IMF staff calculations.
[1]An upward movement indicates an appreciation.

sector, which has experienced rapid growth since 1994, and has become by far the dominant export sector (Figure 5.7 and Box 5.1). To a large degree, the Philippines' continued export-led growth is now tied to the success of electronics exports. Food exports (except coconuts) have also kept growing. Other traditional exports, especially garments, have performed less well. The worst performance has been turned in by minerals exports.

Some observers have pointed to the risks inherent in overspecialization, and have noted evidence of competitiveness problems in the comparatively weak performance of traditional exports. The local value added in electronics exports is also still relatively low

(10–30 percent), as they depend considerably on imported raw and processed materials (especially wafers). The World Bank points out that this situation can only be remedied through the upgrading of local technology and growth of domestic firms that can provide a wider array of ancillary services.[17] Support of small and medium-sized enterprises, including better access to finance, should also help in this context. For garments, the key was judged to be better quality of production, distribution, and marketing. Notwithstanding these caveats, it is clear that the dy-

_____
[17]World Bank (1998).

Box 5.3. External Data Issues

External sector data, especially on the trade and external debt side, are generally of high quality and are available in sufficient detail and frequency, but their compilation has become increasingly difficult in recent years. In particular, increased use of foreign currency deposit units and of offshore banking units has made it difficult to correctly allocate the transactions between current/financial account categories, given banking secrecy laws. As a result, the estimates of services are affected by large uncertainties, and possibly include a sizable amount of capital account transactions.

Significant improvements have been made in recent years. In particular, the Bangko Sentral ng Pilipinas has included in external debt reports of several items previously excluded (most notably of credit lines to banks extended from headquarter banks located abroad). A simplified and more informative foreign exchange reporting form has been introduced, and the Bangko Sentral ng Pilipinas is working on a number of improvements to the reporting system on derivatives. Much of this work is in progress. It is also apparent, however, that the strict bank secrecy provisions prevent substantial progress on improving the estimates of transactions through foreign currency deposit unit accounts.

namism of electronics exports could not have come at a better time for the Philippines, sustaining growth and export earnings at a time of crisis.

Medium-Term Outlook and Issues

Over the medium term, the current account is expected to return to a deficit that is consistent with the medium-term investment norm (2–3 percent of GDP). The speed with which the norm is reached depends on the projected paths for output and the real effective exchange rate. The extent to which exports continue to gain market share is an additional uncertainty. Given the outlook for continued foreign direct investment and rising portfolio inflows, financing the current account deficit and projected debt amortization should not pose a problem. Reserves are expected to continue to increase, to the equivalent of four months of imports by the end of the projection period (2004). Although external debt would continue to increase in absolute terms, it would decline relative to GNP (to 67 percent, from 76 percent in 1998).

In support of such a scenario, a challenging policy agenda remains:

- Macroeconomic policies will need to combine prudent demand management with exchange rate flexibility, to preserve competitiveness and prevent the buildup of excessive leverage and

Figure 5.3. Current Account and Real Exchange Rate[1]

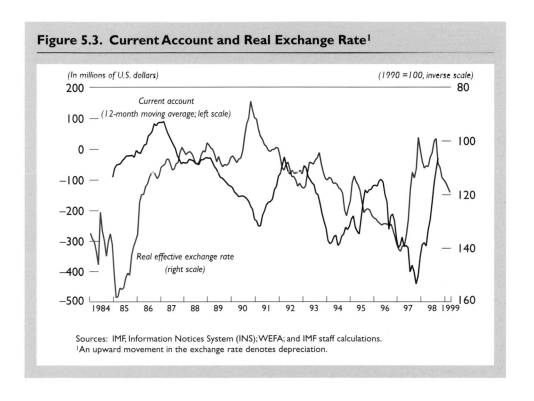

Sources: IMF, Information Notices System (INS); WEFA; and IMF staff calculations.
[1]An upward movement in the exchange rate denotes depreciation.

Figure 5.4. Merchandise Trade Volume

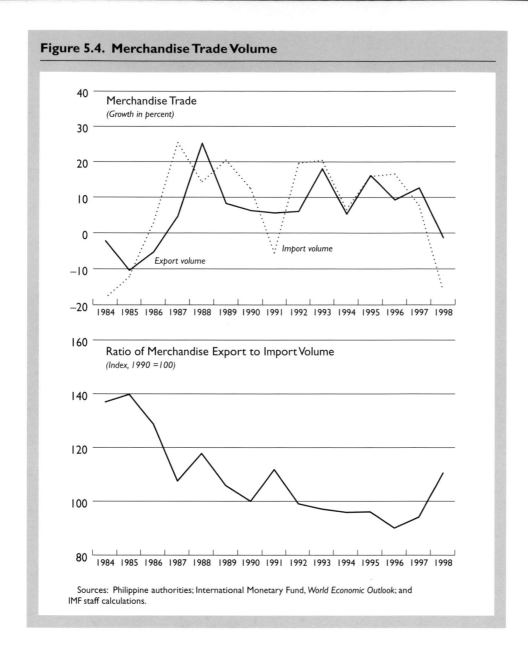

Sources: Philippine authorities; International Monetary Fund, *World Economic Outlook*; and IMF staff calculations.

debt (especially short term). Continued upgrading of prudential and supervisory standards in the banking system will also be necessary for the successful management of the "capital inflows problem."

• Continued trade and investment liberalization will be crucial for the Philippines to fully partake in the benefits of globalization. Average import tariffs are set to come down to 5 percent by 2004, an objective that should be maintained. In addition, protection in agriculture should be reduced to enhance productivity growth in that sector, and to permit dynamic export growth in this area of apparent comparative advantage.

• Support for exports by building up infrastructure, enhancing access to finance for small and medium-sized enterprises, and improvements in services (including in the area of public administration) will also be necessary to sustain gains in market share.

• Debt management should continue to be modernized, to keep pace with rapidly evolving financing techniques and, in particular, to keep on top of all forms of short-term exposures.

• Balance of payments statistics need to improve further to prevent reliable estimates of current account developments. This should include the use of source data on transactions through for-

Figure 5.5. Goods and Services Trade Volume

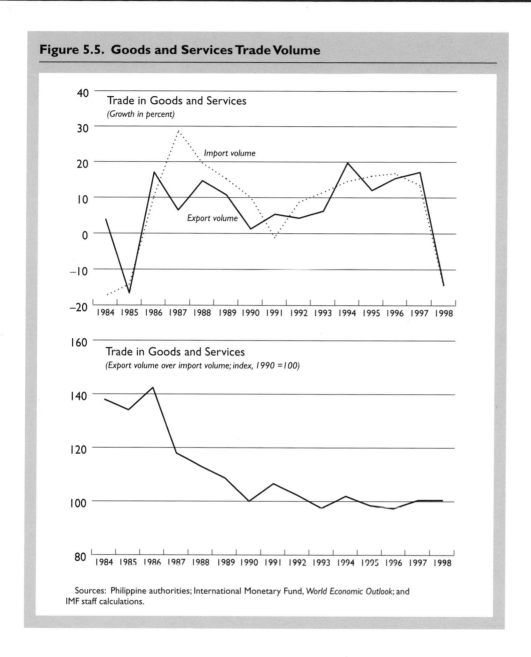

Sources: Philippine authorities; International Monetary Fund, *World Economic Outlook*; and IMF staff calculations.

eign currency deposit unit accounts (even if provided by banks in appropriate form, to accommodate the laws on bank secrecy), or the development of reliable alternatives (survey methods).

Appendix 5.1. External Competitiveness: A Macroeconomic Balance Approach Applied to the Philippines

Analysis of external competitiveness suggests that the peso was overvalued prior to the Asian crisis, then "overshot" in the other direction, and is now close to equilibrium. Analysis based on a macroeco-

nomic balance methodology suggests that prior to the crisis, the peso was overvalued by 10–15 percent in real effective terms.[18] Following the float, the peso depreciated by more than 30 percent, resulting in undervaluation to about 10–15 percent. Since late 1998, the peso has appreciated, bringing it close to its equilibrium level.[19]

---

[18]See Isard and Faruqee (1998) for a general description of the macroeconomic balance approach and how it has been applied at the IMF.

[19]The analysis is based on *medium-term* estimates of the equilibrium exchange rate, and should not be taken as indicators of imminent short-term movements.

Figure 5.6. Asian Export Competitiveness

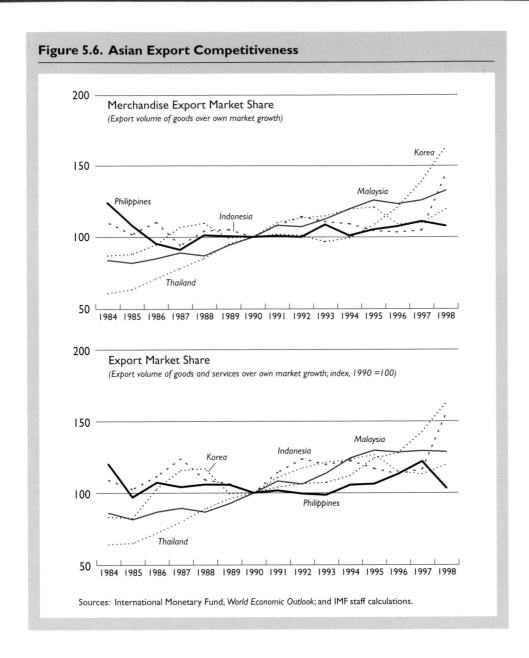

Sources: International Monetary Fund, *World Economic Outlook*; and IMF staff calculations.

Over the medium term, it is expected that the current account (now in surplus of 2 percent of GNP) will return to a deficit of about 2–3 percent of GNP. Such a position would be consistent with a medium-term savings–investment norm estimated using the macroeconomic balance methodology.

The Macroeconomic Balance Approach

The macroeconomic approach is adapted to the Philippines through the use of econometric techniques to provide quantitative estimates of the extent of exchange rate over/undervaluation. The starting point for the econometric investigation is a version of

the equation 5.1 (given in Chapter V of Isard and Faruqee (1998), reproduced below with a few minor adaptations):[20]

$$CA_t = a - b(c_0 R_t + c_1 R_{t-1} + c_2 R_{t-2}) + mR_t - mdYGAP_t,$$

where *CA* denotes the current account to nominal GDP ratio, *R* the logarithm of the real effective exchange rate (in *levels*), and *YGAP* the domestic out-

---

[20]This equation also excludes a term for the foreign output gap of the Philippines' trading partners, for which data was not available.

Figure 5.7. Selected Export Components

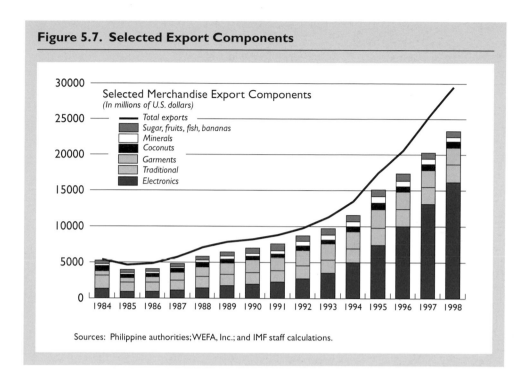

Sources: Philippine authorities; WEFA, Inc.; and IMF staff calculations.

put gap.[21] Some of the parameters given here in summary form have structural interpretations. Notable are b, which is the weighted sum of the (goods and nonfactor) import and export relative price elasticities, representing the trade volume effects of the real exchange rate and related to the Marshall-Lerner condition, and m, which is the import-output ratio—representing the value effect from full pass-through in import prices. The c_i coefficients provide a lag structure with which the exchange rate influences the current account, and are assumed to sum to one (so that the full impact of the exchange rate is assumed to feed through, although the precise lag structure is likely to depend on country-specific characteristics). It is assumed (although this assumption is not qualitatively essential) that two lags (corresponding to two years, for annual data) are sufficient to allow for the exchange rate effect to pass through. Given estimates of the relevant parameters, one can then construct an estimate of the *underlying* current account, or the current account that would prevail at a zero output gap (a "cyclical" adjustment) and once the impact of lagged exchange rates has fully worked itself through (equivalent to past exchange rates being set equal to the current exchange rate). Written out, the equation defining the underlying current account balance is:

$$CA_{ut} = a - bR_{ct} + mR_{ct},$$

with definitions as above, and with u denoting the underlying current account and c the current exchange rate. Once estimates of the coefficients are obtained, one can construct an estimated underlying current account balance. Statistical measures of adequacy of the estimated regression equation can also be used to partly gauge the validity of the whole procedure.

However, as it stands, the equation determining the current account is difficult to estimate directly, because of the presence of the R_t term twice together with the restriction on the lag structure coefficients. To proceed, a certain transformation is applied to the model that exploits (imposes *a priori*) the restriction that the lag structure coefficients (the c_i) sum to one, resulting in the following equation[22]:

$$CA_t = a - (b - m) R_t + b [(c_0 - 1)\Delta R_t \\ + (c_0 + c_1 - 1)\Delta R_{t-1}] - mdYGAP_t.$$

The transformation results in the isolation of the level of the exchange rate (the R_t), and the introduction of terms in the current and lagged change of the

---

[21]As estimated using a Hodrick-Prescott filter.

[22]The transformation used here is analogous to a transformation often used to explore issues of *cointegration,* which transforms an equation that links *levels* of dependent and independent variables that are assumed to be of the same order of integration to an equation that links the *level* of the dependent variable to the *changes* in the independent variable (plus lags) and to the *level* of a lagged dependent variable (depending on the version of the transformation used, the lagged dependent variable can occur either at the first or the last lag).

exchange rate (the ΔR_t which, being logarithmic changes, approximate percent changes). [Note that the R_{t-2} term is embodied in the lagged change.]

With these preliminaries, a regression equation can be fitted directly to the equation immediately above. Of course, there are several issues to contend with, including the quality of the data, the fact that a regression over a given, relatively short sample (here, taken to be 1982–98) may fail to capture well the long-run tendencies, and simultaneity (the current account balance will tend to influence the output gap as well as be influenced by it). Hence, the estimates to be presented below should always be interpreted cautiously, although an attempt will be made to deal with the issue of simultaneity through the use of an instrumental variables estimation technique. A first attempt to fit the above equation results in the following (t-statistics in parentheses):

$$CA_t = -1.85 - 0.001R_t - 0.15\Delta R_t - 0.13\Delta R_{t-1}$$
$$(0.05) \quad (0.02) \quad (2.02) \quad (2.06)$$

$$- 0.55YGAP_t,$$
$$(1.23)$$

$$\sigma_\varepsilon = 2.07, D.W. = 2.05, R^2 - BAR = 0.58,$$

where the estimation is conducted using an instrumental variables technique, and where a constant, R_t, ΔR_t, ΔR_{t-1}, and $YGAP_{t-1}$ are used as instruments (note the lagged output gap term, intended to avoid the simultaneity problem between the current account and the contemporaneous output gap term).[23] Clearly, the equation generally works well, with the exception that the coefficient on the exchange rate level is extremely small and statistically insignificant (it is also surprising that the constant is insignificantly different from zero; one would expect a developing country to have a fairly robust negative average estimate for the current account balance).

Theoretically, a zero estimate for the term $(b - m)$ most likely corresponds to a rather small export price elasticity. To demonstrate, write the structural interpretation of $(b - m)$ in obvious notation as $(M/Y)(b_m - 1) + (X/Y)b_x$—where b_x, b_m represent individual export and import price elasticities. For the Philippines, M/Y is slightly more than ⅓, and X/Y is about ¼. Using the estimates for developing countries quoted in Isard and Faruqee, 0.69 for imports and 0.53 for exports (smaller than for industrial countries, but still satisfying the Marshall-Lerner condition), one would expect $(b - m)$ to equal about 0.03. For $(b - m)$ to equal zero, and holding the import elasticity constant, the export elasticity would

have to equal about 0.4. So, the Marshall-Lerner condition is still satisfied, although just barely, but the nominal trade balance is insensitive to the exchange rate level as volume effects are broadly offset by the value effect on import prices.

Imposing the (statistically valid) restriction that $(b - m)$ is zero, we reestimate the equation using instrumental variables (and dropping R_t from the instruments list) for the current account as follows (t-statistics in parentheses):

$$CA_t = -2.51 - 0.15\Delta R_t - 0.13\Delta R_{t-1} - 0.56*YGAP_t,$$
$$(4.68) \quad (2.76) \quad (2.32) \quad (1.26)$$

$$\sigma_\varepsilon = 1.97, D.W. = 2.05, R^2 - BAR = 0.62$$

The equation has superior statistical properties to that earlier estimated, and is used in what follows. A chart of the actual against the (within sample) predicted current account confirms the statistical tests, as it shows that the predicted current account tracks the actual current rather well, especially during the recent sharp turnaround in the current account.

The next step in the macroeconomic balance approach is to construct an estimate for the underlying current account. Following the exposition in Isard and Faruqee, the underlying current account can be written in terms of the actual current account and the estimated terms. However, the *statistically* derived restriction $(b - m = 0)$ results in a considerably simplified expression, as follows:[24]

$$CA_{ut} = CA_t + b[(c_0 - 1)\Delta R_t + (c_0 + c_1 - 1)\Delta R_{t-1}] + mdYGAP_t$$

The underlying current account for the Philippines is constructed using the estimated coefficients.[25]

A "Warranted" Current Account and the Equilibrium Exchange Rate

The next step is to construct a benchmark, or a medium-term norm, against which the underlying current account estimated above can be compared. This "warranted" current account can be constructed using the Faruqee-Debelle methodology described in Isard and Faruqee (1998) for estimating a savings-investment norm. The procedure was operationalized taking into account the influence of demographic,

---

[23]This procedure is preferred even though it results in ostensibly a lower statistical significance for the output gap term; however, the coefficient itself does not seem too sensitive to the difference in estimation technique.

[24]A comparison between Isard and Faruqee equation 5.3 and the one given here will show that the main effect of the restriction $b - m = 0$ is to negate the impact of the term involving the difference between the current and the year average exchange rates.

[25]Note that by constructing the underlying current account based on the *actual* current account rather than the *predicted* current account from the regression, we include the implicit residual from that estimated equation in our calculation of the underlying current account. As this is an unobservable error term, no obvious choice can be made as to its treatment.

fiscal, and output variables for the Philippines relative to the equivalent variables in a set of industrial economies. The norm is found to fluctuate, but to be significantly less volatile than either the actual or the underlying current accounts. For 1998, for example, the norm indicates a deficit slightly above 2 percent of GDP, while the actual current account position was a surplus of 1.8 percent and the underlying current account surplus about 1 percent.

To finally draw the implications of this analysis for the exchange rate, one needs to know the long-run sensitivity of the current account to the exchange rate. Conceptually, the exchange rate is deemed overvalued (undervalued) when the underlying current account is less than (more than) the savings-investment norm. However, the above analysis has not resulted in a reliable estimate of this sensitivity. Reasonable numbers used for other crisis-affected Asian economies range from 0.25 to 0.3. Using a number in this range for the Philippines, one can estimate the degree of exchange rate adjustment that would be required to equate the underlying and warranted current accounts. Based on this analysis, the exchange rate became undervalued by 10–15 percent during 1998.[26]

The norm is consistent with the indications from the real effective exchange rate measures that the peso was overvalued during the period prior to the Asian crisis. The norm also indicates that the actual current account was closest to the "warranted" level in 1991, and not in 1993, as is sometimes assumed. In 1998, the current account overshot its warranted level, as it moved into sizable surplus. Corresponding to the shifts in the relationship between the cyclically adjusted and the "warranted" current accounts, the real effective exchange rate in 1998 overshot the equilibrium level, becoming undervalued (as earlier indicated) by about 10–15 percent.

References

Aguilar, Rosemarie, 1995, "The Filipino Worker: Leading the Way to Global Competitiveness," *Philippine Development,* Vol. 22, No. 1, pp. 1–2.

---

[26]The Faruqee-Debelle procedure produces an estimate for a "normal" current account (the "savings-investment norm") by using a panel set of countries that are used as comparators (see Isard and Faruqee (1998)). The procedure allows for a "recalibration" of the result, to introduce a "fixed-effect" correction intended to help match the predicted savings-investment norm with some historical average for the country. For the Philippines, the correction was made to match the average current account up to 1993 (later years were excluded so as not to contaminate what should be a medium-term estimate without the effect of recent events).

Anthony Myrvin, and Andrew Hughes Hallett, 1992, "How Successfully Do We Measure Capital Flight? The Empirical Evidence from Five Developing Countries," *The Journal of Development Studies,* Vol. 28, No. 3, pp. 538–56.

Baig, Taimur, and Ilan Goldfajn, 1998, "Financial Market Contagion in the Asian Crisis," IMF Working Paper 98/155 (Washington: International Monetary Fund).

Borras, P., 1994, "Foreign Currency Deposit Units: Beginnings and Current Developments," *Bangko Sentral Review,* Vol. 2, No. 8.

Dolan, Roland, 1993, "Philippines: A Country Study," *Area Country Series* (Washington: Library of Congress).

García, Roberto, 1991, "Foreign Exchange and Payments Arrangements in the Philippines and Eastern European Countries," *Central Bank Review,* Vol. 43, No. 7, pp. 16–24.

GATT (General Agreements on Tariffs and Trade), 1993, *The Philippines: Trade Policy Review,* Volumes 1–2 (Geneva).

International Monetary Fund, 1995, Background Paper SM/95/253, Chapter I (September) (Washington).

Isard, Peter, and Hamid Faruqee, 1998, *Exchange Rate Assessment: Extensions of the Macroeconomic Balance Approach,* IMF Occasional Paper 167 (Washington: International Monetary Fund).

Kajiwara, Hirokazu, 1994, "The Effects of Trade and Foreign Investment Liberalization Policy on Productivity in the Philippines," *The Developing Economies,* Vol. 32, No. 4, pp. 492–508.

Lamberte, Mario, 1995, "Managing Surges in Capital Inflows: The Philippine Case," *Journal of Philippine Development,* Vol. 22 (first semester), No. 1, pp. 43–88.

Mercado-Aldaba, Rafaelita, 1994, *Foreign Direct Investment in the Philippines: A Reassessment,* Philippine Institute for Development Studies, Research Paper Series, No. 94–10, pp. 1–87.

Parlade, Claro, 1997, *Foreign Direct Investment in the Philippines* (Hong Kong: Sweet & Maxwell Asia).

Sikorski, Trevor, 1994, "Limits to Financial Liberalization: The Experiences of Indonesia and the Philippines," *Savings and Development Review,* Vol. 18, No. 4, pp. 393–426.

Tecson, Gwendolyn, 1995, "APEC and Economic Liberalization in the Philippines," *Philippine Review of Economics and Business,* Vol. 32, No. 2, pp. 134–47.

Villasin, B., 1995, "The Changing Structure of Philippine Foreign Trade," *Bangko Sentral Review,* Vol. 3, No. 1.

Vos, Rob, 1992, "Private Foreign Asset Accumulation, Not Just Capital Flight: Evidence from the Philippines," *The Journal of Development Studies,* Vol. 28, No. 3, pp. 500–37.

World Bank, 1998, *Philippines: Country Economic Review* (Washington: World Bank).

Zialcita, Edgardo, 1991, "The Antecedents and After-Effects of Four Major Devaluations in the Philippines," *Central Bank Review,* Vol. 43, No. 10, pp. 13–18.

VI Banking System Reform

Enrique G. de la Piedra

Major improvements in financial and structural policies have played a key role in promoting the emergence of a modern banking system. Historically, the banking sector in the Philippines has suffered from the strong cyclical movements of the economy, and numerous structural problems have acted as obstacles to efficient financial intermediation. This situation, however, has improved noticeably in recent years. As the Philippine economy emerged in the 1990s, from a long period of stagnation and macro imbalances, the banking sector also became more efficient and more resilient against shocks. In particular, financial sector reforms since the mid-1980s have improved the system's ability to perform its basic functions of financial intermediation and facilitation of payment flows. Those reforms were directed mainly at encouraging greater competition, strengthening supervisory and regulatory systems, and streamlining the tools of monetary policy.

Reforms of recent years have also helped shield the Philippine banking system from the worst effects of the Asian crisis in 1997–98. Even so, the banks came under significant stress. The authorities responded with a program of further reforms to strengthen the capacity of banks to face adverse shocks and to reinforce the institutional framework to deal with troubled banks.

This section describes the Philippine banking sector, provides an overall assessment of its soundness, followed by an overview of previous efforts at financial sector reform. It then discusses the authorities' current reform program put in place in response to the regional crisis, and finally summarizes the agenda for further reform.

Philippine Banking System

Size of the Banking System

The banking system in the Philippines comprises 53 commercial banks,[1] 117 thrift banks, and 826

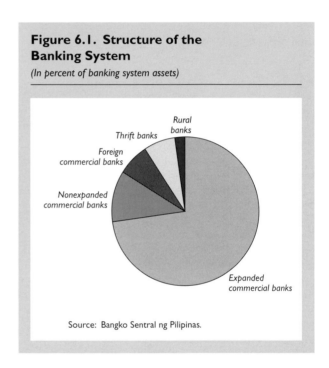

Figure 6.1. Structure of the Banking System
(In percent of banking system assets)

Source: Bangko Sentral ng Pilipinas.

rural banks (see Box 6.1 for a description of the structure of the banking system). Total assets of the banking system amounted to more than ₱2.8 trillion by the end of 1998, roughly equivalent to annual GNP. Commercial banks as a whole (expanded, nonexpanded, and foreign commercial banks) currently represent 90 percent of the banking system, up from 87 percent in 1991; thrift banks and rural banks account for 8 percent and 2 percent, respectively (Figure 6.1). There are also several kinds of nonbank financial intermediaries (Box 6.2), although their importance is smaller than that of the banking sector. The central bank—Bangko Sentral ng Pilipinas—is the main supervisory agency of the banking system (Box 6.3).

Trends in Banking System Activity

With the liberalization of the banking environment and improvement in the business environment during

---

[1]Excluding one small commercial bank—Orient Bank—now under receivership and not operating.

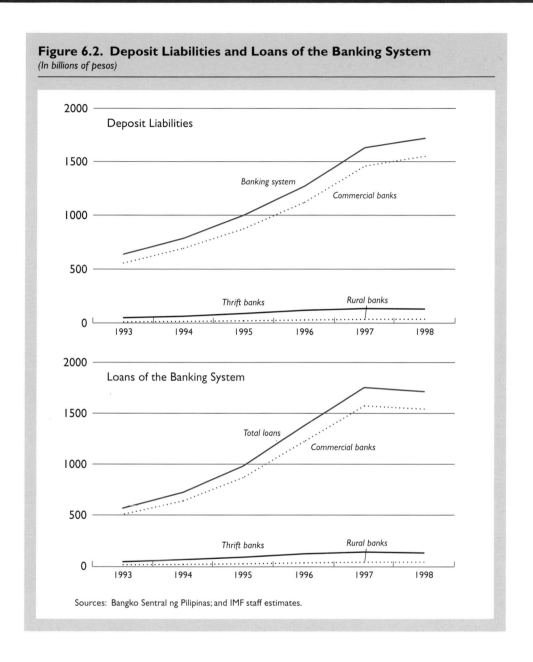

Figure 6.2. Deposit Liabilities and Loans of the Banking System
(In billions of pesos)

Sources: Bangko Sentral ng Pilipinas; and IMF staff estimates.

the 1990s, banking activity increased at a brisk pace until the onset of the 1997 regional financial crisis. Total deposits and loans of the banking system increased about 25 percent and 35 percent a year, respectively, during 1993 to mid-1996 (Figure 6.2). Thus, financial intermediation has deepened significantly in the Philippines, with the ratio of broad money to GDP nearly doubling from 34 percent in 1991 to 61 percent in 1997, and claims on the private sector rising from 18 percent of GDP to 56 percent of GDP during the same period. Nevertheless, the degree of financial deepening in the Philippines remains relatively low compared with other Asian countries affected by the regional crisis (Figure 6.3).

From mid-1997, the growth of banking activity decelerated sharply and came to a virtual halt in 1998 (with total banking system loans contracting by 2 percent and deposits expanding by only 5 percent). The financial crisis and measures to strengthen the banking system prompted a more conservative lending posture of banks as they complied with new minimum capital and loan loss provisioning requirements in particular. Also, demand for credit slowed sharply with the slowdown of economic activity and higher interest rates.

Mirroring the overall trends in banking activity, financial intermediation in foreign currency grew significantly—owing in part to the prevailing institu-

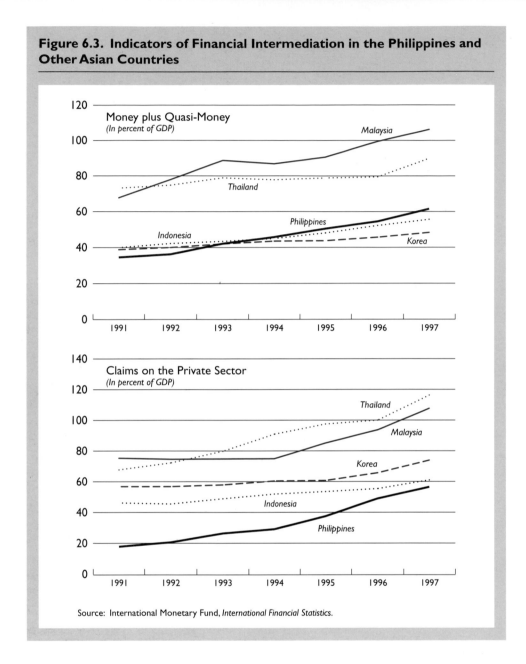

Figure 6.3. Indicators of Financial Intermediation in the Philippines and Other Asian Countries

Source: International Monetary Fund, *International Financial Statistics.*

tional advantages for bank operations in foreign currency[2]—followed by deceleration thereafter. Total

foreign currency deposits in the banking system expanded at an annual rate of 38 percent during 1994–96, reaching over $16 billion in June 1997 (Figure 6.4). As a result, foreign currency deposits represented more than half of total bank liabilities, up from only 3 percent in 1990. Following the onset of the regional crisis, foreign currency deposits started to contract, falling by 17 percent between June 1997 and June 1998. Most of the banks' foreign

---

[2]See Nellor (1998). After a long period in which interest income from foreign currency operations was fully tax exempt, it is now subject only to a 7.5 percent withholding tax (compared with 20 percent in the case of peso deposits). At the same time, profits from the bank's foreign currency deposit units operations are taxed at a 10 percent preferential rate on gross income, compared to the standard tax rate of 35 percent on net profit from other operations. Also, domestic banking activity is subject to the gross receipts and documentary stamp taxes, while transactions in foreign currency with nonresidents and with other foreign currency deposit units are exempt. Finally, while peso deposits are subject

to significant reserve requirements, largely unremunerated, foreign currency deposits are not subject to reserve requirements.

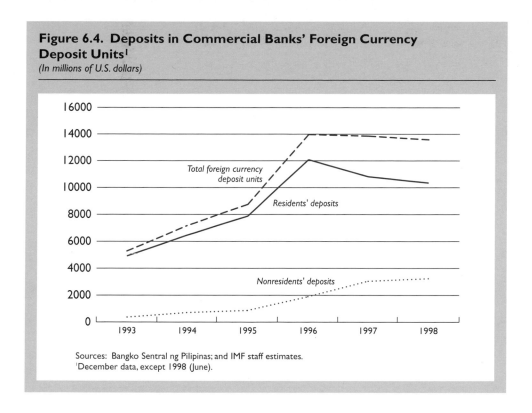

Figure 6.4. Deposits in Commercial Banks' Foreign Currency Deposit Units¹
(In millions of U.S. dollars)

Sources: Bangko Sentral ng Pilipinas; and IMF staff estimates.
¹December data, except 1998 (June).

currency liabilities are to domestic residents, which could make the system less vulnerable to capital flight than the banking systems of other Asian countries. Although nonresidents' deposits grew by 70 percent a year during 1994–97 and continued growing in the first half of 1998, they still accounted for less than 25 percent of total foreign currency deposits by June 1998.

Banks' derivative activity also grew rapidly in recent years, although it remains concentrated in relatively simple contracts; about two-thirds of such activity is conducted by foreign banks. Derivatives transactions of the banks in their regular books and their foreign currency deposit units reached about $8 billion and $1.6 billion, respectively, as of May 1998; almost the entire volume of banks' derivative transactions were foreign exchange derivatives, mainly nondeliverable forward contracts.

Concentration and Competition in the Banking System

The Philippine commercial banking system is highly concentrated. The 10 largest banks (which include nine domestic banks and one foreign bank) account for more than 55 percent of the banking systems' resources and demand liabilities. Domestically owned private banks in the Philippines have been traditionally owned by family-run industrial

groups;[3] these families also have major interests in the nonfinancial sectors. The larger thrift banks are in some cases controlled by commercial banks; smaller thrifts are usually family-owned. Rural banks are either family-owned or run as cooperatives.

To increase competition in the banking sector, the authorities licensed 10 new foreign bank branches in 1995. As a result, competition increased in certain areas, such as project and trade finance, top-tier corporate customers, and wholesale portfolios. However, owing in part to limitations on the activities of foreign banks,[4] domestic banks remain dominant in the retail banking sector, although they face some degree of competition from the smaller thrift and rural banks, which enjoy tax and reserve requirement advantages.

Soundness of the Banking System

The Philippine banking system is, on average, well capitalized. Nonetheless, banks have suffered significant stress following the onset of the regional crisis in mid-1997. After a brief description of the main ef-

---

[3]See Fry (1988) and Tan (1993).
[4]The number of branches that foreign banks are authorized to open cannot exceed six, while their borrowing from head offices cannot exceed $4 for every $1 of domestically held capital.

Box 6.1. Structure of the Philippine Banking Sector

There are five types of banks in the Philippines: universal banks (also called "expanded commercial banks"), commercial banks, thrift banks, rural banks, and government-owned banks. The difference between universal banks and commercial banks is that the former—which are the most important component of the banking sector—may perform the functions of an investment house (which includes underwriting securities), own equity in nonallied undertakings, and own a majority or all of the equity of a financial intermediary except a commercial bank. Among universal and commercial banks, only one bank—the Philippine National Bank—is partly owned by the government. Thrift banks—which include savings and mortgage banks, private development banks, and stock and savings associations—service mainly to the consumer retail market and small and medium-sized enterprises. The rural banking system services the needs of the agricultural sector, farmers, and rural cooperatives; rural banks are not allowed to issue mortgage certificates.

In general, foreign banks may operate in the Philippines at any time by acquiring up to 60 percent of the voting stock of an existing domestic bank or by investing in up to 60 percent of the voting stock of a new institution incorporated locally. In addition, foreign banks may set up branches in the Philippines, although the number of such branches has been capped at 14 since 1995, when 10 foreign banks were authorized to set up new branches. One of the 10 foreign bank branches, however, converted into a subsidiary in September 1998. The authorities have proposed a legislative amendment that, if approved, would allow foreign banks to invest in up to 100 percent of the voting stock of local banks in distress, although they would be required to reduce their ownership to 85 percent of the bank's stock after five years and to 70 percent after 10 years. (This amendment may be further modified in the legislative process.) On average, foreign equity was just under one-fifth of total equity for universal banks, about 13 percent for commercial banks, and negligible in the case of thrift banks.

There are three fully government-owned banks, including the Land Bank of the Philippines, the Development Bank of the Philippines, and the Al Amanah Islamic Investment Bank of the Philippines. The Land Bank of the Philippines and the Development Bank of the Philippines are specialized development banks, although they also undertake some commercial banking functions (mainly for their traditional clients). The mandate of the Land Bank of the Philippines is to promote the growth of the agricultural sector. The main activities of the Development Bank of the Philippines are the on-lending, on a wholesale basis, of official development assistance funds (which amounts to 60 percent of its funds available for lending) and retail lending in certain areas not attended by commercial banks—mainly environmentally oriented investment projects. Both banks provide financial services to the government and to other official financial institutions, such as the Philippine Deposit Insurance Corporation.

fects of the Asian crisis on the banking sector, this section discusses the soundness of banks based on three indicators: capital adequacy, the quality of the asset portfolio, and earnings and profitability.

The Banking Sector in the Wake of the Asian Crisis

The banking sector came under stress during 1997–98. Owing to the effects of the regional crisis and major drought, starting in 1997, economic growth in the Philippines slowed, the peso depreciated, interest rates increased, and corporate profits declined. As a result, since mid-1997, the quality of bank assets deteriorated, capital adequacy weakened, and bank lending slowed sharply. Banks' recourse to central bank emergency lending increased from ₱4.5 billion at end-1997 to a peak of ₱14.3 billion in May 1998. The external shock of the crisis interacted with domestic vulnerabilities that had built up in the years preceding the crisis. In particular, there was rapid credit growth with growing exposure of the banking sector to real estate activities and un-

hedged foreign currency borrowing. These problems were particularly acute in the case of smaller commercial banks, thrift banks, and rural banks, owing to the characteristics of their asset portfolio,[5] weak credit management systems, and generally slower response to the rapidly changing environment.

Owing in part to past reforms (described below), the financial condition of the Philippine banking system has remained better than in several of the neighboring countries, and major bank failures have been avoided.[6] The recent tightening of prudential standards has helped improve this even further. Compared with countries in the region, banks in the

---

[5]Real estate loans, lending to small businesses, and consumer loans figure more prominently in the portfolio of these banks, compared with bigger banks, which tend to have a more diversified portfolio.

[6]Since the start of the current difficulties in the financial sector in 1998, one small commercial bank, six thrift banks, and 33 rural banks were closed; the combined size of these banks' assets, however, is small and thus their problems have not had any systemic implications.

Box 6.2. Nonbank Financial Intermediaries

The nonbank financial system in the Philippines comprises a number of different institutions, including investment houses, financing companies, investment companies, securities dealers and brokers, fund managers, pawnshops, lending investors, nonstock savings and loan associations, building and loans associations, venture capital corporations, cooperatives, credit unions, and insurance companies (Lirio, 1998). As of mid-1998, the nonbank financial intermediaries accounted for 18 percent of the financial system's assets and 8 percent of its liabilities (excluding the Bangko Sentral ng Pilipinas). Of all these institutions, only financing companies and investment houses may be authorized by the Monetary Board to engage in quasi-banking business and are then referred to as quasi banks; in this case, they are authorized to borrow funds for purposes of relending or purchasing of receivables, but are not permitted to issue deposit liabilities.

According to the provisions of the Bangko Sentral ng Pilipinas Act, only the following will ultimately remain under Bangko Sentral ng Pilipinas supervision: nonbank financial intermediaries with quasi-banking functions, trust or investment management authority, building and loan associations, nonstock savings and loan associations, trust companies, nonbank financial intermediaries that are subsidiaries or affiliates of banks or quasi banks, and nonbank financial intermediaries, such as pawnshops, placed under Bangko Sentral ng Pilipinas supervision in accordance with special laws. The supervision of insurance companies engaged in securities dealership or brokerage is the responsibility of the Office of the Insurance Commission and the Securities and Exchange Commission, although the Bangko Sentral ng Pilipinas has supervisory authority over those insurance companies and dealers or brokers that are subsidiaries or affiliates of other supervised institutions.

Box 6.3. Prudential Framework for the Banking System

According to the Bangko Sentral ng Pilipinas Act, the ultimate authority in the area of bank licensing and supervision in the Philippines is the seven-member Monetary Board of the Bangko Sentral ng Pilipinas, which is chaired by the Governor of the Bangko Sentral ng Pilipinas. Within the Bangko Sentral ng Pilipinas, the Supervision and Examination Sector, headed by a Deputy Governor who reports directly to the Governor, is charged with the supervision of all banks operating in the country as well as all nonbank financial intermediaries authorized to perform quasi-banking functions. Bangko Sentral ng Pilipinas guidelines require that all head offices of banks operating in the country, at least 50 percent of the branches of a bank, and at least 85 percent of a bank's total resources be examined annually.

In addition, the Philippine Deposit Insurance Corporation—which is charged with insuring deposits and rehabilitating or liquidating banks closed and placed under receivership by the Monetary Board—is empowered by its charter to examine banks and to require them to submit relevant information. In the normal course of events, however, the Philippine Deposit Insurance Corporation makes extensive use of the supervisory information and findings of the Bangko Sentral ng Pilipinas.

reappraised lending strategies, which should support an early recovery of bank lending.

Capital Adequacy

The banking system's overall capital adequacy increased during 1998, reaching 17.6 percent by end-December. This increase reflected the slowdown in asset growth, concentration of new lending in zero-risk assets (government paper), and new minimum capital requirements (see below). This improvement followed a gradual decline of capital adequacy ratios since 1992 that had reflected the rapid growth of bank assets during the period. The current level of capital adequacy is well above the minimum regulatory requirement of 10 percent,[8] which is somewhat higher than in most Asian countries (Figure 6.5). On average, all classes of banks enjoyed healthy capital

Philippines are better capitalized—especially at the top end of the market—the corporate sector is less leveraged, and the real estate boom was not as long or as pronounced.[7] At the same time, following the onset of the crisis, banks have stepped up credit collection efforts, reduced higher-risk exposures, and

---

[7]Property demand in the Philippines was flat during 1989–94, which in turn prevented a boom and subsequent oversupply of real estate projects (the office vacancy rate in Manila by early 1997 was about 2 percent, compared with about 12 percent in Jakarta and Bangkok). At the same time, the prevalence of presold projects helped limit large-scale reliance on bank finance for real estate purposes. In addition, the Bangko Sentral ng Pilipinas in 1997 took measures to limit bank lending for real estate projects.

[8]For capital adequacy, the Bangko Sentral ng Pilipinas has adopted a net worth-to-risk asset ratio, which measures capital in relation to the degree of risk of different categories of assets. The risk weighting methodology includes two weights: zero for highly liquid assets and 100 percent for the remainder of the balance sheet items, that is, fixed assets, loans, and investments.

Figure 6.5. Selected Asian Countries: Capital Adequacy Requirements
(In percent)

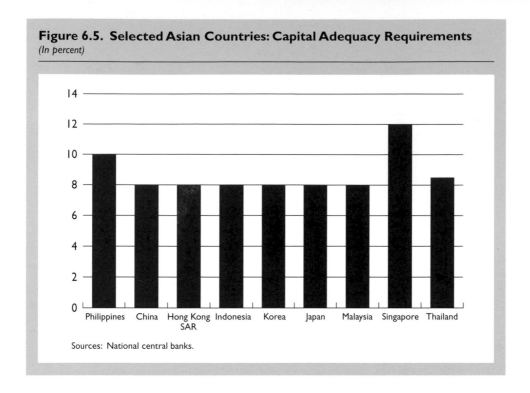

Sources: National central banks.

adequacy ratios; among large banks, all except one have capital adequacy ratios in excess of 10 percent.

Asset Quality

The ratio of nonperforming loans to total loans reached 11 percent in December 1998,[9] compared with only 4 percent in June 1997. The ratio is much higher among thrift banks and rural banks than in the case of commercial banks. The worsening of prudential indicators over the past two years reflects both the deterioration in asset quality as a result of weakening economic conditions, and the tightening of prudential standards, which has made the degree of loan portfolio impairment more transparent (Figure 6.6).

Earnings and Profitability

Bank earnings have declined significantly since 1997, reflecting both the general slowdown in the business environment as well as the need to meet the new general and specific loan loss provisioning requirements. For the banking system as a whole, the average return on equity declined to 0.37 percent in June 1998, from 1.66 percent in 1997, and an average of more than 2.3 percent during 1990–96. At the

same time, the ratio of operating expenses to operating income reached 90 percent.

Financial Sector Reforms Prior to 1997

After a major financial and balance of payments crisis of the early 1980s, the authorities started a process of financial sector reform that intensified in the early 1990s and set the stage for the dynamic expansion of the financial sector since then. These measures were aimed at strengthening the operations of the banking system by improving the regulatory environment, enhancing competition, and liberalizing the financial environment. In the initial stage, interest rates were liberalized, controls on foreign currency operations were eased, and the central bank streamlined its monetary policy instruments. At the same time, universal banking was introduced and minimum capital requirements were raised.

Throughout the 1980s, the financial sector suffered from the lingering effects of the 1982–83 crisis. The crisis had severely affected the health of the financial system,[10] and led to a contraction of almost 55 percent in real terms of banks' credit to the private sector between 1982 and 1986. In turn, the cen-

---

[9]The ratio increased further to 13.1 percent in March 1999.

[10]See Nascimento (1991).

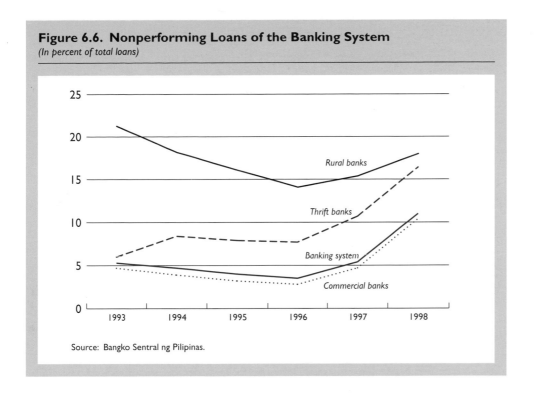

Figure 6.6. Nonperforming Loans of the Banking System
(In percent of total loans)

Source: Bangko Sentral ng Pilipinas.

tral bank provided significant levels of financial as-sistance to troubled banks. Also, weak financial and nonfinancial institutions were taken over by the gov-ernment-owned banks, while the Philippine National Bank and the Development Bank of the Philippines were rehabilitated and restructured, in part by trans-ferring their nonperforming assets to an agency cre-ated especially for this purpose.

Starting in the early 1990s, the authorities intensi-fied the reform effort. A centerpiece of this effort was the restructuring and recapitalization in 1993 of the central bank, which had become technically in-solvent following the crisis of the 1980s. The new central bank (the Bangko Sentral ng Pilipinas) also was granted independence from other branches of government. In addition, the authorities eased re-strictions on the entry and operation of banks to in-crease competition and strengthen the banking sys-tem. In 1995, 10 new foreign banks were licensed to operate in the country (in addition to the four already operating) and foreign banks were authorized to pur-chase up to 60 percent of the equity of local banks; and the bank branching policies were liberalized. The authorities also tightened prudential regulations, including through higher minimum capital require-ments and a liquid asset requirement on foreign cur-rency deposit unit loans. Finally, several measures were adopted to reinforce the legal framework, in-cluding in the areas of banks' derivatives trading, thrift banks, and rural banks.

1998–99 Reform Program

Banking sector reforms were strengthened to face the problems arising from the regional crisis that broke out in 1997. The authorities in early 1998 adopted a comprehensive banking sector reform pro-gram aimed at strengthening banks' capacity to withstand shocks and enhancing the authorities' abil-ity to deal with banks in financial difficulties. The strategy, developed in collaboration with the IMF and the World Bank,[11] envisaged a decentralized pri-vate-sector led improvement of bank balance sheets and risk management practices, encouraged by a tightening of prudential and supervisory standards and development of a more transparent bank exit and resolution strategy. A separate (government led) plan was designed to deal with the Philippine Na-tional Bank (the largest bank in distress, with 46 per-cent government ownership).

Bank Supervision and Regulation

Despite significant improvements in the supervi-sory framework prior to the onset of the Asian crisis, serious weaknesses undermined the effectiveness of

---

[11]Banking sector reform is a major component of the program supported by the current Stand-By Arrangement with the IMF; and the World Bank in December 1998 approved a Banking Sec-tor Reform Loan.

bank supervision. The main issues related to the prudential standards in place, supervisory skills and practices, and enforcement of the bank regulatory and supervisory framework. In particular:

- Even if average bank capital levels remained adequate, capital adequacy ratios had been declining since 1992. At the same time, average capital adequacy levels disguised the presence of individual institutions—especially smaller ones—which suffered from low capital levels.
- Loan classification and provisionary standards deviated from best supervisory practice in several respects. In particular, collateralized substandard loans were not being provisioned for, and banks were not required to make general loan loss provisions.
- The supervisory and risk assessment methodologies used by the Bangko Sentral ng Pilipinas were not in full agreement with best international practice.
- Additional shortcomings were present in other areas of supervisory responsibility, including disclosure of information, bank licensing, and bank accounting practices.

To address the weaknesses in the regulatory and supervisory framework, the authorities took measures to strengthen the position of the banks as well as the ability of the Bangko Sentral ng Pilipinas to supervise them, along the lines of best international practice. The full implementation of these measures will be of key importance in ensuring the continued soundness of the banking system.

Minimum Capital and Loan Loss Provisioning Requirements

To strengthen the ability of banks to deal with adverse shocks, the authorities announced an ambitious plan to increase bank capital and enhance provisioning by banks against substandard loans.

- An increase in minimum capital requirements for banks through end-2000, with intermediate levels for end-1998 and end-1999, was announced in March 1998.[12] At the same time, the lower capital adequacy ratio of 8 percent (instead of the usual 10 percent) in place for certain universal banks was phased out in January 1999.[13]
- New loan loss provisioning requirements, following the tightening of loan classification

guidelines, were announced on October 1997.[14] The new provisioning requirements are generally in line with best international practice and those in place in other Asian countries. Banks are now required to make a general loan loss provision (gradually rising to 2 percent by October 1999)[15] as well as specific loan loss provisions for "especially mentioned" and collateralized substandard loans.

Supervision Methodologies

Fundamental changes have been initiated in the focus and methodology of bank supervision to enhance the capacity to assess the health of individual banks and to detect cases of bank distress early on.

- The Bangko Sentral ng Pilipinas is changing the focus of supervision from a purely compliance-based and check list-driven process to a forward-looking and risk-based framework. This change has been well received by banks. The examination process is being reoriented to assess the various elements of risk, and the systems used by banks to manage those risks (including liquidity, interest rate, and foreign exchange risks, as well as risks arising from off-balance-sheet activities).
- Improvements have also been made in bank rating methodologies. The CAMEL rating system[16] has been revised to ensure that the composite rating will never be better than a bank's individual factor rating for capital adequacy.[17] In addition, as of July 1998, "sensitivity to market risk" has been added to the traditional CAMEL rating system. Also, the composite rating system[18] will be based on the weighted sum of the component ratings, with weights depending on the size, complexity of activities, and risk profile of the institution being rated. Examiners are also starting to use qualitative analysis to determine the component ratings.[19] Finally, a revised examination format has been introduced,[20] to replace the detailed examination report in use until recently.

---

[12]Circular 156 of March 19, 1998, Bangko Sentral ng Pilipinas, Office of the Governor.

[13]Circular 168 of July 3, 1998, Bangko Sentral ng Pilipinas, Office of the Governor.

[14]Monthly installment loans are now to be considered nonperforming after three months in arrears rather than six, whereas quarterly installment loans are to be treated as nonperforming after one quarter in arrears rather than two.

[15]In April 1999, as a measure to encourage new lending by banks, the stock of loans above the end-March 1999 level was exempted from the general loan loss provision.

[16]"CAMEL" stands for Capital, Assets, Management, Earnings, and Liquidity.

[17]Supervision and Examination Sector Order 3, of March 6, 1998.

[18]The rating system is now called CAMELS.

[19]Supervision Guidelines No. 98–7, of May 22, 1998.

[20]Supervision and Examination Sector Order No. 10 of November 28, 1997.

- The authorities have initiated action to undertake consolidated supervision of financial conglomerates. An amendment of the General Banking Act has been submitted to Congress that would impose consolidated capital requirements and extend consolidated supervision of financial institutions to include their interests in nonfinancial ventures. As a preliminary step, the Bangko Sentral ng Pilipinas is conducting consolidated supervision of banks and quasi banks based on the inclusion of their financial subsidiaries and affiliates.[21] The authorities have also started to compile a list of the laws and regulations that would need to be modified to fully implement consolidated supervision.
- External auditors have been required to report to the Bangko Sentral ng Pilipinas all matters that could adversely affect the financial condition of a bank. In this regard, the authorities will begin a system of accreditation of external auditing firms that banks are authorized to hire for the examination of their balance sheets. If an auditing firm fails to properly inform the Bangko Sentral ng Pilipinas on the problems of a bank, it would be "blacklisted" by the Monetary Board (for a period during which banks would not be permitted to engage its services).

Other Supervisory Issues

Several other initiatives have been taken to strengthen the soundness of the banking system and the Bangko Sentral ng Pilipinas' ability to monitor it.

- To enhance transparency and market discipline, banks listed by the Philippine Stock Exchange are now required to disclose publicly, on a quarterly basis, the level of nonperforming loans, the ratio of nonperforming loans to the total loan portfolio, the amount of classified assets and other risk assets, and the extent of specific and general loan loss reserves.[22]
- Stricter licensing guidelines for new banks have been in place since July 1998.[23] Also, the Bangko Sentral ng Pilipinas has announced that it will impose higher profitability guidelines on thrift banks and rural banks wishing to set up additional branches.

---

[21]Monetary Board Decision 553 of April 15, 1998, Bangko Sentral ng Pilipinas.
[22]Circular 157 of March 19, 1998.
[23]Monetary Board Resolution 832 of June 10, 1998, Bangko Sentral ng Pilipinas.

- To improve banks' accounting practices, the Bangko Sentral ng Pilipinas has required them to mark to market their trading securities portfolio.[24]

Bank Exit and Resolution

Traditionally, there have been several impediments to a smooth process of bank exit in the Philippines. Bank supervisors have been hampered by the lack of immunity for actions related to the discharge of their responsibilities and by bank secrecy regulations. The Monetary Board typically has not been subjected to specific time limitations governing the different steps that it must take before placing a bank under receivership. Also, the Bangko Sentral ng Pilipinas could suffer financial losses if a decision is taken to close a bank.[25] Finally, the Philippine Deposit Insurance Corporation has been constrained in its role as *receiver* (because it cannot dispose of the assets of a bank under receivership as soon as it is closed), in its role as *insurer* (because the secrecy law prevents it from accessing vital deposit information before a bank is closed), and in its role as *liquidator* (because it cannot proceed rapidly and on a timely basis mainly because of the inefficiency of the judicial system).

Recent Measures to Enhance Bank Resolution

A number of measures have been adopted to enhance the Bangko Sentral ng Pilipinas' ability to deal with troubled banks. As a result, the Bangko Sentral ng Pilipinas is now better prepared to identify early on cases of bank distress, and have better instruments to deal with banks that develop problems. Also, steps have been taken to enhance the role of the Philippine Deposit Insurance Corporation as receiver, and to reduce the financial risk for the Bangko Sentral ng Pilipinas associated with bank closures.

- To permit early detection of problems, the Bangko Sentral ng Pilipinas has compiled a list of banks in potential distress.[26] On the basis of this list, which is updated regularly, the Bangko Sentral ng Pilipinas has adopted a program of intensified monitoring and special examinations

---

[24]Circular 161 of March 30, 1998.
[25]Such losses may arise from three sources: uncollateralized overdraft lending to a troubled bank; inability by the Bangko Sentral ng Pilipinas to execute the collateral backing emergency loans to banks—in part owing to valuation problems; and the fact that, in the event of insufficient resources, the Philippine Deposit Insurance Corporation has unlimited access to Bangko Sentral ng Pilipinas credit.
[26]The list is compiled on the basis of forward- as well as backward-looking indicators.

of selected banks. The Monetary Board has allowed the supervision services of the Bangko Sentral ng Pilipinas to conduct such special examinations without the need for specific previous authorization.[27]

- The Bangko Sentral ng Pilipinas has issued a matrix of sanctions and a matrix of corrective actions to be taken according to the degree of capital shortfall of individual banks.[28] Also, the Bangko Sentral ng Pilipinas has issued harsher nonmonetary penalties to deal with banks that are in violation of supervisory rules, and has submitted draft legislation to allow for a 10-fold increase in the current value of monetary penalties. The Bangko Sentral ng Pilipinas has formulated contingency plans to deal with any systemic bank problems, in cooperation with the Philippine Deposit Insurance Corporation and the Department of Finance.

- To improve the ability of the Philippine Deposit Insurance Corporation to act as the receiver of banks, it has been determined that once the Philippine Deposit Insurance Corporation recommends that a bank be liquidated, the Monetary Board will approve the liquidation within 10 days. Also, the authorities are proposing legislation that would allow it to sell distressed bank assets to pay for the administration costs related to receivership.

- The Monetary Board has approved additional guidelines for emergency loans to banks. These guidelines—which restrict the activities of the bank concerned, halt the distribution of dividends, and impose certain obligations on the banks' owners and officers—reaffirm the fully collateralized nature of emergency loans, and represent an important step forward in insulating the Bangko Sentral ng Pilipinas from the risk of financial loss. The Bangko Sentral ng Pilipinas is also aware of the risk of financial loss arising from uncollateralized overdrafts to banks, and has submitted a proposal to amend the Bangko Sentral ng Pilipinas Act to eliminate this practice. In the meantime, the Bangko Sentral ng Pilipinas has issued regulations to require thrift banks to provide collateral against all Bangko Sentral ng Pilipinas overdrafts,[29] and

---

[27]In principle, no bank can be inspected more than once a year without authorization of the Monetary Board. However, the Monetary Board has granted a blanket authorization to conduct bank inspections on a rolling six-month basis. An amendment to the Bangko Sentral ng Pilipinas Act has been proposed to make this authorization permanent.

[28]Circular 176 of September 7, 1998, and Circular 181 of November 15, 1998.

[29]Circular 163 of April 8, 1998, and Implementing Guidelines of September 3, 1998.

intends to issue similar regulations for commercial banks.

Philippine National Bank

Strengthening the Philippine National Bank on a sustainable basis is an important part of the authorities' banking reform program. The Philippine National Bank, the second largest bank in the country and partially owned by the government, suffered to a greater degree than other banks from the fallout of the regional crisis (see Box 6.4). The authorities have announced publicly their intention to privatize the bank by mid-2000, at the latest. In the meantime, the Philippine National Bank has moved to write down its capital from ₱22 billion to ₱15 billion to reflect the impairment of its assets, while at the same time instituting additional loan loss provisions and phasing out obsolete information systems. The Philippine National Bank management intends to recapitalize the bank through the sale of undervalued assets, and possibly a rights issue to existing owners during 1999.

Initial Results and Agenda for Further Reform

Implementation of the banking reform program adopted in early 1998 has been largely on track, and initial results are positive. Banks are seeking market-based solutions to capital deficiencies (including fresh capital infusions and merges), and loan loss provisions have been strengthened significantly. Corrective supervisory action, supported by appropriate sanctions, has encouraged the pace of resolution. These measures included memoranda of understandings with noncompliant banks (regarding minimum capital requirements), supervision of certain banking activities, downgrading of licenses, and closure of banks. As a result, while the financial condition of banks had deteriorated over the past year, the situation is under control.

Looking ahead, to further strengthen the soundness of the system and reinforce supervisory capabilities, continued reforms should focus on (1) reducing distortions in financial intermediation; (2) further strengthening the prudential framework; (3) streamlining the process of bank exit and resolution; and (4) the Philippine National Bank.

Reducing Distortions in Financial Intermediation

Although important steps to improve the efficiency of financial intermediation have been taken, further progress is needed. In particular, the authorities should:

- Eliminate the bias in the tax system and in the regulatory framework against financial intermediation in pesos.[30] This would help reduce vulnerability to exchange rate volatility and lower costs of peso intermediation.
- Reduce and avoid frequent changes in reserve requirements. Since reserve requirements are mostly nonremunerated, they impose a tax on financial intermediation. In addition, their frequent modification imposes a cost for banks as they adapt their balance sheets, and could result in banks' permanently holding excess reserves.[31]
- Eliminate mandatory credit allocation programs to avoid misallocation of resources.[32] Currently, banks are required to lend 25 percent of their credit to agriculture and agroprocessing industries and 10 percent to small and medium-sized enterprises.
- Allow further foreign participation in the banking sector. Additional top-rated international banks should be allowed to open branches in the Philippines, and existing limits to the expansion of such branches should be liberalized (including limits on foreign ownership of local banks, the number of branches that foreign banks can open, and restrictions on financing from abroad for foreign banks).

Strengthening the Prudential Framework

The Bangko Sentral ng Pilipinas should continue to implement the strengthened prudential framework rigorously. In particular, it should:

- Enforce full and prompt compliance with minimum capital and loan provisioning requirements. Noncompliant banks should be subject to the procedures for prompt corrective action approved by the Monetary Board.
- Prudential forbearance and pressures to dilute the new standards for loan provisioning, classification standards, and disclosure requirements should be resisted. The 2-percent general provision requirement, and the recent exemption of incremental loans, should be reviewed at an early date.
- Specific loans loss provisions should be made tax deductible, and in accordance with best international practice.[33]

---

[30]See footnote 2.

[31]See Hardy (1997) for a discussion of the drawbacks of reserve requirements as an instrument of monetary control.

[32]See Alexander, Baliño, and Enoch (1995) for an analysis of the adverse effects of directed credit and other direct instruments of monetary policy.

[33]See Escolano (1997) for an analysis of the tax treatment of loan losses and loan reserves of banks.

Box 6.4. The Philippine National Bank

The Philippine National Bank, established in 1916, has more than 320 branches and accounts for about 10 percent of the banking sector's assets. It is the country's largest bank in terms of liabilities and the second largest in terms of assets. It lags behind industry leaders in a number of areas, however, including credit and risk management policies and the degree of automation of its operations. In June 1996, the government reduced its ownership in the Philippine National Bank from 100 percent to 45.6 percent. The stock in private hands is widely dispersed.

The Philippine National Bank's financial performance has deteriorated significantly in the past few years, following a series of large corporate loan defaults (including Philippine Airlines). Return on assets remains the lowest among the large banks in the country. The difficulties of the Philippine National Bank were exacerbated by the onset of the 1997 regional financial crisis and the accompanying devaluation of the peso and economic downturn. The Philippine National Bank was particularly vulnerable because it had lent aggressively in foreign currency; at about 35 percent of total loans, it had the highest proportion of credit in foreign currency among the large banks. Also, the bank is highly exposed to the property sector (14 percent of its loan portfolio). After a drop in net income of 75 percent in 1997, compared with an average increase of 10 percent in the net income of the four other largest banks in the Philippines, financial results in 1998 continued to worsen.

In early 1999, provisions of ₱8.9 billion (about 7 percent of the loan book) were constituted retroactively for 1998; obsolete information systems were written off; the cost of unfunded pensions and retrenchment packages were explicitly allowed for; and capital was written down from ₱22 billion to about ₱15 billion, reducing the capital adequacy ratio to about one-half the required 10 percent. Management of the bank has indicated its intention to remedy the capital shortfall through the sale of undervalued assets (including its headquarters building) and a rights issue.

Banks' Vulnerability to Exchange Rate Volatility

Continued strengthening of prudential standards will be critical to the management of cross-border flows and associated risk. Banks are subject to caps on their overbought and oversold foreign exchange positions and to cover requirements for their foreign currency liabilities. In addition, banks should maintain adequate assets to cover for all foreign currency liabilities, as well as appropriate control and reporting systems regarding their foreign exchange exposure. Banks should be asked regularly to submit detailed information on their foreign exchange transactions, including positions by currency and maturity of the spot and forward books. At the same time, additional prudential requirements should be market-based and compatible with maintaining an open capital account.

Supervisory Resources and Training

Bangko Sentral ng Pilipinas supervisory resources should be focused on supervision of large banks. Although expanded commercial banks make up more than two-thirds of the banking system's assets, only about one-fourth of Bangko Sentral ng Pilipinas supervisory staff is involved in their supervision (while more than one-third is dedicated to supervising rural banks—which account for 2 percent of total assets). Of course, the necessary focus of resources on larger potential problem banks needs to be balanced against the need to enforce prompt corrective action vis-à-vis all noncompliant banks.

To ensure the successful implementation of modern supervisory methodologies, Bangko Sentral ng Pilipinas and the Philippine Deposit Insurance Corporation supervisory staff should continue to receive intensive training in the area of risk-based supervision, including assessment of risk, appraisal of banks' risk management, and forward-looking assessment of banks.

Legal Protection for Bank Supervisors

It would be desirable to clarify the protection for bank supervisors by way of clear and explicit legal statute. Although in principle no public officer in the Philippines is civilly liable for official acts, unless there is a clear showing of bad faith, malice, or gross negligence,[34] the courts have allowed civil lawsuits to be brought against individual bank supervisors in connection with such acts.

Bank Secrecy

Current legislation on bank secrecy should be modified to bring bank supervisors within the perimeter of the law. The present situation is at variance with best international practice; it prohibits banks from releasing any information on their deposit accounts, except when the depositor authorizes it or under a court order. As a result, the supervisory authorities do not have detailed information on the banks' primary funding source. The law also im-

pedes speedy resolution of bank failures as the Philippine Deposit Insurance Corporation has no information on individual depositors prior to closure of the bank.

Banks' Trust Activities

The Bangko Sentral ng Pilipinas should clarify the relationship between trust accounts and the bank, including regulations on conflict of interest. There is a widespread perception among bank clients that a bank's trust activities are fully guaranteed by the parent bank.

Streamlining the Process of Bank Exit and Resolution

The framework for bank resolution must be strengthened further.

- As soon as a bank is placed under receivership, the Philippine Deposit Insurance Corporation should be able to resolve it as soon as possible to avoid a further deterioration in the value of the bank's portfolio. In particular, the Philippine Deposit Insurance Corporation should be authorized to swiftly carve out bad assets from a bank under receivership to improve the chances for a quick sale to a new owner.
- To enhance transparency, just as Philippine Deposit Insurance Corporation receivership is subject to time limits (up to 90 days),[35] it would be useful also to set time limits for the Monetary Board's actions in the area of bank resolution.
- Banks should not be allowed unilaterally to declare "bank holidays" (suspension of operations) without full intervention by the supervisory authorities. In line with best international practice, any bank that declares a bank holiday should be immediately placed under receivership or conservatorship.[36]
- To limit the risk for the Bangko Sentral ng Pilipinas arising from financial assistance to troubled banks, all forward emergency assistance should be fully collateralized, and the limit on emer-

---

[34]Executive Order No. 292, July 1987.

[35]Extendable five times by an additional 30 days each, through Monetary Board Resolution.

[36]The Bangko Sentral ng Pilipinas can use two institutional arrangements to oversee operations of banks in trouble that have not yet been closed. A comptroller is named automatically when a bank is granted an emergency loan. The powers of the comptroller are limited, however, involving only reports to the Monetary Board but without authority to override the decisions of the bank's board. Conservatorship is a more powerful arrangement, as the conservator has the authority to override the decisions of the bank's board and management.

gency loans related to the size of a bank's capital rather than deposits.[37]

References

Alexander, William E., Tomás J. T. Baliño, and Charles Enoch, 1995, *The Adoption of Indirect Instruments of Monetary Policy,* IMF Occasional Paper 126 (Washington: International Monetary Fund).

Escolano, Julio, 1997, "Tax Treatment of Loan Losses of Banks," in *Banking Soundness and Monetary Policy,* ed. by Charles Enoch and John H. Green (Washington: International Monetary Fund).

Fry, Maxwell J., 1988, *Money, Interest and Banking in Economic Development* (Baltimore: The Johns Hopkins University Press).

Hardy, Daniel C., 1997, "Reserve Requirements and Monetary Management: An Introduction," in *Instruments of Monetary Management: Issues and Country Experiences,* ed. by Tomás J. T. Baliño and Lorena M. Zamalloa (Washington: International Monetary Fund).

Lirio, Ricardo P., 1998, "The Central Bank and Non-Bank Financial Intermediaries," in *Philippine Financial Almanac 1997/98* (Manila).

Nascimento, Jean-Claude, 1991, "Crisis in the Financial Sector and the Authorities' Reaction: The Philippines," in *Banking Crises: Cases and Issues,* ed. by V. Sundararajan and Tomás J. T. Baliño (Washington: International Monetary Fund).

Nellor, David C. L., 1998, "Tax Policy and the Asian Crisis" (Washington: International Monetary Fund).

Tan, Edita A., 1993, "Interlocking Directorates of Commercial Banks, Other Financial Institutions and Bon-Financial Corporations," in *Philippine Review of Economics and Business,* Vol. 30, No. 1 (Manila: June).

World Bank, 1998, Banking Sector Reform Loan (Washington: World Bank).

———, 1998, Country Economic Memorandum (Washington: World Bank).

---

[37]Currently, emergency loans are capped at 50 percent of deposits. There is a strong element of moral hazard because a bank in distress has an incentive to increase its deposits by any means possible—and thus further complicate its difficulties—before approaching the Bangko Sentral ng Pilipinas for an emergency loan.

VII Corporate Governance

Prakash Loungani

Good "corporate governance"—the system by which corporations are directed and controlled—is critical in building market confidence and encouraging stable, long-term investment flows, particularly foreign capital flows. In addition, good corporate governance practices with respect to debt restructuring improve economic dynamism by facilitating the transfer of capital from weak firms to stronger ones.

This section examines how Philippine corporate governance practices compare with those of other countries, particularly a group of Asian comparators. The comparison covers four basic aspects of governance: shareholder rights; creditor rights; accounting, disclosure, and enforcement; and ownership and control. The main findings are the following.

- Shareholder rights are afforded about the same degree of legal protection in the Philippines as in most other Asian countries.
- There is scant legal protection for creditor rights, making the Philippines a clear outlier among the comparator countries. In addition, the process for debt resolution works in a manner that is highly prejudicial to the interest of creditors, particularly secured creditors.
- Philippine accounting standards compare favorably with those of other Asian countries, but enforcement appears to be weak.
- The dominance of a few families is a notable feature of the Philippine corporate sector; for instance, about 17 percent of total market capitalization can be traced to the ultimate control of a single family, much higher than in other Asian countries. The linkages between (nonfinancial) corporations and banks also appear to be tighter in the Philippines than in the other countries.

While no two countries' laws are identical, they are sufficiently similar in some critical respects to permit a classification of countries into legal "families." Building on the work of legal scholars, La Porta, Lopez-de-Silanes, Shleifer, and Vishny (1998; henceforth La Porta and others) identify four such families: English, French, German, and Scandinavian. English law is common law (made by judges and subsequently incorporated into legislation), whereas the other three follow civil-law tradition, which dates back to Roman law (laws made by scholars and legislators). La Porta and others show that the legal rules from these traditions differ in the extent to which they provide protection to shareholder and creditor rights, and in the degree of ownership concentration.

The Philippines belongs to the French family under this classification. The Asian comparator countries are distributed over the first three families.

English origin:	Hong Kong SAR, Malaysia, Singapore, and Thailand
French origin:	Indonesia, Philippines
German origin:	Japan, Korea, and Taiwan Province of China

Shareholders' Rights

Shareholders' rights are exercised through voting for directors and on major corporate issues. La Porta and others measure—on a scale of 0 to 6—how strongly the legal system favors minority shareholders against managers or dominant shareholders in the corporate decision-making process by (1) allowing proxy votes by mail (rather than in person); (2) not blocking selling of shares prior to a shareholders' meeting; (3) allowing cumulative voting for directors and proportional representation on the board of directors; (4) giving minority shareholders legal mechanisms against perceived oppression by directors; (5) granting shareholders a preemptive right to buy new issues of stock; and (6) setting a high percentage of share capital needed to call an extraordinary shareholders' meeting.

On average, English-origin countries offer the best protection to minority shareholders, while French-origin countries offer the least; the Philippines is a little above the average within its category (Table 7.1). In practice, the legal safeguards in the Philippines do not always secure the rights of minority shareholders. The high concentration of ownership in a few hands (described below) provides opportunity for self-dealing at the expense of outsiders.

Table 7.1. Shareholders' Rights

English-origin average	4.00
Hong Kong SAR	5.00
Malaysia	4.00
Singapore	4.00
Thailand	2.00
French-origin average	2.33
Indonesia	2.00
Philippines	*3.00*
German-origin average	2.33
Japan	4.00
Korea	2.00
Taiwan Province of China	3.00
Scandinavian-origin average	3.00
Sample average (49 countries)	3.00

Source: La Porta, Lopez-de-Silanes, Shleifer, and Vishny (1998).
Note: Shareholders' rights are measured on a scale of 0 to 6, with 0 indicating low protection of these rights.

The lack of effective enforcement and noncompliance and light penalties for violations of the law often lead to expropriation of minority shareholders' interests.[1]

Creditor Rights and Debt Restructuring

The most basic right of a senior collateralized creditor is the right to repossess—and then liquidate or keep—collateral when a loan is in default. Alternatively, creditors may have powers against borrowers through their votes in decisions on a reorganization of the company. La Porta and others measure—on a scale of 0 to 4—how strongly countries protect creditor rights by (1) not imposing an automatic stay on assets (which would prevent secured creditors from getting possession of loan collateral); (2) assuring secured creditors the right to collateral in reorganization, as opposed to giving priority to other groups, such as government and workers; (3) placing restrictions on filings for reorganization, such as creditor consent; and (4) replacing management by a party appointed by the court or the creditors during the reorganization process.

The Philippines stands out as a clear outlier in affording scant protection to creditor rights. In the

sample given in La Porta and others, about 80 percent of the countries require that secured creditors be paid first, whereas roughly one-half do not have an automatic stay on assets, restrict unilateral filings of reorganization, and remove management in reorganization proceedings. In the Philippines, none of these rights are given to secured creditors, placing it below the French-origin average for creditor rights, and far below the sample average for all countries (Table 7.2).

In some countries (for example, Taiwan Province of China), a legal reserve requirement forcing firms to maintain a certain level of capital to avoid automatic liquidation serves as an alternate measure of protecting creditor rights. This alternative, however, is not available in the Philippines (Table 7.2). The Philippines also stands as an exception to the finding that creditor rights tend to be stronger in poorer than in richer countries.[2]

The formal framework for debt restructuring in the Philippines leaves much to be desired. In 1976, the Securities and Exchange Commission supplanted the court system as the venue for resolving the debts of distressed companies.[3] The Securities and Exchange Commission has the power to impose stays of actions by creditors against corporate debtors; permit debtors to suspend payments to their creditors; decide whether a debtor should be liquidated or permitted to attempt rehabilitation; and appoint receivers, members of management committees, and liquidators. The manner in which debt suspension cases are handled by the Securities and Exchange Commission appears highly prejudicial to the interests of creditors and seldom leads to the rehabilitation of distressed firms.[4] Of the 93 cases filed between 1982 and 1998, 41 had ongoing hearings, and 12 had ongoing rehabilitation—including 2 cases dating back to the 1980s (Table 7.3). There have been no instances of the existing procedures leading to the successful rehabilitation of the companies concerned.

---

[1]Claessens, Djankov, Fan, and Lang (1999) attempt to measure the extent of expropriation of minority shareholders' interests in East Asian countries, including the Philippines.

[2]La Porta and others suggest that this finding arises because poorer countries adapt their laws to facilitate secured lending to compensate for a lack of other financing opportunities.

[3]Creditor-debtor relations can be regulated by the courts (under the Civil Code and the Insolvency Law, enacted in 1909) or by the Securities and Exchange Commission (under Presidential Decree No. 902-A, proclaimed in 1976). As a result of the decree, and two important court decisions in 1994 and 1998, the Securities and Exchange Commission has supplanted the courts as the venue for decisions on debt resolution.

[4]The Asian Development Bank (1999) states: "The process is quite remarkable for a number of reasons. In effect, it has shifted what was once a judicial process into a quasi-judicial process. There appear to be few, if any, but the most basic rules to govern the process. It gives the appearance of being far from a transparent process. The involvement of creditors appears problematic."

Table 7.2. Creditors' Rights

	No Automatic Stay on Assets	Secured Creditors Paid First	Restrictions on Going into Reorganization	Management Does Not Stay in Reorganization	Creditors' Rights	Legal Reserve Required as a Percentage of Capital
English-origin average	0.72	0.89	0.72	0.78	3.11	0.01
Hong Kong SAR	1	1	1	1	4	0.00
Malaysia	1	1	1	1	4	0.00
Singapore	1	1	1	1	4	0.00
Thailand	1	1	0	1	3	0.10
French-origin average	0.26	0.65	0.42	0.26	1.58	0.21
Indonesia	1	1	1	1	4	0.00
Philippines	*0*	*0*	*0*	*0*	*0*	*0.00*
German-origin average	0.67	1.00	0.33	0.33	2.33	0.41
Japan	0	1	0	1	2	0.25
Korea	1	1	0	1	3	0.50
Taiwan Province of China	1	1	0	0	2	1.00
Scandinavian-origin average	0.25	1.00	0.75	0.00	2.00	0.16
Sample average	0.49	0.81	0.55	0.45	2.30	0.15

Source: La Porta, Lopez-de-Silanes, Shleifer, and Vishny (1998).
Note: Creditors' rights are measured on a scale of 0 to 4 by summing up the scores in the four previous columns.

Lim and Woodruff (1998) and World Bank (1999) identify several deficiencies in the process that need to be addressed:

- Without due process or indemnification against loss, secured creditors are prevented from exercising their contractual rights.
- The process lacks clear and coherent rules and time-bound procedures.
- There is no prohibition against assigning fiduciary powers and responsibilities for the management of distressed enterprises to individuals who have serious conflicts of interest.

Accounting, Disclosure, and Enforcement

Accounting plays a critical role in corporate governance. Contracts between managers and investors typically rely on the verifiability in court of some measures of firms' income or assets. In addition, basic accounting standards are needed to make company disclosures of information meaningful to potential investors.

Philippine accounting standards, including those dealing with consolidation, are comprehensive and appear to adequately cover all basic accounting prin-

Table 7.3. Suspension of Payments Cases Filed with Securities and Exchange Commission

	Number of Cases	Ongoing Hearings	Ongoing Rehabilitation or Liquidation	Dismissed or Withdrawn
1980s	3	0	2	1
1990 to 1996	34	13	7	14
1997	20	4	3	13
1998	36	24	0	12
Total	93	41	12	40

Source: Securities and Exchange Commission.

Table 7.4. Rating on Accounting Standards	
English-origin average	70
Hong Kong SAR	69
Malaysia	76
Singapore	78
Thailand	64
French-origin average	51
Indonesia	n.a.
Philippines	*65*
German-origin average	63
Japan	65
Korea	62
Taiwan Province of China	65
Scandinavian-origin average	74
Sample average (49 countries)	61

Source: La Porta, Lopez-de-Silanes, Schleifer, and Vishny (1998).
Note: Accounting standards are measured on a scale of 0 to 100 based on examination of company reports from the different countries.

Table 7.5. Average Ownership of Ten Largest Nonfinancial Domestic Firms by Three Largest Shareholders	
English-origin average	0.43
Hong Kong SAR	0.54
Malaysia	0.54
Singapore	0.49
Thailand	0.47
French-origin average	0.54
Indonesia	0.58
Philippines	*0.57*
German-origin average	0.34
Japan	0.18
Korea	0.23
Taiwan Province of China	0.18
Scandinavian-origin average	0.37
Sample average (49 countries)	0.46

Source: La Porta, Lopez-de-Silanes, Schleifer, and Vishny (1998).

ciples. In addition, the rules require disclosure of all matters that might affect the decision of an investor to buy or sell the securities of the company. All companies with quarterly sales in excess of ₱100,000 must have their financial statements audited and signed by a certified public accountant.

While Philippine accounting standards compare favorably with those of other Asian countries, enforcement appears to be weak. In a survey of 41 countries used by La Porta and others, the quality of Philippine accounting standards is rated above the sample average (Table 7.4). Lim and Woodruff (1998) report that according to users of financial statements, including banks and investment banks, accounting and disclosure standards compare favorably with those in many Asian countries. However, the same users report that enforcement by regulators is weak and auditors seldom issue caveats that might raise questions about the reliability of the information contained in client financial statements. In addition, there is no tradition of legal actions by investors and lenders against company officers or auditors in connection with cases of deficient or misleading financial reporting. The use of light penalties and extensions of amnesty on violation of disclosure requirements appear to have led to significant noncompliance.

Over time, assuming improvements in the efficiency and fairness of the judicial system, investors and shareholders may become more willing in seeking compensation for losses resulting from violations of disclosure rules and misleading financial

statements. However, in the meantime, the Securities and Exchange Commission could add teeth to its regulations by imposing fines large enough to deter noncompliance. The Securities and Exchange Commission could also facilitate class actions by providing lawyers willing to represent investors, on a contingency fee basis, with access to any evidence of noncompliance by the defendants in such actions.

Ownership and Control

Concentration of ownership is the norm around the world. In the La Porta and others sample of countries, the average ownership of the three largest shareholders is 46 percent (Table 7.5). The highest concentration of ownership tends to be found in the French civil-law countries; the Philippines is close to the average for the French-origin countries.

The ultimate control of corporations is largely concentrated in the hands of families and the state, even in some of the most developed countries. La Porta, Lopez-de-Silanes, and Shleifer (1999) study the extent to which corporations in 29 rich countries are controlled by a few shareholders, that is, they trace the chain of ownership to identify the ultimate owners of capital and of voting rights in firms. In particular, they classify firms into either (1) a widely held corporation or (2) corporations with ultimate owners; the latter is divided further into four categories: family-controlled, state-controlled, con-

Table 7.6. Control of Publicly Traded Companies in East Asia
(In percent of total)

	Widely Held Corporations	Corporations with Ultimate Owners			
		Family-controlled	State-controlled	Controlled by widely held financial institution	Controlled by widely held corporation
Hong Kong SAR	7	67	1	5	20
Indonesia	5	72	8	2	13
Japan	80	10	1	6	3
Korea	43	48	2	1	6
Malaysia	10	67	13	2	7
Philippines	19	45	2	7	27
Singapore	5	55	24	4	12
Taiwan Province of China	26	48	3	5	17
Thailand	7	62	8	9	15

Source: Claessens, Djankov, and Lang (1998).

trolled by a widely held financial institution, and controlled by a widely held corporation.

There are large differences in the distribution of ultimate control across East Asian countries. Applying the La Porta, Lopez-de-Silanes, and Shleifer methodology to nine East Asian countries, Claessens, Djankov, and Lang (1998) find that family-controlled corporations form the largest category in each case, with the exception of Japan (Table 7.6). Relative to other ASEAN countries, the Philippines has a higher share of widely held corporations (19 percent) and a lower share of family-controlled corporations (45 percent).

Despite the lower overall share of family-controlled firms, the dominance of a few families is a notable feature of the Philippine corporate sector (Table 7.7). About 17 percent of total market capitalization can be traced to the ultimate control of a single family. The largest 10 families in Indonesia, the Philippines, and Thailand control one-half of the corporate sector in terms of market capitalization.

Some other findings of the Claessens, Djankov, and Lang study with respect to the Philippines are:

• The share of family-controlled firms increases for smaller-size firms, but to a lesser extent than in most other countries (for instance, the share of family-controlled firms is 40 percent for the largest 20 firms and 45 percent for the smallest 50 firms).

• The Philippines does not stand out as an outlier among the East Asian countries in the use of various other mechanisms to enhance corporate control, such as deviations from one-share-one-

vote voting rights; use of pyramid structures; cross-holdings; absence of a second controlling owner; and lack of separation of control and management (Table 7.8).[5]

A high degree of ownership concentration may not necessarily be bad. Economies of scale arguments would suggest some positive correlation be-

[5]The apparent separation of management and control in the case of the Philippines is partly due to the practice of having interlocking directorates and management boards (Tan (1993)).

Table 7.7. Concentration of Family Control

	Percent of Total Market Capitalization That Families Control		
	Top family	Top 5 families	Top 15 families
Hong Kong SAR	6.5	26.2	34.4
Indonesia	16.6	40.7	61.7
Japan	0.5	1.8	2.8
Korea	11.4	29.7	38.4
Malaysia	7.4	17.3	28.3
Philippines	17.1	42.8	55.1
Singapore	6.4	19.5	29.9
Taiwan Province of China	4.0	14.5	20.1
Thailand	9.4	32.2	53.3

Source: Claessens, Djankov, and Lang (1998).

Table 7.8. Means of Enhancing Control in East Asian Corporations
(Percent of total)

	Deviations from One-Share-One-Vote[1]	Pyramids with Ultimate Owners	Cross Holdings	Absence of Second Controlling Owner	Management Is from Controlling Family
Philippines	18.7	40	7	35	42
ASEAN-3 average	18.8	40	6	36	79
East Asia average	19.2	41	9	51	67
Range	18.1 (Malaysia)	13 (Thailand)	1 (Thailand)	19 (Thailand)	37 (Japan)
	19.9 (Japan)	67 (Indonesia)	16 (Singapore)	87 (Japan)	85 (Malaysia)

Source: Claessens, Djankov, and Lang (1998).

[1]This column shows the average minimum percent of the book value required to control 20 percent of the vote.

tween ownership concentration and efficiency of operations as well as higher levels of profitability. In the Philippines, however, the top families also control most of the major banks in the country (in addition to owning and controlling major sectors of the manufacturing and services sector). The high ownership concentration and the tight linkage between the corporate and banking sectors—tighter than in many other Asian countries (Table 7.9)—has also led to a significant concentration of loans outstanding. For instance, the top 100 corporate borrowers account for 30 percent of the loans outstanding in the banking system. Combined with extensive cross-

shareholdings of banks, large firms can easily circumvent prudential controls on commercial bank lending, leading to significantly higher leverage and increased vulnerability to a downturn in the economy. Moreover, controlling shareholders could become so important that they could expropriate wealth from minority shareholders.[6] For instance, in the Philippines, buyers in takeovers can deal only

[6]Morck, Shleifer, and Vishny (1988) show that as ownership becomes more concentrated in U.S. firms, the value of the firm declines, suggesting that wealth is diverted from minority shareholders through various means.

Table 7.9. Aspects of Corporate Relations with Banks

	Indonesia	Korea	Malaysia	Philippines	Taiwan Province of China	Thailand
Sources of banks' permissiveness in credit decisions	Lack of information hinders risk assessment. Central bank support of banks bailing out corporations	Elements other than risk, such as employment, are often involved in credit decisions	Some weakness in risk assessment capability	Strong influence of politicians favoring projects and "relations"	Adequate risk assessment. In case of large corporate distress, Ministry of Finance coordinates grace period	Strong ties between politicians, banks, and conglomerates. Lending to friendly parties without risk assessment
Banks' ownership of equity	Restricted	Restricted, but control is possible	Restricted	Legal	Generally not permitted	Restricted
Banks' representation on corporate boards	Rare	Usual with equity	Rare	Usual even without ownership	No	Usual

Sources: Asian Development Bank (1998); and Hussain and Wihlborg (1999).

with the owners of controlling share blocks and are under no obligation to offer the same purchase price to minority shareholders. The close relationship between banks and corporations has also encouraged both parties to exploit the arbitrage opportunities presented by the considerable distortion in the tax treatment across institutions and currency (see Section IV, Table 4.4), which allows firms to profit more from dollar intermediation through foreign currency deposit units than from peso intermediation. Arbitrage activities in response to these incentives lead to increases in exchange rate risk, credit risk, and market risk in the banking system.

To ensure that firms face proper incentives to prevent a buildup of excessive short-term and unhedged foreign borrowing, the risk and liquidity management practices in the banking system must be strengthened; distortions that have led to significant regulatory and tax arbitrage across institutions, currency, and investors must be reduced; and the supervisory oversight of the Bangko Sentral ng Pilipinas and the Securities and Exchange Commission must be improved to encourage transparency and enforce compliance with prudential regulations.

Until recently, the main prudential measures in place governing bank lending to the corporate sector were limits on the exposure of banks to a single borrower. In particular, the total liabilities of a borrower to a bank were not allowed to exceed 25 percent of the unimpaired capital of the bank; and the direct and indirect lending of banks to directors, officers, stockholders, and other related interests (DOSRI loans) were limited to 15 percent of the total loan portfolio of the bank or 100 percent of the adjusted capital accounts of the bank. Furthermore, the unsecured direct or indirect lending to DOSRIs could not exceed 30 percent of the aggregate ceiling on the outstanding direct and indirect loans, whichever was lower. During the regional financial crisis, however, the Bangko Sentral ng Pilipinas took additional measures to regulate bank lending to corporate borrowers and to level the playing field between dollar and peso intermediation. These measures include, inter alia (1) preventing overexposure to the real estate sector by reducing the limit on property loans from 30 percent to 20 percent of a bank's total loan portfolio; (2) reducing the ratio of loans against acceptable collateral from 70 percent to 60 percent of the appraised value; (3) reducing the statutory reserve requirements on peso deposits to 10 percent from 15 percent, and imposing a 7.5 percent withholding tax on foreign currency deposits; (4) requiring that foreign currency deposit units maintain 100 percent cover on liabilities, with at least 30 percent of the cover required to be in the form of liquid assets; and (5) reducing tax arbitrage opportunities by requiring that interest expense savings be limited to 20 percent.

While these measures are in the right direction, more can still be done. In particular, the tax on peso intermediation remains relatively high while enforcement of prudential regulations can be made stricter by imposing stiffer penalties for noncompliance.

Conclusions

Philippine corporations were able to withstand the Asian crisis fairly well. Unlike corporations in other Asian crisis countries, most corporations in the Philippines entered the crisis period with manageable levels of total indebtedness and exposure to foreign debt. Furthermore, exports remained robust (as discussed in Section V).

Nevertheless, the survey conducted above reveals that much can be done to improve corporate governance in the country. In particular, strong efforts are needed to:

- afford greater protection to creditor rights;
- reform the policy and administrative framework for debt resolution and insolvency;
- improve enforcement of accounting standards and disclosure rules; and
- ensure that banks adhere to high standards for prudential lending, particularly with respect to DOSRI limits and loans to related corporate borrowers.

References

Asian Development Bank, 1998, *Local Study of Insolvency Law Regimes,* Regional Technical Assistance Project, Manila.

———, 1999, *Law and Development at the ADB.*

Claessens, Stijn, Simeon Djankov, and Larry Lang, 1998, "Who Controls East Asian Corporations?" (unpublished working paper; World Bank).

Claessens, Stijn, Simeon Djankov, Joseph Fan, and Larry Lang, 1999, "Expropriation of Minority Shareholders: Evidence from East Asia" (unpublished working paper; World Bank).

Hussain, Qaizar, and Clas Wihlborg, 1999, "Corporate Insolvency Procedures and Bank Behavior: A Study of Selected Asian Countries" (unpublished working paper; International Monetary Fund).

La Porta, Rafael, Florencio Lopez-de-Silanes, Andrei Shleifer, and Robert Vishny, 1998, "Law and Finance," *Journal of Political Economy,* Vol. 106 (No. 6), pp. 1113–54.

La Porta, Rafael, Florencio Lopez-de-Silanes, and Andrei Shleifer, 1999, "Corporate Ownership Around the World," *Journal of Finance,* Vol. LIV (April), pp. 471–517.

Lim, Cheng Hoon, and Charles Woodruff, 1998, "Managing Corporate Distress in the Philippines: Some Policy Recommendations," IMF Working Paper 98/138 (Washington: International Monetary Fund).

Morck, Randall, Andrei Shleifer, and Robert Vishny, 1998, "Management Ownership and Market Valuation: An Empirical Analysis," *Journal of Financial Economics*, Vol. 20, pp. 293–315.

Tan, Edita A., 1993, "Interlocking Directorates of Commercial Banks, Other Financial Institutions and Non-Financial Corporations," *Philippine Journal of Economics and Business*, Vol. 30, No. 1, pp. 1–50.

World Bank, 1999, *Philippines: The Challenge of Economic Recovery*, Report No.18895-PH (February).

VIII   Equity, Growth, and Economic Policies

Prakash Loungani

Equity considerations are playing an increasingly important role in the operational work of the IMF. According to Fischer (1999), this is because "we accept the view that poverty in the midst of plenty is not socially acceptable," and because equitable adjustment programs are more likely to be sustainable. In the case of the Philippines, the importance of equity considerations is heightened by the persistence of significant poverty, in part a consequence of the weak and uneven growth performance discussed in Section II.

This section presents key trends in equity in the Philippines and evidence on how growth and economic policies have influenced these trends.[1] Highlights include measures of poverty incidence, measures of income distribution, human development, and governance to arrive at a broad view of trends in equity. Economic policies are also discussed, with evidence on the impact of economic growth on equity, as well as specific economic policies that can have an impact on equity (in particular, fiscal policies, external sector policies, and policies toward the agricultural sector).

The main conclusion of the section is that while continued economic growth is a sine qua non for gains in equity, more targeted interventions may be needed, particularly in rural areas. The conclusion that growth helps equity is based on consideration of the cross-country evidence as well as an analysis of time-series and cross-regional data for the Philippines. However, this analysis also reveals that growth by itself may not be sufficient to achieve the desired reduction in poverty, particularly in rural areas.

Trends in Equity

Indicators of poverty have shown a decline since 1985, but remain high in absolute terms, particularly in rural areas (Table 8.1).

- Preliminary figures from the recent Family Income and Expenditure Survey indicate that in 1997, incidence of poverty (the percent of families classified as "poor") was 32 percent, and 16.5 percent of families lived below a subsistence threshold. Indicators of poverty in rural areas have shown a much slower rate of decline, and in 1997, remained considerably above the average for all areas.
- Balisacan (1998) calculates an adjusted measure of incidence that embeds a "consistency" feature for a poverty norm, namely that the poverty threshold is the same across various population subgroups and time periods in terms of the implied standard of living. The measures of incidence based on the Family Income and Expenditure Survey, in contrast, are based on poverty thresholds that differ by region, areas, and years. The adjusted measure of incidence (which will be used further in the next section) shows the same broad pattern as the official measure.

The aggregate figures on poverty incidence conceal a great deal of spatial variation. The National Capital Region (Metro Manila) has consistently had the lowest incidence of poverty—7 percent in 1997—and subsistence incidence (less than 1 percent); outside of the capital region, the poverty incidence ranged from 17 percent to 59 percent (Figure 8.1, top panel). As might be expected, there is a strong positive correlation between the incidence of poverty in a region and the share of families in the region that are rural (Figure 8.1, bottom panel).

Income inequality has not changed much over the past two decades, and over the most recent period (1994–1997), inequality has actually increased slightly (Figure 8.2). Over the past two decades, the richest 20 percent of the population has received a little over one-half the country's total income, whereas the poorest 20 percent has received about 5 percent. Understanding the reasons for the recent increase in income inequality requires an analysis of the detailed "raw" data underlying the Family Income and Expenditure Survey (which were only released recently).

---

[1] The discussion draws extensively on the work of IMF staff, particularly Gerson (1998), as well as on manuscripts provided by Philippine scholars Arsenio Balisacan and Solita Collas-Monsod, particularly Balisacan (1998), Collas-Monsod (1998), and Collas-Monsod and Monsod (1998).

Table 8.1. Indicators of Poverty
(All areas and rural areas)

	1985	1988	1991	1994	1997
Incidence of poverty—all areas	44.2	40.2	39.9	35.5	32.1
Rural areas	50.7	46.3	48.6	47.0	44.4
Subsistence incidence—all areas	24.4	20.3	20.4	18.1	16.5
Rural areas	30.0	25.3	26.4	25.6	24.8
Adjusted measure of incidence	41.5	35.0	35.5	32.2	...

Sources: National Statistical Office; and Balisacan (1998).

Recent advances in equity research (Sen (1999)) have emphasized that poverty should be seen as the deprivation of basic capabilities. Premature mortality, significant undernourishment, and widespread illiteracy are examples of deprivations that directly impoverish human life. Hence, the allocation of economic resources as well as arrangements for social provision must give some priority to removing these disadvantages.

A variety of indices have been developed by the United Nations Development Program (UNDP) to measure differences across countries in the degree of human development and material well-being; the Philippines tends to be placed in the middle of the group of developing countries, roughly consistent with its per capita income.

- The Human Development Index, measured on a scale of 0 to 1, is a composite of three measures: health, as proxied by life expectancy; knowledge, as proxied by functional literacy; and standard of living, as proxied by real per capita income. The Philippine Human Development Index for 1995 was 0.672, placing it in the UNDP's "medium" human development category. The Philippines ranks 98th out of 174 countries for which the index is computed and 89th in per capita GDP; the "negative gap" between the GDP rank and the Human Development Index rank suggests that there is some "potential of redirecting resources to human development" (UNDP (1999)).
- A related measure, the Human Poverty Index, attempts to measure the extent of deprivation of the most materially deprived people in the country; it is derived as a composite of the following features: a short life (as proxied by the percentage of people expected to die before age 40); a lack of basic education (proxied by the percentage of adults who are illiterate); and lack of access to

public and private resources (proxied by the percentage of people without access to health services and safe water, and the percentage of underweight children under five). In 1995, the Human Poverty Index calculated for the Philippines indicated that 17.7 percent of the population was affected by the forms of deprivation included in the measure, roughly comparable to the Human Poverty Index for China and Indonesia.

Corruption is inequitable. The benefits from corruption tend to accrue to the better-connected individuals in society, who belong mostly to the high-income groups (Tanzi (1995)). Recent work by IMF staff (Gupta, Davoodi, and Alonso-Terme (1998)) demonstrates that high and rising corruption increases income equality and poverty by (1) reducing economic growth; (2) lowering the progressivity of the tax system; (3) reducing the effectiveness of social spending and the formation of human capital; and (4) perpetuating an unequal distribution of asset ownership and unequal access to education. An important implication of these results is that policies that reduce corruption will also reduce income inequality and poverty.

Cross-country surveys of perceptions of corruption place the Philippines in the middle of the group of emerging market economies. Transparency International's Corruption Perceptions Index measures the level of corruption as perceived by business people, risk analysts, investigative journalists, and the general public. The index focuses on corruption in the public sector and defines corruption as the abuse of public office for private gain. In 1998, the Philippines ranked 55th out of 85 countries for which the index was computed.[2]

---

[2]Coronel (1998) presents nine case studies of the nature and extent of corruption in the Philippines, and the steps being taken to combat it.

Figure 8.1. Poverty Incidence and Rural Share

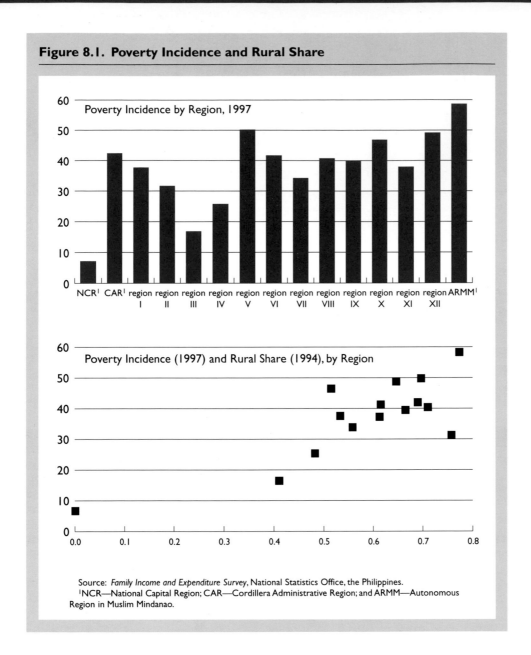

Source: *Family Income and Expenditure Survey*, National Statistics Office, the Philippines.
[1]NCR—National Capital Region; CAR—Cordillera Administrative Region; and ARMM—Autonomous Region in Muslim Mindanao.

Impact of Growth and Economic Policies on Equity

Growth-Oriented Policies and Equity

The relative efficacy of growth-oriented and redistributive policies in promoting equity continues to be a matter of discussion and debate. Countries adopt different strategies to promote equity. Some focus on redistributive policies, for example, by actively promoting the use of public resources to raise the share of income going to the bottom tier of the distribution or by imposing highly progressive taxes to reduce the share going to the top tier. Some of the support for redistributive policies is based on the be-

lief that growth has an adverse effect on equity in the early stages of development (the so-called "Kuznets curve"). Other countries rely largely on growth to help low-income families, without emphasis on redistribution.

Recent cross-country empirical evidence provides little support for the view that growth is detrimental to equity (Summers (1999)); the Philippines, however, appears to be an exception.

- Deininger and Squire (1998) find scant evidence of a Kuznets curve for most countries; indeed, periods of growth are just as likely to improve equity as to reduce it. The study uses a much larger data set, covering 91 countries

Figure 8.2. Income Inequality, 1994 and 1997

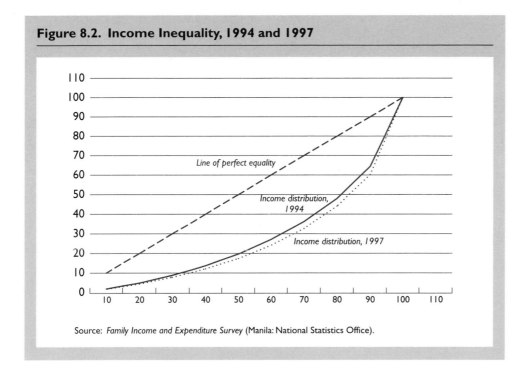

Source: *Family Income and Expenditure Survey* (Manila: National Statistics Office).

over more than 30 years (1960–92), and better econometric methods than many of the previous studies in the literature. The Philippines, however, is one of five countries where the data do support the presence of a Kuznets curve.

* More generally, the cases of Japan, the "Asian tigers," and China provide evidence of enormous reductions in poverty as a result of sustained and rapid growth. Deininger and Squire find that growth produced rising incomes for the bottom fifth of the population in all but a handful of the economies in their study.

In contrast, analysis of Philippine time-series data on poverty incidence points to the importance of growth in improving equity. One way to measure the relative importance of redistributive policies and growth-oriented policies is by performing some counterfactual experiments using the adjusted poverty incidence measure discussed earlier. In particular, the poverty measure can be decomposed into two components:

* the "growth" component is the change in the measure due to a change in per capita income growth, holding the distribution of income constant (at some reference level); and
* the "redistribution" component is the change in the poverty measure due to a change in the distribution of income, holding per capita income constant (at some reference level).

The results of the decomposition for the Philippine case are given in Table 8.2. The results show that over 1985–94 as a whole, the growth component has been responsible for essentially all the decline in poverty; the redistribution component has actually been responsible for a slight increase in poverty over the period. Even for subperiods, the growth component has been dominant in periods when the change in per capita growth has been significant; in these periods, the redistribution component has augmented the favorable impact of growth on poverty.

Philippine regional data also support the view that growth contributes to a reduction in poverty incidence, but the effect is weak in rural areas.

Table 8.2. Decomposition of Poverty Incidence into Growth and Redistribution Components

	Change in Incidence of Poverty	Growth Component	Redistribution Component
1985–88	−6.5	−6.2	−0.3
1988–91	−0.5	−3.1	3.6
1991–94	−3.3	−1.1	−2.2
1985–94	−9.3	−10.3	1.0

Source: Balisacan (1998).

VIII EQUITY, GROWTH, AND ECONOMIC POLICIES

Table 8.3. Regional Poverty Incidence and Regional Growth
(Regression estimates)

Regression #	Sector of the Economy	Independent Variables			
		Intercept	Real income	Year fixed effects?	R^2
1.	All areas	−0.02 (0.03)	−0.44 (0.20)	no	0.11
2.	All areas	0.05 (0.04)	−0.45 (0.25)	yes	0.25
3.	Urban areas	0.06 (0.04)	−0.80 (0.26)	yes	0.46
4.	Rural areas	0.12 (0.05)	−0.23 (0.28)	yes	0.22
5.	Rural areas	0.13 (0.05)	−0.33 (0.28)	yes	0.23

Source: Author's calculations.

Notes: (a) the variables are specified in growth rates; hence, the estimated coefficients can be interpreted as elasticities; and (b) numbers reported in parentheses are standard errors.

- This conclusion is based on panel regression estimates using data on regional poverty incidence and regional real income from the Family Income and Expenditure Survey for 1988, 1991, 1994, and 1997. These data are used to compute the growth in poverty incidence and real income growth for 13 regions over three periods (1998–91, 1991–94, and 1994–97), giving a total of 39 observations. The Family Income and Expenditure Survey also reports poverty incidence for urban and rural areas within each region, which allows for a test of whether the response of poverty to growth is different between the two groups.
- The regression estimates, reported in Table 8.3, show that the higher the real income growth in a region, the faster is the decline in poverty incidence. In particular, a 1 percent increase in regional income leads to about a 0.4 percent decline in poverty incidence (regression 1). This relationship continues to hold after accounting for year-fixed effects, that is, elements that were common to all regions in a given year (regression 2). Poverty responds much more to growth in urban areas than in rural areas. In urban areas, the estimated elasticity is 0.8 (regression 3), whereas in the rural areas, it is only 0.2 and not precisely estimated (regression 4). The use of an alternate, and arguably more relevant, measure of rural income growth—gross value added in agriculture and forestry—raises the estimated

elasticity to 0.3, but once again, it is not estimated precisely.

These results suggest that while growth can be expected to alleviate poverty, it may not be sufficient (as indicated by the relatively low R^2 of the regressions). The remainder of the discussion in this section focuses, therefore, on other economic policies that could have an impact on equity (in particular, policies toward the agricultural sector, fiscal policies, and external sector policies).

Agrarian Reforms and Equity

The poor performance of Philippine agriculture in the past two decades has severely constrained the gains in poverty alleviation. Some of the elements responsible for the poor performance include:

- Heavy regulation of the agricultural sector. As noted in Section II, beginning in the 1970s, price controls on rice and other products were imposed, and imports of wheat and soybeans were monopolized. Controls on the production, marketing, and processing of coconuts—long the country's most important crop in terms of export earnings and employment—were put in place. Fertilizer and pesticide imports were controlled through licensing requirements. While many of these restrictions have been relaxed or eliminated under the administrations of Aquino and Ramos, reforms in this area have not yet been completed, and important regulations remain in effect that restrict the ability of farmers to increase their earnings or acquire inputs at the lowest possible prices.

- Uncertainty concerning the implementation of land ownership reform under the government's Comprehensive Agrarian Reform Program. Launched in 1987, the reform program was intended to redistribute about three-fourths of all agricultural land to landless farmers and farm workers. The program, however, has been plagued by bottlenecks owing to a lack of financing for the enormous costs of the program as well as cumbersome administrative requirements. Uncertainty about the program has discouraged planting and the flow of private investments into agriculture, and encouraged conversion of agricultural lands into nonagricultural uses; agricultural land increased at an annual rate of 3.6 percent a year in the 1970s, but only 0.8 percent a year in the 1980s and early 1990s. Since the government is now the only buyer and seller of a large chunk of agricultural land subject to agrarian reform in the country, the agricultural land market is distorted and the collateral value of agricultural land has been adversely affected, thus further reducing the already inadequate access to formal credit in rural areas (World Bank (1999)).

- A sharp fall in investments in agriculture, both private (as a consequence of the bias against agriculture introduced by the overvalued real exchange rate and the heavy regulation of the sector) and public (especially rural roads, irrigation, and agricultural research and development).[3]

Equitable Fiscal Policies

Fiscal policies can contribute to improvements in equity. The main ingredients of equitable fiscal policy are (1) implementation of a fair and efficient system of taxation—ideally a system of easily administered taxes, moderate tax rates, and a minimum number of exemptions; and (2) provision of adequate social expenditures, particularly on education and health, to increase equality of opportunity.

In the Philippines, the Comprehensive Tax Reform Program and expansion of the VAT are likely to increase the contribution of the tax system to equity. While there is little evidence to date of the effects on these tax changes on equity, they are likely to improve equity for the following reasons:

- The extension of the VAT has increased the taxation of many services that are consumed largely by the upper income groups of the population.
- The reform of the income tax system is intended to ensure that families living below the poverty line have no income tax liability. In addition, the reform is intended to bring into the tax net many individuals, mostly wealthy individuals, who were previously outside the net.
- The net impact of corporate tax reforms on equity is difficult to predict. Certain features of the reform, such as the tax on employee fringe benefits, would improve the progressivity of the system. Other features, such as elimination of corporate tax breaks and investment incentives, may have an impact on equity only through their likely impact on growth.
- The impact of the increase in excise taxes on cigarettes and alcohol is likely to be regressive, though the effect is dampened to some extent by the higher tax imposed on premium brands.

In addition, better tax administration can be expected to improve equity by ensuring sufficient revenues for critical social expenditures, and providing a more transparent and uniform treatment of taxpayers.

Education has gained a larger share of total expenditures in recent years; however, concerns about poor quality of educational resources and lack of equity in their distribution remain valid. Since 1994, the share of education in total expenditures has risen—to about 25 percent at present—roughly the same share as in Malaysia and Thailand (Figure 8.3). However, concerns about the intrasectoral and regional allocation of educational resources, as well as the efficiency of educational expenditures remain as valid as ever. In particular:

- The increased expenditures have gone largely for higher personnel costs, while expenditures on maintenance and other operating expenditures have remained at levels that are incompatible with the provision of quality education (World Bank (1999)).
- There are significant differences in the regional distribution of educational resources and consequently in educational outcomes. For instance, in 1997, the National Capital Region accounted for about 10 percent of total enrollment in public educational institutions, but received 34 percent of the education budget. As a consequence of this uneven distribution of resources, poorer regions tend to have higher proportions of inexperienced teachers and lower completion rates.
- The share of educational resources devoted to elementary education has declined sharply over time, whereas the share devoted to tertiary edu-

---

[3]In general, the amount of budget spending devoted to agriculture is quite moderate (1–2 percent of GNP in recent years). However, agriculture is supported through substantial tax privileges and by the National Food Authority (which regulates the rice market and protects domestic farmers from being undercut by cheaper imports).

Figure 8.3. Share of Education and Health Expenditures

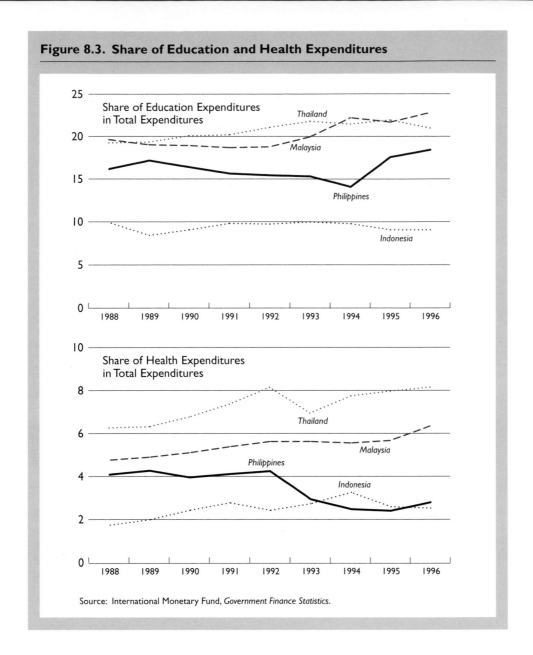

Source: International Monetary Fund, *Government Finance Statistics*.

cation has increased. A reallocation of spending toward elementary education could contribute to a significant improvement in the quality of schooling and higher retention rates for lower-income students, especially in rural areas, and in the process help equity.

Spending on health and nutrition is relatively low in the Philippines by ASEAN standards, biased toward personal health care (rather than preventive care interventions), and inefficient in its interregional allocation of resources.

- Health is underfunded in the Philippines relative to other ASEAN countries (Figure 8.3, bottom panel).

- Despite the conventional wisdom that preventive care interventions should have the first claim on resources because of their substantial positive externalities, such programs receive only between 10–15 percent of the Department of Health's budget.
- Spending is allocated in a manner that does not target the poorest segments of the population.

External Sector Policies and Equity

In principle, realistic exchange rates and an outward-oriented trade policy are presumed to be consistent with growth, reduced poverty, and improved equity in the medium to long run. Evidence from a recent cross-country study by Sarel (1997) finds partial support for this view. He finds that real exchange rate overvaluation leads to a more unequal income distribution, especially in poorer countries. He concludes that the government should try at least not to contribute to such overvaluation, and be prepared to take corrective measures when such overvaluation occurs. Sarel does not find any link between openness to international trade and changes in the income distribution.

In the Philippines, exchange and trade policies historically have contributed to inequity through a number of channels; changes in many of these policies during the 1990s should have a favorable impact on equity, at least in the medium to long run.

- As noted in Section II, the Philippines followed a policy favoring import substitution until the tariff reforms of the early 1990s. Trade policies over this period penalized the primary and agricultural sectors—where the poor are predominantly employed—in favor of the manufacturing sector. For instance, estimates of the effective rate of protection indicate that in 1985, the average effective rate of protection for manufacturing was 43 percent higher than that of agriculture.
- Even within manufacturing, an overvalued exchange rate coupled with fiscal and other incentives encouraged the substitution of capital for labor.

The shift toward outward-oriented policies and market determination of exchange rates should, in principle, contribute to a increase in equity; however, there is as yet little reliable evidence on this issue.

Conclusions

Sustained growth, combined with targeted interventions in some areas, are required to make further gains in equity in the Philippines. Poverty rates remain high, particularly in the rural areas, and the income distribution is highly unequal. While poverty is responsive to growth, attaining the government's targets for poverty alleviation (poverty incidence of 25–28 percent by 2004) is likely to require targeted interventions in the rural areas, as well as equitable fiscal and external sector policies.

References

Balisacan, Arsenio, 1998, "What Do We Really Know—or Don't Know—about Economic Inequality and Poverty in the Philippines?" (unpublished manuscript).

Collas-Monsod, Solita, 1998, "The War Against Poverty: A Status Report," in *The Philippines: New Directions in Domestic Policy and Foreign Relations,* edited by David G. Timberman (Washington: The Asia Society).

———, and Toby C. Monsod, 1998, "International and Intranational Comparisons of Philippine Poverty" (unpublished manuscript).

Coronel, Sheila (ed.), 1998, *Pork and Other Perks,* Philippine Center for Investigative Journalism.

Deininger, Klaus, and Lyn Squire, 1998, "New Ways of Looking at Old Issues: Inequality and Growth," *Journal of Development Economics,* Vol. 57, pp. 259–87.

Fischer, Stanley, 1999, "A View from the IMF," in *Economic Policy and Equity,* edited by Vito Tanzi, Ke-young Chu, and Sanjeev Gupta (Washington: International Monetary Fund).

Gerson, Phil, 1998, "Poverty, Income Distribution, and Economic Policy in the Philippines," *Philippines—Selected Issues* (Washington: International Monetary Fund).

Gupta, Sanjeev, Hamid Davoodi, and Rosa Alonso-Terme, 1998, "Does Corruption Affect Income Inequality and Poverty?" IMF Working Paper 98/76 (Washington: International Monetary Fund).

Monsod, Toby C., 1998, "Social Reform: Doable but Not Done?" in *The State and the Market: Essays on a Socially Oriented Philippine Economy,* edited by Filomeno S. Sta. Ana III (Manila: Ateneo de Manila University Press).

Sarel, Michael, 1997, "How Macroeconomic Factors Affect Income Distribution: The Cross-Country Evidence," IMF Working Paper 97/152 (Washington: International Monetary Fund).

Sen, Amartya, 1999, "Economic Policy and Equity: An Overview," in *Economic Policy and Equity,* edited by Vito Tanzi, Ke-young Chu, and Sanjeev Gupta (Washington: International Monetary Fund).

Summers, Lawrence, 1999, "Equity in a Global Economy," in *Economic Policy and Equity,* edited by Vito Tanzi, Ke-young Chu, and Sanjeev Gupta (Washington: International Monetary Fund).

Tanzi, Vito, 1995, "Corruption: Arm's-Length Relationships and Markets," in *The Economics of Organized Crime,* edited by Gianluca Fiorentini and Sam Peltzman (Cambridge, England: Cambridge University Press).

United Nations Development Programme, 1999, *Human Development Indicators* (New York: United Nations Development Programme).

World Bank, 1999, *Philippines: Promoting Equitable Rural Growth* (Washington: World Bank).

Recent Occasional Papers of the International Monetary Fund

187. Philippines: Toward Sustainable and Rapid Growth, Recent Developments and the Agenda Ahead, by Markus Rodlauer, Prakash Loungani, Vivek Arora, Charalambos Christofides, Enrique G. de la Piedra, Piyabha Kongsamut, Kristina Kostial, Victoria Summers, and Athanasios Vamvakidis. 2000.

186. Anticipating Balance of Payments Crises: The Role of Early Warning Systems, by Andrew Berg, Eduardo Borensztein, Gian Maria Milesi-Ferretti, and Catherine Pattillo. 1999.

185. Oman Beyond the Oil Horizon: Policies Toward Sustainable Growth, edited by Ahsan Mansur and Volker Treichel. 1999.

184. Growth Experience in Transition Countries, 1990–98, by Oleh Havrylyshyn, Thomas Wolf, Julian Berengaut, Marta Castello-Branco, Ron van Rooden, and Valerie Mercer-Blackman. 1999.

183. Economic Reforms in Kazakhstan, Kyrgyz Republic, Tajikistan, Turkmenistan, and Uzbekistan, by Emine Gürgen, Harry Snoek, Jon Craig, Jimmy McHugh, Ivailo Izvorski, and Ron van Rooden. 1999.

182. Tax Reform in the Baltics, Russia, and Other Countries of the Former Soviet Union, by a Staff Team Led by Liam Ebrill and Oleh Havrylyshyn. 1999.

181. The Netherlands: Transforming a Market Economy, by C. Maxwell Watson, Bas B. Bakker, Jan Kees Martijn, and Ioannis Halikias. 1999.

180. Revenue Implications of Trade Liberalization, by Liam Ebrill, Janet Stotsky, and Reint Gropp. 1999.

179. Dinsinflation in Transition: 1993–97, by Carlo Cottarelli and Peter Doyle. 1999.

178. IMF-Supported Programs in Indonesia, Korea, and Thailand: A Preliminary Assessment, by Timothy Lane, Atish Ghosh, Javier Hamann, Steven Phillips, Marianne Schulze-Ghattas, and Tsidi Tsikata. 1999.

177. Perspectives on Regional Unemployment in Europe, by Paolo Mauro, Esawar Prasad, and Antonio Spilimbergo. 1999.

176. Back to the Future: Postwar Reconstruction and Stabilization in Lebanon, edited by Sena Eken and Thomas Helbling. 1999.

175. Macroeconomic Developments in the Baltics, Russia, and Other Countries of the Former Soviet Union, 1992–97, by Luis M. Valdivieso. 1998.

174. Impact of EMU on Selected Non–European Union Countries, by R. Feldman, K. Nashashibi, R. Nord, P. Allum, D. Desruelle, K. Enders, R. Kahn, and H. Temprano-Arroyo. 1998.

173. The Baltic Countries: From Economic Stabilization to EU Accession, by Julian Berengaut, Augusto Lopez-Claros, Françoise Le Gall, Dennis Jones, Richard Stern, Ann-Margret Westin, Effie Psalida, Pietro Garibaldi. 1998.

172. Capital Account Liberalization: Theoretical and Practical Aspects, by a staff team led by Barry Eichengreen and Michael Mussa, with Giovanni Dell'Ariccia, Enrica Detragiache, Gian Maria Milesi-Ferretti, and Andrew Tweedie. 1998.

171. Monetary Policy in Dollarized Economies, by Tomás Baliño, Adam Bennett, and Eduardo Borensztein. 1998.

170. The West African Economic and Monetary Union: Recent Developments and Policy Issues, by a staff team led by Ernesto Hernández-Catá and comprising Christian A. François, Paul Masson, Pascal Bouvier, Patrick Peroz, Dominique Desruelle, and Athanasios Vamvakidis. 1998.

169. Financial Sector Development in Sub-Saharan African Countries, by Hassanali Mehran, Piero Ugolini, Jean Phillipe Briffaux, George Iden, Tonny Lybek, Stephen Swaray, and Peter Hayward. 1998.

168. Exit Strategies: Policy Options for Countries Seeking Greater Exchange Rate Flexibility, by a staff team led by Barry Eichengreen and Paul Masson with Hugh Bredenkamp, Barry Johnston, Javier Hamann, Esteban Jadresic, and Inci Ötker. 1998.

167. Exchange Rate Assessment: Extensions of the Macroeconomic Balance Approach, edited by Peter Isard and Hamid Faruqee. 1998

166. Hedge Funds and Financial Market Dynamics, by a staff team led by Barry Eichengreen and Donald Mathieson with Bankim Chadha, Anne Jansen, Laura Kodres, and Sunil Sharma. 1998.

165. Algeria: Stabilization and Transition to the Market, by Karim Nashashibi, Patricia Alonso-Gamo, Stefania Bazzoni, Alain Féler, Nicole Laframboise, and Sebastian Paris Horvitz. 1998.

164. MULTIMOD Mark III: The Core Dynamic and Steady-State Model, by Douglas Laxton, Peter Isard, Hamid Faruqee, Eswar Prasad, and Bart Turtelboom. 1998.

163. Egypt: Beyond Stabilization, Toward a Dynamic Market Economy, by a staff team led by Howard Handy. 1998.

162. Fiscal Policy Rules, by George Kopits and Steven Symansky. 1998.

161. The Nordic Banking Crises: Pitfalls in Financial Liberalization? by Burkhard Dress and Ceyla Pazarbaşıoğlu. 1998.

160. Fiscal Reform in Low-Income Countries: Experience Under IMF-Supported Programs, by a staff team led by George T. Abed and comprising Liam Ebrill, Sanjeev Gupta, Benedict Clements, Ronald McMorran, Anthony Pellechio, Jerald Schiff, and Marijn Verhoeven. 1998.

159. Hungary: Economic Policies for Sustainable Growth, Carlo Cottarelli, Thomas Krueger, Reza Moghadam, Perry Perone, Edgardo Ruggiero, and Rachel van Elkan. 1998.

158. Transparency in Government Operations, by George Kopits and Jon Craig. 1998.

157. Central Bank Reforms in the Baltics, Russia, and the Other Countries of the Former Soviet Union, by a staff team led by Malcolm Knight and comprising Susana Almuiña, John Dalton, Inci Otker, Ceyla Pazarbaşıoğlu, Arne B. Petersen, Peter Quirk, Nicholas M. Roberts, Gabriel Sensenbrenner, and Jan Willem van der Vossen. 1997.

156. The ESAF at Ten Years: Economic Adjustment and Reform in Low-Income Countries, by the staff of the International Monetary Fund. 1997.

155. Fiscal Policy Issues During the Transition in Russia, by Augusto Lopez-Claros and Sergei V. Alexashenko. 1998.

154. Credibility Without Rules? Monetary Frameworks in the Post–Bretton Woods Era, by Carlo Cottarelli and Curzio Giannini. 1997.

153. Pension Regimes and Saving, by G.A. Mackenzie, Philip Gerson, and Alfredo Cuevas. 1997.

152. Hong Kong, China: Growth, Structural Change, and Economic Stability During the Transition, by John Dodsworth and Dubravko Mihaljek. 1997.

151. Currency Board Arrangements: Issues and Experiences, by a staff team led by Tomás J.T. Baliño and Charles Enoch. 1997.

150. Kuwait: From Reconstruction to Accumulation for Future Generations, by Nigel Andrew Chalk, Mohamed A. El-Erian, Susan J. Fennell, Alexei P. Kireyev, and John F. Wilson. 1997.

149. The Composition of Fiscal Adjustment and Growth: Lessons from Fiscal Reforms in Eight Economies, by G.A. Mackenzie, David W.H. Orsmond, and Philip R. Gerson. 1997.

148. Nigeria: Experience with Structural Adjustment, by Gary Moser, Scott Rogers, and Reinold van Til, with Robin Kibuka and Inutu Lukonga. 1997.

147. Aging Populations and Public Pension Schemes, by Sheetal K. Chand and Albert Jaeger. 1996.

146. Thailand: The Road to Sustained Growth, by Kalpana Kochhar, Louis Dicks-Mireaux, Balazs Horvath, Mauro Mecagni, Erik Offerdal, and Jianping Zhou. 1996.

145. Exchange Rate Movements and Their Impact on Trade and Investment in the APEC Region, by Takatoshi Ito, Peter Isard, Steven Symansky, and Tamim Bayoumi. 1996.

144. National Bank of Poland: The Road to Indirect Instruments, by Piero Ugolini. 1996.

143. Adjustment for Growth: The African Experience, by Michael T. Hadjimichael, Michael Nowak, Robert Sharer, and Amor Tahari. 1996.

Note: For information on the title and availability of Occasional Papers not listed, please consult the IMF Publications Catalog or contact IMF Publication Services.